STUDY GUIDE

for use with

First Canadian Edition

Psychology

Includes text-specific CD-ROM inside

a journey

Coon • Brown • Malik • McKenzie

PREPARED BY

Dennis Coon

Madeleine Côté
Dawson College

THOMSON
NELSON

Australia   Canada   Mexico   Singapore   Spain   United Kingdom   United States

THOMSON

NELSON

Study Guide for
Psychology: A Journey,
First Canadian Edition

by Dennis Coon, Patrick Brown,
Rajesh Malik, and Susanne McKenzie

Prepared by Dennis Coon and
Madeleine Côté

Editorial Director and Publisher:
Evelyn Veitch

Executive Editor:
Joanna Cotton

Marketing Manager:
Murray Moman

Senior Developmental Editor:
Joanne Sutherland

Managing Production Editor:
Susan Calvert

Production Coordinator:
Hedy Sellers

Creative Director:
Angela Cluer

Cover Design:
Katherine Strain

Cover Image:
Anne Bradley

National Library of Canada
Cataloguing in Publication Data

Coon, Dennis
Study guide for Psychology: a
journey, first Canadian edition /
Dennis Coon, Madeleine Côté.

Includes bibliographical references
and index.
ISBN 0-17-622543-9

1. Psychology—Problems,
exercises, etc. I. Côté, Madeleine,
1960- II. Title.

BF121.P8323 2003 Suppl. 1   150
C2003-900562-3

TABLE OF CONTENTS

Chapter 1: Psychology: The Search for Understanding   1

Chapter 2: Brain and Behaviour   26

Chapter 3: Human Development   47

Chapter 4: Sensation and Perception   69

Chapter 5: States of Consciousness   98

Chapter 6: Conditioning and Learning   121

Chapter 7: Memory   143

Chapter 8: Cognition, Intelligence, and Creativity   164

Chapter 9: Motivation and Emotion   188

Chapter 10: Personality   212

Chapter 11: Health, Stress, and Coping   233

Chapter 12: Psychological Disorders   253

Chapter 13: Therapies   277

Chapter 14: Social Behaviour   302

How to Use this Study Guide

This *Study Guide* for *Psychology: A Journey* is designed to help you learn more, study efficiently, and get better grades. The exercises in this guide are closely coordinated with text chapters so that you can practice and review what you have read.

Each *Study Guide* chapter contains the following sections:

- Chapter Overview
- Learning Objectives
- Recite and Review
- Connections
- Check Your Memory
- Final Survey and Review
- Mastery Test
- Solutions

A brief description of each section follows along with suggestions for using them.

Chapter Overview

The Chapter Overview is a highly focused summary of major ideas in the text. By boiling chapters down to their essence, the Chapter Overview will give you a framework to build on as you learn additional ideas, concepts, and facts. Before you work on any other sections of this guide, read the Chapter Overview. In fact, it would be a good idea to re-read the Chapter Overview each time you use the *Study Guide*.

Learning Objectives

The Learning Objectives will show you, in detail, if you have mastered a reading assignment. To use them, you may want to write brief responses for each objective after you finish reading a chapter of the text. As an alternative, you may want to just read the Learning Objectives, pausing after each to see if you can respond in your own words. Then, after you have completed all of the other exercises in the *Study Guide* you can return to the Learning Objectives. At that time, you can either respond verbally or in writing. In either case, give special attention to any objectives you can't complete.

Recite and Review

This section will give you a chance to review major terms and concepts. Recite and Review is organized with the same Survey Questions found in the textbook chapters. This exercise will help you actively process information, so that it becomes more meaningful. Recite and Review also gives you a chance to practice recalling ideas from your reading.

As you work through Recite and Review, don't worry if you can't fill in all of the blanks. Go search for the answer in your text. The searching will help you review the information and increase the chances that the new knowledge will be memorized. All of the solutions are listed at the end of each *Study Guide* chapter. Page numbers are provided for each section of Recite and Review so you can return to the text to clarify any points that you missed.

Connections

This section contains matching-type items. It will help you build associations between related terms, facts, concepts, and ideas. Where appropriate, art is reproduced from the text so that you can match to images, rather than words. This is a good way to add links to your memory networks. Again, solutions are listed at the end of the chapter.

Check Your Memory

The true-false statements in Check Your Memory highlight facts and details that you may have overlooked when you read the text. It's easy to fool yourself about how much you are remembering as you read. If you answered wrong for any of the items in Check Your Memory, you should return to the textbook to find out why. Page numbers listed for each group of items will make it easy for you to locate the relevant information in the textbook.

Final Survey and Review

This exercise might seem like a repeat of the Recite and Review section, but it's not. This time, you must supply a different set of more difficult terms and concepts to complete the review. The Final Survey and Review challenges you to consolidate your earlier learning and to master key concepts from the text. The Final Survey and Review is not a test. Don't be upset if you can't fill in some of the blanks. But do give missing ideas extra practice when you check your solutions. Indeed, try to learn more each time you complete a *Study Guide* exercise, check your solutions, or return to the text for review and clarification.

Mastery Test

The multiple-choice items of the Mastery Test are at least as difficult as those found on typical in-class tests. If you do well on the Mastery Test, you can be confident that you are prepared for in-class tests. On the other hand, a low score is a clear signal that further study and review are needed. However, don't expect to always get perfect scores on the Mastery Tests. In some cases, the questions cover information that was not reviewed in any of the preceding *Study Guide* sections. The Mastery Tests are designed to continue the learning process, as well as to give you feedback about your progress.

Solutions

Solutions for all of the preceding exercises are listed at the end of each *Study Guide* chapter. Solutions for the Mastery Test include page numbers so you can locate the source of the question in the textbook.

A Five-Day Study Plan

There is no single "best" way to use this guide. Getting the most out of the *Study Guide* depends greatly on your personal learning style and study habits. Nevertheless, as a starting point, you might want to give the following plan a try.

Days 1 and 2

Read the assigned chapter in the textbook. As you do, be sure to make use of the Knowledge Builders and all the steps of the SQ4R method described in the textbook.

Day 3

Review the textbook chapter and any notes you made as you read it. Read the Chapter Overview in the *Study Guide* and read the Learning Objectives. Now do the Recite and Review section.

Day 4

Read the margin definitions in the textbook and the Chapter Overview in the *Study Guide*. Do the Connections and Check Your Memory sections of the *Study Guide*. Return to the textbook and make sure you understand why any items you missed were wrong.

Day 5

Review the textbook chapter and any notes you made as you read it. Read the Chapter Overview in the *Study Guide*. Then do the Final Survey and Review section, and check your solutions. Return to the textbook and clarify any items you missed. Now take the Mastery Test. If you miss any questions, review appropriate sections of the textbook again. To really consolidate your learning, say or write responses to all of the Learning Objectives.

Summary

The close ties between *Psychology: A Journey* and the *Study Guide* make it possible for the *Study Guide* to be used in a variety of ways. You may prefer to turn to the *Study Guide* for practice and review after you have completed a reading assignment, as suggested in the Five-Day Plan. Or, you might find it more helpful to treat the *Study Guide* as a reading companion. In that case, you would complete appropriate *Study Guide* sections from each type of exercise as you progress through the text. In any event, it is nearly certain that if you use the *Study Guide* conscientiously, you will retain more, learn more efficiently, and perform better on tests. Also, don't forget that the CD-ROM that came with your textbook has additional exercises and test questions to enrich your explorations of psychology. I hope you enjoy your journey into the fascinating realm of human behaviour.

Chapter 1

Psychology: The Search for Understanding

Chapter Overview

Psychology is the scientific study of behaviour and mental processes. Psychology's goals are to describe, understand, predict, and control behaviour. Psychologists answer questions about behaviour by applying the scientific method and gathering empirical evidence.

Psychology grew out of philosophy. The first psychological laboratory was established by Wilhelm Wundt, who studied conscious experience. The first school of thought in psychology was structuralism, a kind of "mental chemistry." Structuralism was followed by the rise of functionalism, behaviourism, Gestalt psychology, psychoanalytic psychology, and humanistic psychology. Five main streams of thought in modern psychology are behaviourism, humanism, the psychodynamic approach, biopsychology, and cognitive psychology.

The training of psychologists differs from that of psychiatrists, psychoanalysts, counsellors, and social workers. Clinical and counselling psychologists specialize in doing psychotherapy. Other specialties are industrial-organizational, educational, consumer, school, developmental, engineering, medical, environmental, forensic, psychometric, and experimental psychology.

Scientific investigation involves observing, defining a problem, proposing a hypothesis, gathering evidence/testing the hypothesis, publishing results, and forming a theory.

Many psychological investigations begin with naturalistic observation, which is informative despite its limitations. In the correlational method, the strength of the relationship between two measures is investigated. Correlations allow predictions, but they do not demonstrate cause-and-effect connections.

Experiments show whether an independent variable has an effect on a dependent variable. This allows cause-and-effect connections to be identified.

The clinical method employs detailed case studies of single individuals. In the survey method, people in a representative sample are asked a scrics of questions. This provides information on the behaviour of large groups of people.

A key element of critical thinking is an ability to weigh the evidence bearing on a claim and to evaluate the quality of that evidence.

Belief in various pseudo-psychologies is based in part on uncritical acceptance, the fallacy of positive instances, and the Barnum effect.

Information in the popular media varies greatly in quality and accuracy. It is wise to approach such information with skepticism regarding the source of information, uncontrolled observation, correlation and causation, inferences, over-simplification, single examples, and unrepeatable results.

Learning Objectives

1. List two reasons for studying psychology.

2. Define psychology.

3. Define the term *behaviour* and differentiate overt from covert behaviour.

4. Explain the term *empirical evidence* and give an example of it.

5. Explain the term *scientific observation*.

6. Give two reasons why the study of some topics in psychology is difficult.

7. Write a brief summary of each of the following areas of specialization in psychology:
   a. developmental
   b. learning
   c. personality
   d. sensation and perception
   e. comparative
   f. biopsychology
   g. social
   h. cultural

8. Explain why animals are used in research and define the term *animal model* in your discussion.

9. Explain the four goals of psychology.

10. Describe the school of psychology known as structuralism, including:
    a. where and when it was established
    b. who established it (the "father" of psychology)
    c. the focus of its study
    d. research method and its major drawback
    e. goal
    f. who brought structuralism to the United States

11. Describe the functionalist school of psychology, including:
    a. its founder
    b. its goal
    c. major interests

12. Describe behaviourism, including:
    a. its founder
    b. why its founder could not accept structuralism or functionalism
    c. its emphasis
    d. Skinner's contribution and his concept of a "designed culture."
    e. the new importance of cognitive behaviourism

13. Describe the Gestalt school of psychology, including:
    a. who founded it
    b. its goal
    c. its slogan
    d. topics it has influenced

14. Describe the contribution of women in the early history of psychology and contrast the representation of women in psychology then and now. Name the first woman to receive her doctorate in psychology.

15. Describe the psychodynamic school of psychology, including:
    a. who founded it
    b. its major emphasis
    c. the concept of repression
    d. its method of psychotherapy

16. Describe the humanistic school of psychology including:
    a. how its approach differs from psychoanalytic and behaviouristic thought
    b. who its major representatives are
    c. its position on "free will" (as contrasted with determinism)
    d. its focus on psychological needs
    e. its stress of subjective factors rather than a scientific approach
    f. the concept of self-actualization

17. Describe the eclectic approach.

18. List and briefly describe the 5 major perspectives in modern psychology.

19. Briefly tell why biopsychology and cognitive psychology have become more important in recent years.

20. Explain how understanding human diversity may help us better understand ourselves and the behaviour of others. Define the terms *cultural relativity* and *norms*.

21. Characterize the differences in training, emphasis, and/or expertise among psychologists, psychiatrists, psychoanalysts, counsellors, psychiatric social workers, and psychiatric nurses. Describe the roles of clinical and counselling psychologists, and define the term *scientist-practitioner model*.

22. Identify the largest areas of specialization among psychologists. List the 23 divisions of the Canadian Psychological association. Name the major sources of employment for psychologists.

23. Differentiate basic from applied research.

24. List the six steps of the scientific method.

25. Define the term *hypothesis* and be able to identify one. Explain what an operational definition is.

26. Explain the purpose of theory building and the importance of publication.

27. Describe the technique of naturalistic observation including both the advantages and limitations of this method. Explain what the anthropomorphic fallacy is and how it can lead to problems in psychological research.

28. Describe what a correlational study is and list any advantages and disadvantages of this method. Explain what a correlation coefficient is, how it is expressed, what it means, and how it is related to causation.

29. List and describe the three essential variables of the experimental method.

30. Explain the nature and the purpose of the control group and the experimental group in an experiment.

31. Explain the purpose of randomly assigning subjects to either the control or the experimental group.

32. Identify the advantages and disadvantages of the experimental method.

33. Explain what a placebo is, how effective it is, how it probably works, and what its purpose is in an experiment.

34. Explain what single-blind and double-blind experimental arrangements are.

35. Explain the nature of the experimenter effect and how it is related to the self-fulfilling prophecy.

36. Briefly describe the clinical method of research including advantages and disadvantages. Give an example of a case in which the clinical method would be used.

37. Briefly describe the survey method of investigation including the importance of a representative sample, and an advantage and a disadvantage of the method. Define the term *courtesy bias*.

38. Define the term *critical thinking*. Describe each of the four principles which form the foundation of critical thinking.

39. Briefly describe each of the following pseudo-psychologies:
    a. palmistry
    b. graphology
    c. phrenology
    d. astrology

40. List and explain the three reasons why pseudo-psychologies continue to thrive even though they have no scientific basis.

41. List eight suggestions that your author gives to help you become a more critical reader of psychological information in the popular press.

Practice Quizzes

Recite and Review

- *What is psychology? What are its goals?*

Recite and Review: Pages 1−6

1. Psychology is both a science and a _____ .

2. Psychology is defined as the scientific study of behaviour and _____ processes.

3. Psychologists study overt and covert _____

4. Psychologists seek empirical _____ based on scientific observation.

5. Scientific observation is _____ so that it answers questions about the world.

6. Answering psychological questions requires a valid _____ _____ .

7. Developmental psychologists study the course of human _____ .

8. Learning theorists study how and why _____ occurs.

9. Personality _____ study personality traits and dynamics.

10. Sensation and perception psychologists study the _____ organs and perception.

11. Comparative psychologists study different species, especially _____ .

12. Biopsychologists study the connection between biological processes and _____ .

13. Social psychologists study _____ behaviour.

14. Cultural psychologists study the ways that culture affects _____ .
15. Other species are used as _____ models in psychological research to discover principles that apply to human behaviour.
16. Psychology's goals are to describe, _____ , predict, and control behaviour.

• How did psychology emerge as a field of knowledge?

Recite and Review: Pages 6—11

17. Historically, psychology is an outgrowth of philosophy, the study of _____ , reality, and human nature.
18. The first psychological _____ was established in Germany by Wilhelm Wundt.
19. Wundt tried to apply scientific methods to the study of conscious _____ .
20. Functionalism was concerned with how the mind helps us _____ to our environments.
21. Behaviourism was launched by John B. _____ .
22. Behaviourists objectively study the relationship between stimuli and _____ .
23. The modern behaviourist B.F. Skinner believed that most behaviour is controlled by _____ reinforcers.
24. Cognitive behaviourism combines _____ , reinforcement, and environmental influences to explain behaviour.
25. Gestalt psychology emphasizes the study of _____ units, not pieces.
26. According to the Gestalt view, in psychology the whole is often _____ than the sum of its parts.
27. The psychoanalytic approach emphasized the _____ origins of behaviour.
28. Psychoanalytic psychology, developed by Austrian physician Sigmund _____ , is an early psychodynamic approach.
29. Humanistic psychology emphasizes free will, subjective experience, human potentials, and personal _____ .
30. Psychologically, humanists believe that self- _____ and self-evaluation are important elements of personal adjustment.
31. Humanists also emphasize a capacity for self-actualization—the full development of personal _____ .

• What are the major trends and specialties in psychology?

Recite and Review: Pages 11—16

32. Five main streams of thought in modern psychology are behaviourism, _____ the psychodynamic approach, biopsychology, and cognitive psychology.
33. Much of contemporary psychology is an eclectic _____ of the best features of various viewpoints.
34. To fully understand behaviour, psychologists must be aware of human _____ as well as human universals.
35. Our behaviour is greatly affected by cultural _____ and by social norms (_____ that define acceptable behaviour).
36. Psychologists who treat emotional problems specialize in _____ or counselling psychology.
37. Psychiatrists typically use both _____ and psychotherapy to treat emotional problems.
38. Freudian psychoanalysis is a specific type of _____ .

39. Counsellors have either a _____ degree or a doctoral degree. Many psychiatric social workers hold a _____ degree.

40. Some major _____ in psychology are clinical, counselling, industrial-organizational, developmental, environmental, military, family, health, and criminal justice.

41. Scientific research in psychology may be either _____ or applied.

• *Why is the scientific method important to psychologists?*

Recite and Review: Pages 16—19

42. Scientific investigation in psychology is based on reliable evidence, accurate description and _____ , precise definition, controlled observation, and repeatable results.

43. The scientific method involves observing, defining a _____ , proposing a hypothesis, gathering evidence/testing the hypothesis, publishing _____ , and forming a theory.

44. To be scientifically _____ a hypothesis must be testable.

45. Psychological concepts are given operational _____ so that they can be observed.

46. A _____ is a system of ideas that interrelates facts and concepts.

47. Published research reports usually include the following sections: an _____ , an introduction, a methods section, a _____ sections, and a final discussion.

• *How do psychologists collect information?*

Recite and Review: Pages 18—21

48. The tools of psychological research include naturalistic observation, the correlation method, the experimental method, the _____ method, and the survey method.

49. Naturalistic observation refers to actively observing behaviour in _____ settings.

50. Two problems with naturalistic studies are the effects of the observer on the observed (the observer _____) and _____ bias.

51. The anthropomorphic fallacy is the error of attributing human qualities to _____ .

52. Problems with naturalistic studies can be minimized by keeping careful observational _____ .

53. In the correlation method, the _____ between two traits, responses, or events is measured.

54. Correlation coefficients range from +1.00 to -1.00. A correlation of _____ indicates that there is no relationship between two measures.

55. Correlations of +1.00 and -1.00 reveal that _____ relationships exist between two measures.

56. The closer a correlation coefficient is to plus or _____ 1, the stronger the measured relationship is.

57. A positive correlation shows that _____ in one measure correspond to decreases in a second measure.

58. In a negative correlation, _____ in one measure correspond to decreases in a second measure.

59. Correlations allow us to make _____ , but correlation does not demonstrate causation.

60. _____ -and-effect relationships in psychology are best identified by doing a controlled experiment.

- ## *How is an experiment performed?*

Recite and Review: Pages 22—25

61. In an experiment, conditions that might affect behaviour are intentionally _____ . Then, changes in behaviour are observed and recorded.

62. In an experiment, a variable is any condition that can _____ , and that might affect the outcome of the experiment (the behaviour of subjects).

63. Experimental conditions that are intentionally varied are called _____ variables.

64. _____ variables measure the results of the experiment.

65. Extraneous variables are conditions that a researcher wishes to _____ from affecting the outcome of the experiment.

66. Subjects exposed to the independent variable are in the experimental _____ . Those not exposed to the independent variable form the control _____ .

67. Extraneous variables that involve personal _____ , such as age or intelligence, can be controlled by randomly assigning subjects to the experimental and control groups.

68. If all extraneous variables are _____ for the experimental group and the control group, any differences in behaviour must be caused by differences in the independent variable.

69. Experiments involving drugs must control for the placebo _____ .

70. In a single- _____ study, subjects don't know if they are getting a drug or a placebo. In a double- _____ study, neither experimenters nor subjects know who is receiving a real drug.

71. Researchers must minimize the experimenter effect (the tendency for people to do what is _____ of them).

- ## *What other research methods do psychologists use?*

Recite and Review: Pages 25—27

72. Clinical psychologists frequently gain information from _____ studies.

73. Case studies may be thought of as _____ clinical tests.

74. In the survey method, information about large populations is gained by asking people in a representative _____ a series of carefully worded questions.

75. The value of surveys is lowered when the sample is biased and when replies to questions are _____ .

- ## *What is critical thinking?*

Recite and Review: Pages 27—28

76. Critical thinking is the ability to _____ , compare, analyze, critique, and synthesize information.

77. In psychology, _____ thinking skills help evaluate claims about human behaviour.

78. Critical thinking involves a willingness to _____ evaluate _____ .

79. Scientific observations usually provide the highest quality _____ about various claims.

- ## *How does psychology differ from false explanations of behaviour?*

Recite and Review: Pages 28—31

80. Palmistry, phrenology, graphology, and astrology are _____ systems or pseudo-psychologies.

81. Belief in pseudo-psychologies is encouraged by uncritical acceptance, the fallacy of positive instances, and the _____ effect, named after a famous showman who had "something for everyone".

- ## *How good is psychological information found in the popular media?*

Recite and Review: Psychology in Action, Pages 31−35

82. _____ and critical thinking are called for when evaluating claims in the popular media.

83. You should be on guard for _____ or biased sources of information in the media.

84. Many claims in the media are based on unscientific observations that lack control _____ .

85. In the poplar media, a failure to distinguish between correlation and _____ is common.

86. Inferences and opinions may be reported as if they were _____ observations.

87. Single cases, unusual _____ , and testimonials are frequently reported as if they were valid generalizations.

Connections

1.	_____ covert behaviour	a.	hidden from view
2.	_____ EEG	b.	brain waves
3.	_____ scientific observation	c.	systematic observation
4.	_____ comparative psychology	d.	animal behaviour
5.	_____ description	e.	detailed record
6.	_____ psychology	f.	human and animal behaviour
7.	_____ understanding	g.	"why" questions
8.	_____ biopsychology	h.	brain and behaviour
9.	_____ empirical evidence	i.	direct observation
10.	_____ personality theorist	j.	traits, dynamics, individual differences

11.	_____ psychometrics	a.	father of psychology
12.	_____ control	b.	natural selection
13.	_____ Wundt	c.	behaviourism
14.	_____ Titchener	d.	mental measurement
15.	_____ James	e.	functionalism
16.	_____ Darwin	f.	conditioned responses
17.	_____ Skinner	g.	Gestalt
18.	_____ Pavlov	h.	colour vision
19.	_____ Wertheimer	i.	introspection
20.	_____ Ladd-Franklin	j.	influencing behaviour

21.	_____ Freud	a.	self-actualization
22.	_____ Maslow	b.	self-image
23.	_____ psychodynamic view	c.	psychoanalysis
24.	_____ behaviouristic view	d.	information processing
25.	_____ humanistic view	e.	Ph.D.,Psy.D.,Ed.D.
26.	_____ biopsychology	f.	M.D.
27.	_____ cognitive view	g.	internal forces
28.	_____ psychologist	h.	physiological process
29.	_____ psychiatrist	i.	controlled observation
30.	_____ scientific method	j.	environmental forces

31.	_____ common sense	a.	tentative explanation
32.	_____ hypothesis	b.	formal log
33.	_____ operational definition	c.	measure of variables
34.	_____ Clever Hans	d.	related traits, behaviours
35.	_____ observational record	e.	math errors
36.	_____ correlational study	f.	head signals
37.	_____ correlation of +3.5	g.	effect on behaviour
38.	_____ identify causes of behaviour	h.	experimental method
39.	_____ independent variable	i.	unscientific information
40.	_____ dependent variable	j.	varied by experimenter

41.	_____ extraneous variables	a.	Phineas Gage
42.	_____ control group	b.	done by using chance
43.	_____ random assignment to groups	c.	participation is voluntary
44.	_____ lobotomy	d.	excluded by experimenter
45.	_____ placebos	e.	clinical method
46.	_____ endorphins	f.	representative of population
47.	_____ case studies	g.	inaccurate answers
48.	_____ valid sample	h.	chemical
49.	_____ courtesy bias	i.	reference for comparison
50.	_____ ethical research	j.	sugar pills

Check Your Memory

Check your Memory: Pages 1—6

1. Psychology can best be described as a profession, not a science.
   True or False

2. Psychology is defined as the scientific study of human behaviour.
    True or False

3. Although it is a covert activity, dreaming is a behaviour.
    True or False

4. The term empirical evidence refers to the opinion of an acknowledged authority.
    True or False

5. The term data refers to a systematic procedure for answering scientific questions.
    True or False

6. Naming and classifying are the heart of psychology's second goal, understanding behaviour.
    True or False

Check your Memory: Pages 6—11

7. In 1879, Wundt established a lab to study the philosophy of behaviour.
    True or False

8. Wundt used introspection to study conscious experiences.
    True or False

9. Edward Titchener is best known for promoting functionalism in America.
    True or False

10. The functionalists were influenced by the ideas of Charles Darwin.
    True or False

11. Behaviourists define psychology as the study of conscious experience.
    True or False

12. Watson and Pavlov's concept of conditioned responses to explain most behaviour.
    True or False

13. The "Skinner Box" is used primarily to study learning in animals.
    True or False

14. Cognitive behaviourism combines thinking and Gestalt principles to explain human behaviour.
    True or False

15. Margaret Washburn was the first woman in America to be awarded a Ph.D. in psychology.
    True or False

16. Mary Calkins did early research on memory.
    True or False

17. According to Freud, repressed thoughts are held out of awareness, in the unconscious.
    True or False

18. Humanists generally reject the determinism of the behaviourist and psychodynamic approaches.
    True or False

19. The first Canadian psychology lab was established at the University of Toronto in 1948.
    True or False

Check Your Memory: Pages 11—16

20. The five major perspectives in psychology today are behaviourism, humanism, functionalism, biopsychology, and cognitive psychology.
    True or False

21. Humanism offers a positive, philosophical view of human nature.
    True or False

22. The cognitive view explains behaviour in terms of information processing.
    True or False

23. To understand behaviour, psychologists must be aware of the cultural relativity of standards for evaluating behaviour.
    True or False

24. Most psychologists work in private practice.
    True or False

25. The differences between clinical and counselling psychology are beginning to fade.
    True or False

26. To enter the profession of psychology today you would need to earn a doctorate degree
    True or False

27. The Psy.D. degree emphasizes scientific research skills and is offered at most Canadian universities.
    True or False

28. The majority of all psychologists specialize in clinical or counselling psychology.
    True or False

29. A psychologist that seeks for solutions to help people deal with daily stresses does basic research.
    True or False

30. Studying ways to improve the memories of eyewitnesses to crimes would be an example of applied research.
    True or False

Check Your Memory: Pages 16—19

31. The scientific method involves testing a proposition by systematic observation.
    True or False

32. An operational definition states the exact hypothesis used to represent a concept.
    True or False

33. Clever Hans couldn't do math problems when his owner left the room.
    True or False

34. Operational definitions link concepts with concrete observations.
    True or False

35. Most research reports begin with an abstract.
    True or False

Check Your Memory: Pages 18—21

36. Jane Goodall's study of chimpanzees made use of the clinical method.
    True or False

37. Concealing the observer helps reduce the observer effect.
    True or False

38. A correlation coefficient of +.100 indicates a perfect positive relationship.
    True or False

39. Strong relationships produce positive correlation coefficients; weak relationships produce negative correlations.
    True or False

40. Perfect correlations demonstrate that a causal relationship exists.
    True or False

41. The best way to identify cause-and-effect relationships is to perform a case study.
    True or False

Check Your Memory: Pages 22—25

42. Extraneous variables are those that are varied by the experimenter.
    True or False

43. Independent variables are suspected causes for differences in behaviour.
    True or False

44. In an experiment to test whether hunger affects memory, hunger is the dependent variable.
    True or False

45. Independent variables are randomly assigned to the experimental and control groups.
    True or False

46. A person who takes a drug may be influenced by his or her expectations about the drug's effects.
    True or False

47. Placebos appear to reduce pain because they cause a release of endogenous Dexedrine.
    True or False

48. In a single-blind experiment, the experimenter remains blind as the to whether
    she or he is administering a drug.
    True or False

49. Subjects in psychology experiments can be very sensitive to hints about what is expected of them.
    True or False

Check Your Memory: Pages 25—27

50. Phineas Gage is remembered as the first psychologist to do a case study.
    True or False

51. Case studies may be inconclusive because they lack formal control groups.
    True or False

52. Representative samples are often obtained by randomly selecting people to study.
    True or False

53. A tendency to give socially desirable answers to questions can lower the accuracy of surveys.
    True or False

Check Your Memory: Pages 27—28

54. Critical thinking is the ability to make a good use of intuition and mental imagery.
    True or False

55. Critical thinkers actively evaluate claims, ideas, and propositions
    True or False

56. A key element of critical thinking is evaluating the quality of evidence related to the claim.
    True or False

57. Critical thinkers recognize that the opinions of experts and authorities should
    be respected without questions.
    True or False

Check Your Memory: Pages 28—31

58. Pseudo-scientists test their concepts by gathering data.
    True or False

59. Phrenologists believe that lines on the hands reveal personality traits.
    True or False

60. Graphology is only valid if a large enough sample of handwriting is analyzed.
    True or False

61. Astrological charts consisting of positive traits tend to be perceived as "accurate" or true, even if they are not.
    True or False

62. The students that rated their daily horoscope to be accurate were displaying the Barnum Effect.
    True or False

Check Your Memory: Psychology in Action, Pages 31—35

63. The existence of dermo-optical perception was confirmed by recent experiments.
    True or False

64. Psychological courses and services offered for profit may be misrepresented, just as some other products are.
    True or False

65. At least some psychic ability is necessary to perform as a stage mentalist.
    True or False

66. Successful fire walking requires neurolinguistic programming.
    True or False

67. Violent crime rises and falls with lunar cycles.
    True or False

68. If you see a person crying, you must infer that he or she is sad.
    True or False

69. Individual cases and specific examples tell us nothing about what is true in general.
    True or False

Final Survey and Review

• *What is psychology? What are its goals?*

1. Psychology is both a _____ and a _____ .
2. Psychology is defined as the scientific study of _____ and _____ _____ .
3. Psychologists study both overt and _____ behaviour.
4. Psychologists seek _____ evidence based on scientific observation. They settle disputes by collecting _____ .
5. _____ observation is structured and systematic.
6. Answering psychological questions requires a valid _____ _____ .
7. _____ psychologists study the course of human development.
8. Learning _____ study how and why learning occurs.
9. _____ theorists study personality traits and dynamics.
10. _____ and perception psychologists study the sense organs and perception.
11. _____ psychologists study different species, especially animals.
12. _____ study biological processes and behaviour.
13. Social psychologists study _____ _____ .

13

14. _____ psychologists study the ways that culture affects behaviour.

15. Other species are used as _____ _____ in psychological research to discover principles that apply to human behaviour.

16. Psychology's goals are to describe, understand, _____ and _____ behaviour.

• *How did psychology emerge as a field of knowledge?*

17. Historically, psychology is an outgrowth of _____ .

18. The first psychological laboratory was established in Germany by _____ _____ .

19. His goal was to apply scientific methods to the study of _____ _____ .

20. The first school of thought in psychology was _____ , a kind of "mental chemistry."

21. _____ was concerned with how the mind helps us adapt to our environments. William _____ was one of its proponents.

22. _____ was launched by John B. Watson, who wanted to study the relationship between _____ and responses.

23. The modern behaviourist B.F. _____ believed that most behaviour is controlled by positive _____ .

24. _____ behaviourism combines thinking and environmental influences to explain behaviour.

25. _____ psychology emphasizes the study of whole experiences, not elements or pieces.

26. According to Max _____ and other _____ psychologists, the whole is often greater than the _____ of its parts.

27. The _____ approach emphasizes the unconscious origins of behaviour.

28. The Austrian physician, Sigmund _____ , developed a psychodynamic system called _____ .

29. _____ psychology emphasizes free will, subjective experience, human _____ , and personal growth.

30. Psychologically, humanists believe that _____ , self-evaluation, and one's _____ of reference are important elements of personal adjustment.

31. Humanists also emphasize a capacity for _____ – the full development of personal potential.

• *What are the major trends and specialties in psychology?*

32. Five main streams of thought in modern psychology are _____ , _____ , the psychodynamic approach, _____ , and cognitive psychology.

33. Much of contemporary psychology is an _____ blend of the best features of various viewpoints.

34. To fully understand behaviour, psychologists must be aware of human _____ , as reflected in personal and _____ differences.

35. Psychologists who treat emotional problems specialize in _____ or _____ psychology.

36. _____ are medical doctors who typically use both drugs and _____ to treat emotional problems.

37. Freudian _____ is a specific type of psychotherapy.

38. _____ can have either a masters or doctoral degree while _____ _____ workers could hold a masters degree.

39. _____ psychologists specialize in the growth of children; _____ psychologists help design machines; psychologists in _____ study classroom dynamics.

40. Scientific research in psychology may be either basic or _____ .

• *Why is the scientific method important to psychologists?*

41. Scientific investigation in psychology is based on reliable _____ , accurate description and _____ , precise definition, controlled observation, and repeatable results.

42. The scientific method involves observing, defining a problem proposing a _____ gathering evidence/testing the hypothesis, publishing results, and forming a _____ .

43. To be _____ valid a hypothesis must be _____ .

44. Psychological concepts are given _____ definitions so that they can be observed. Such definitions state the exact _____ used to represent a concept.

45. A _____ is a system of ideas that interrelates facts and concepts. In general, good _____ summarize existing _____ , explain them, and guide further research.

46. The results of scientific studies are _____ in professional _____ so they will be publicly available.

• *How do psychologists collect information?*

47. The tools of psychological research include naturalistic observation, the correlational method, the _____ method, the clinical method, and the _____ method.

48. Naturalistic observation refers to actively observing behaviour in _____ _____ which are the typical _____ in which people and animals live.

49. Two problems with naturalistic observation are the effects of the observer on the _____ and observer _____ .

50. The _____ fallacy is the error of attributing human qualities to animals.

51. Problems with naturalistic observation can be minimized by keeping careful _____ _____ .

52. In the _____ method, the strength of the relationship between two measures.

53. A correlation of _____ indicates that there is no relationship between two measures. Correlations of +1.00 and -1.00 reveal that _____ relationships exist between two measures.

54. The _____ a correlation coefficient is to plus or minus 1.00, the stronger the measured relationship is.

55. A _____ correlation or relationship shows that increases in one measure correspond to increases in a second measure.

56. In a negative correlation, _____ in one measure correspond to _____ in a second measure.

57. Correlations allow prediction, but correlation does not demonstrate _____ .

58. Cause-and-effect relationships in psychology are best identified by doing a _____ _____ .

• *How is an experiment performed?*

59. In an experiment, conditions that might affect behaviour are intentionally varied. Then, changes in behaviour are _____ and _____ .

60. In an experiment a _____ is any condition that can change, and that might affect the outcome of the experiment.

61. Experimental conditions that are intentionally varied are called _____ variables; they are potential _____ of changes in behaviour.

62. _____ variables measure the results of the experiment; they reveal any _____ on behaviour.

63. _____ variables are conditions that a researcher wishes to prevent form affecting the _____ of the experiment.

64. Extraneous variables are _____ by making sure that they are the same for all subjects in an experiment.

65. Subjects exposed to the independent variable are in the _____ group. Those not exposed to the independent variable form the _____ group.

66. Extraneous variables that involve _____ characteristics, such as age or intelligence, can be controlled by _____ assigning subjects to the experimental and control groups.

67. If all extraneous variables are identical for the experimental group and the control group, any differences in behaviour must be caused by differences in the _____ variable.

68. Experiments involving drugs must control the _____ effect.

69. In a _____ study, subjects don't know if they are getting a drug or a placebo. In a _____ study, neither experimenters nor subjects know who is receiving a real drug.

70. Researchers must also minimize the _____ _____ (the tendency for people to do what is expected of them).

71. In many situations, the experimenter effect leads to _____ prophecies.

- ## *What other research methods do psychologists use?*

72. Clinical psychologists frequently gain information from _____ _____ , which focus on all aspects of a single _____ .

73. Case studies may be thought of as natural _____ _____ of the effects of brain tumors, accidental poisonings, and other unusual conditions.

74. In the survey method, information about large _____ is gained by asking people in a _____ sample a series of carefully worded questions.

75. The value of surveys is lowered when the sample is _____ and when replies to _____ are inaccurate or untruthful.

- ## *What is critical thinking?*

76. Critical thinking is the ability to evaluate, compare, analyze, _____ , and _____ information.

77. In psychology, critical thinking skills help _____ claims about human behaviour.

78. Critical thinking involves evaluating the quality of the _____ used to support various claims.

79. _____ observations usually provide the highest quality evidence about various claims.

- ## *How does psychology differ from false explanations of behaviour?*

80. Palmistry, _____ , graphology, and astrology are _____ -psychologies.

81. Belief in false psychologies is encouraged by _____ acceptance, the fallacy of _____ instances, and the _____ effect.

- ## *How good is psychological information found in the popular media?*

82. _____ and _____ thinking are called for when evaluating claims in the popular media.

83. You should be on guard for unreliable or _____ sources of information in the media.

84. Many claims in the media are based on unscientific observations that lack _____ groups.

85. _____ does not demonstrate causation. In the popular media, a failure to distinguish between _____ and causation is common.

86. Inferences and opinions may be reported as if they were objective _____ .

87. Single _____ , unusual examples, and testimonials are frequently reported as if they were valid _____ .

Mastery Test

1. Data in psychology are typically gathered to answer questions about
   a. clinical problems
   b. human groups
   c. human cognition
   d. overt or covert behaviour

2. Who among the following would most likely study the behaviour of gorillas?
   a. developmental psychologist
   b. comparative psychologist
   c. environmental psychologist
   d. forensic psychologist

3. An engineering psychologist helps redesign an airplane to make it safer to fly. The psychologist's work reflects which of psychology's goals?
   a. understanding
   b. control
   c. prediction
   d. description

4. Who among the following placed the greatest emphasis on introspection?
   a. Watson
   b. Wertheimer
   c. Washburn
   d. Wundt

5. Which pair of persons had the most similar ideas?
   a. Titchener–Skinner
   b. James–Darwin
   c. Watson–Rogers
   d. Wertheimer–Maslow

6. The behaviourist definition of psychology clearly places great emphasis on
   a. overt behaviour
   b. conscious experience
   c. psychodynamic responses
   d. introspective analysis

7. As a profession, psychology is fully open to men and women, a fact that began with the success of
   a. O'Sullivan–Calkins
   b. Tyler–James
   c. Ladd–Franklin
   d. Neal–Collins

8. The idea that threatening thoughts are sometimes repressed would be of most interest to a
   a. structuralist
   b. psychoanalyst
   c. humanist
   d. Gestaltist

9. "A neutral, reductionistic, mechanistic view of human nature." This best describes which viewpoint?
   a. psychodynamic
   b. cognitive
   c. psychoanalytic
   d. biopsychological

10. Which of the following professional titles usually requires a doctorate degree?
    a. psychologist
    b. psychiatric social worker
    c. counsellor
    d. all of the preceding

11. The majority of all psychologists specialize in what branches of psychology?
    a. counselling and comparative
    b. applied and counselling
    c. psychodynamic and clinical
    d. counselling and clinical

12. When critically evaluating claims about behaviour it is important to also evaluate
    a. the source of anecdotal evidence
    b. the credentials of an authority
    c. the quality of the evidence
    d. the strength of one's intuition

13. Which of the following pairs is most different?
    a. pseudo-psychology–critical thinking
    b. graphology–pseudo-psychology
    c. palmistry–phrenology
    d. psychology–empirical evidence

14. The German anatomy teacher Franz Gall popularized
    a. palmistry
    b. phrenology
    c. graphology
    d. astrology

15. A tendency to believe flattering descriptions of oneself is called
    a. the Barnum effect
    b. the astrologer's dilemma
    c. the fallacy of positive instances
    d. uncritical acceptance

16. Descriptions of personality that contain both sides of several personal dimensions tend to create
    a. an illusion of accuracy
    b. disbelieve and rejection
    c. the astrologer's dilemma
    d. a system similar to phrenology

17. If an entire population is surveyed, it becomes unnecessary to obtain a
    a. control group
    b. random comparison
    c. random sample
    d. control variable

18. Control groups are most often used in
    a. naturalistic observation
    b. the clinical method
    c. Para science
    d. experiments

19. Concealing the observer can be used to minimize the
    a. observer bias effect
    b. double-blind effect
    c. observer effect
    d. effects of extraneous correlations

20. A psychologist studying lowland gorillas should be careful to avoid the
    a. anthropomorphic fallacy
    b. Gestalt fallacy
    c. psychodynamic fallacy
    d. fallacy of positive instances

21. Testing the hypothesis that frustration encourages aggression would require
    a. a field study
    b. operational definitions
    c. adult subjects
    d. perfect correlations

22. In experiments involving drugs, experimenters remain unaware of who received placebos in a _____ arrangement.
    a. zero-blind
    b. single-blind
    c. double-blind

    d.   control-blind

23. In psychology, the _____ variable is suspected cause of differences in _____ .
    a.   independent, the control group
    b.   dependent, the experimenter effect
    c.   independent, behaviour
    d.   dependent, correlations

24. A person who is observed crying may not be sad. This suggests that it is important to distinguish between
    a.   individual cases and generalizations
    b.   correlation and causation
    c.   control groups and experimental groups
    d.   observation and inference

25. In an experiment on the effects of hunger on the reading scores of elementary school children, reading scores are the
    a.   control variable
    b.   independent variable
    c.   dependent variable
    d.   reference variable

26. Which of the following correlation coefficients indicates a perfect relationship?
    a.   1.00
    b.   100.0
    c.   -1
    d.   both a and c

27. Jane Goodall's studies of chimpanzees in Tanzania are good examples of
    a.   field experiments
    b.   experimental control
    c.   correlation studies
    d.   naturalistic observations

28. To equalize the intelligence of members of the experimental group and the control group in an experiment, you could use
    a.   extraneous control
    b.   random assignment
    c.   independent control
    d.   subject replication

29. Which method would most likely be used to study the effects of tumors in the frontal lobes of the brain?
    a.   sampling method
    b.   correlation method
    c.   clinical method
    d.   experimental method

30. The release of endorphins by the pituitary gland helps explain the
    a.   experimenter effect
    b.   placebo effect

c. multiple-personality effect

d. gender-bias effect

31. Cause is to effect as _____ variable is to _____ variable.

    a. extraneous, dependent

    b. dependent, independent

    c. independent, extraneous

    d. independent, dependent

32. The specific procedures used to gather data are described in which section of a research report?

    a. introduction

    b. abstract

    c. method

    d. discussion

33. Which of the following correlations demonstrates a cause-effect relationship?

    a. .980

    b. 1.00

    c. .50

    d. none of the preceding

Solutions

Recite and Review

1. profession
2. mental
3. behaviour
4. evidence
5. planned or structured
6. research, method
7. development
8. learning
9. theorists
10. sense (or sensory)
11. animals
12. behaviour
13. social
14. behaviour
15. animal
16. understand
17. knowledge
18. laboratory
19. experience
20. adapt
21. Watson
22. responses
23. positive
24. thinking
25. whole
26. greater
27. unconscious
28. Freud
29. growth
30. image
31. potentials
32. humanism
33. blend
34. diversity (or differences)
35. values, rules
36. clinical
37. drugs
38. psychotherapy
39. masters, masters
40. divisions
41. basic
42. measurement
43. problem, results
44. valid (or useful)
45. definitions
46. theory
47. abstract, results
48. clinical
49. natural
50. effect, observer
51. animals
52. records
53. correlation (or relationship)
54. zero
55. perfect
56. minus
57. increases
58. increases
59. predictions
60. Cause
61. varied
62. change
63. independent
64. Dependent
65. prevent
66. group, group
67. characteristics
68. identical
69. effect
70. blind, blind
71. expected
72. case
73. natural
74. sample
75. untruthful (or inaccurate)
76. evaluate
77. critical
78. actively, ideas
79. evidence
80. false
81. Barnum
82. Skepticism
83. unreliable (or inaccurate)
84. groups
85. causation
86. valid (or scientific)
87. examples

Connections

1. A
2. B
3. C
4. D
5. E
6. F
7. G
8. H
9. I
10. J
11. D
12. J
13. A
14. I

15. E

16. B

17. C

18. F

19. G

20. H

21. C

22. A

23. G

24. J

25. B

26. H

27. D

28. E

29. F

30. I

31. I

32. A

33. C

34. F

35. B

36. D

37. E

38. H

39. J

40. G

41. D

42. I

43. B

44. A

45. J

46. H

47. E

48. F

49. G

50. C

Check Your Memory

1. F

2. F

3. T

4. F

5. F

6. F

7. F

8. T

9. F

10. T

11. F

12. T

13. T

14. F

15. T

16. T

17. T

18. T

19. F

20. F

21. T

22. T

23. T

24. F

25. T

26. F

27. F

28. T

29. F

30. T

31. T

32. F

33. F

34. T

35. T

36. F

37. T

38. F

39. F

40. F

41. F

42. F

43. T

44. F

45. F

46. T

47. F

48. F

49. T

50. F

51. T

52. T

53. T

54. F

55. T

56. T

57. F

58. F

59. F

60. F

61. T

62. T

63. F

64. T

65. F

66. F

67. F
68. F
69. T

Final Survey and Review

1. science, profession
2. behaviour, mental, processes
3. covert
4. empirical, data
5. Scientific
6. research, method
7. Developmental
8. theorists
9. Personality
10. Sensation
11. Comparative
12. Biopsychologists
13. social, behaviour
14. Cultural
15. animal, models
16. predict, control
17. philosophy
18. Wilhelm, Wundt
19. conscious, experience
20. structuralism
21. Functionalism, James
22. Behaviourism, stimuli
23. Skinner, reinforcers
24. Cognitive
25. Gestalt
26. Wertheimer, Gestalt, sum
27. psychoanalytic (or psychodynamic)
28. Freud, psychoanalysis
29. Humanistic, potentials

30. self-image, frame
31. self-actualism
32. behaviourism, humanism, biopsychology
33. eclectic
34. diversity, cultural
35. clinical, counselling
36. Psychiatrists, psychotherapy
37. psychoanalysis
38. Counsellors, psychiatric, social
39. Developmental, industrial, education
40. applied
41. evidence, measurements
42. hypothesis, theory
43. scientifically, testable
44. operational, procedures
45. theory, theories, observations
46. published, journals
47. experimental, survey
48. natural, settings, environments
49. observed, bias
50. anthropomorphic
51. observational, records
52. correlation
53. zero, perfect
54. closer
55. positive
56. increases, decreases
57. causation
58. controlled, experiment
59. observed, recorded
60. variable
61. independent, causes
62. Dependent, effects
63. Extraneous, outcome

64. controlled
65. experimental, control
66. personal, randomly
67. independent
68. placebo
69. single-blind, double-blind
70. experimenter, effect
71. self-fulfilling
72. case, studies, subject
73. clinical, tests
74. populations, representatives
75. biased, questions
76. critique, synthesize
77. evaluate
78. evidence
79. Scientific
80. phrenology, pseudo
81. uncritical, positive, Barnum
82. Skepticism, critical
83. biased
84. control
85. Correlation, correlation
86. observations
87. cases, generalizations

Mastery Test

1. D (p. 2)
2. B (p. 2)
3. B (p. 5)
4. D (p. 6)
5. B (p. 7)
6. A (p. 7)
7. C (p. 9)
8. B (p. 10)
9. D (p. 12)

10. A (p. 14)

11. D (p. 14)

12. C (p. 17)

13. A (p. 27)

14. B (p. 29)

15. D (p. 30)

16. A (p. 30)

17. C (p. 26)

18. D (p. 22)

19. C (p. 19)

20. A (p. 19)

21. B (p. 16)

22. C (p. 24)

23. C (p. 22)

24. D (p. 16)

25. C (p. 22)

26. D (p. 20)

27. D (p. 19)

28. B (p. 23)

29. C (p. 25)

30. B (p. 24)

31. D (p. 22)

32. C (p. 18)

33. D (p. 20)

Chapter 2

Brain and Behaviour

Chapter Overview

The brain and nervous system are made up of networks of neurons. Nerve impulses are basically electrical. Communication between neurons is chemical in that neurons release neurotransmitters which affect other neurons. Rather than merely carrying messages, neuropeptides regulate the activity of neurons in the brain. Neurogenesis is a process that grows new cells in the nervous system both in children and adults. Using stem cells to repair brain damage is a new method.

The nervous system includes the central nervous system (CNS), consisting of the brain and spinal cord, and the peripheral nervous system (PNS). The PNS includes the somatic system and the autonomic system, with its sympathetic and parasympathetic branches.

Conventional brain research relies on dissection, staining, ablation, deep lesioning, electrical recording, electrical stimulation, micro-electrode recording, EEG recording, and clinical studies. Newer methods make use of computer-enhanced images of the brain and its activities.

The basic functions of the lobes of the brain are as follows: occipital lobes—vision; parietal lobes—bodily sensation; temporal lobes—hearing and language; frontal lobes—motor control, speech, and abstract thought. Association areas of the cortex are related to complex abilities such as language, memory, and problem solving. The left and right cerebral hemispheres have different specialized abilities.

The brain is subdivided into the forebrain, midbrain, and hindbrain. The subcortex includes important brain structures at all three levels. These are: the medulla ("vegetative" functions), the cerebellum (coordination), the reticular formation (sensory and motor messages and arousal), the thalamus (sensory information), and the hypothalamus (basic motives). The limbic system is related to emotion.

The endocrine system provides chemical communication in the body through the release of hormones into the bloodstream.

Hand dominance ranges from strongly left- to strongly right-handed, with mixed handedness and ambidexterity in between. In general, the left-handed are less strongly lateralized in brain function than are right-handed persons.

Learning Objectives

1. Name the basic unit of the nervous system, state what it is specifically designed to do, and list and describe its four parts.

2. Explain how a nerve impulse (action potential) occurs and how it is an all-or-nothing event.

3. Describe the difference between the nature of a nerve impulse and the nature of the communication between neurons.

4. Explain how nerve impulses are carried from one neuron to another at the synapse.

5. Explain what determines whether a neuron will have an action potential triggered.

6. Explain the function of neuropeptides.

7. Differentiate a nerve from a neuron.

8. Describe the effect of myelin on the speed of the nerve impulse.

9. Explain what determines whether a nerve will regenerate. Briefly tell what the term *neurogenesis* means.

10. Explain what stem cells are and why they are used to repair some types of brain damage.

11. Chart the various subparts of the human nervous system and generally explain their functions.

12. Differentiate between the two branches of the autonomic nervous system.

13. Explain the mechanism of the reflex arc.

14. List and describe five techniques for studying the brain. Briefly describe how EEG works.

15. Describe each of the three scanning techniques for studying the entire brain as it functions.

16. Describe the main difference between the brains of lower and higher animals. Name what appears to be the foundation of human intellectual superiority. Describe the main difference between the brains of people who score high versus low on mental tests.

17. Define the term "hemispheres" and explain the function of the corpus callosum. Describe the problem known as spatial neglect.

18. Explain how and why a brain is "split" and describe what the resulting effects are.

19. Differentiate the abilities of the two hemispheres of the cerebral cortex. Describe what is known about their working together as well as how they process information.

20. Describe the function(s) of each of the following:
    a. occipital lobes
    b. parietal lobes (include the somatosensory areas)
    c. temporal lobes
    d. frontal lobes (include the motor cortex)
    e. associative areas (include Broca's and Wernicke's areas)

21. Explain the relationship between the size of the various parts of the somatosensory and motor areas of the cortex and the degree of sensitivity or importance of the corresponding body parts.

22. Describe the cause and effect of the two disorders aphasia and agnosia. Explain why there may be gender differences in aphasia following brain injuries.

23. List and be able to recognize the three areas of the subcortex.

24. Explain the function of each of the following parts of two of the three areas of the subcortex:
    a. hindbrain (brainstem)
        i)   medulla
        ii) cerebellum
        iii) reticular formation
    b. forebrain
        i)   thalamus
        ii) hypothalamus

25. Name the structures that comprise the limbic system and explain its function (include a description of the function of the amygdala and the hippocampus). Briefly describe the significance of "pleasure" and "aversive" areas in the limbic system.

26. Briefly explain the purpose of the endocrine system. Describe the action of hormones in the body.

27. Describe the effect that the following glands have on the body and behaviour:
    a. pituitary (include a description of giantism, hypopituitary dwarfism, and acromegaly)
    b. pineal
    c. thyroid (include a description of hyperthyroidism and hypothyroidism)
    d. adrenal medulla
    e. adrenal cortex (include a description of virilism, premature puberty, and the problems of anabolic steroids)

28. Describe the debate surrounding the assertion that the different hormones found in male and female fetuses are responsible for the different abilities in adult males and females.

29. Describe the relationship among handedness, brain dominance, and speech. Describe the element of handedness that appears to be inherited.

30. Explain how a person can determine which hemisphere is dominant.

31. State the incidence of left-handedness and discuss the relative advantages and/or disadvantages of being right-handed versus left-handed.

Practice Quizzes

Recite and Review

- ### *How do nerve cells operate and communicate?*

Recite and Review: Pages 41–45

1. The _____ and nervous system are made up of linked nerve cells called _____ , which pass information from one to another through synapses.

2. The basic conducting fibres of neurons are _____ , but dendrites (a receiving area), the soma (the cell body) and also a receiving area), and _____ terminals (the branching ends of a neuron) are also involved in communication.

3. The firing of an action potential (_____) is basically electrical, whereas communication between neurons is chemical.

4. An action potential occurs when the _____ potential is altered enough to reach the threshold for firing. At that point, sodium _____ flow into the axon, through _____ channels.

5. After each action potential, the neuron has a brief _____ after-potential. Next, potassium ions flow out of the _____ , restoring the resting potential.

6. The _____ potential is an all-or-nothing event.

7. Neurons release a _____ substance called neurotransmitters at the synapse. These cross to _____ sites on the receiving cell, causing it to be excited or inhibited. For example, the transmitter chemical acetylcholine activates _____ .

8. Chemicals called neuropeptides do not carry messages directly. Instead, they _____ the activity of other neurons.

9. Opiate-like neural regulators called enkephalins and endorphins are released in the brain to relieve _____ and stress.

• *What are the functions of major parts of the nervous system?*

Recite and Review: Pages 45−49

10. Nerves are made of large bundles of _____ and dendrites. Neurons and nerves in the peripheral nervous system can often regenerate; damage in the central nervous system is usually _____ , unless a repair is attempted by grafting or implanting healthy tissue.

11. The layer of fatty tissue coating the axon is called _____ .

12. The nervous system can be divided into the _____ nervous system (the _____ and spinal cord) and the peripheral nervous system.

13. While we lose many brain cells everyday, it is now believed that _____ neurons grow to replace some of them.

14. A new method to treat some types of brain damage involve _____ stem cells. These are _____ cells that will team up with existing cells in the damaged area.

15. The PNS includes the somatic (_____) and autonomic (_____) nervous systems.

16. The autonomic system has two divisions: the sympathetic (emergency, activating) _____ and the parasympathetic (sustaining, conserving) _____ .

17. Thirty-one pairs of spinal _____ leave the spinal cord. Twelve pairs of cranial _____ leave the brain directly. Together, they carry sensory and motor messages between the brain and the body.

18. The simplest _____ is a reflex arc, which involves a sensory neuron, a connector neuron, and a _____ neuron.

• *How do we know how the brain works?*

Recite and Review: Pages 49−52

19. Conventional brain research relies on dissection, staining, ablation, deep lesion-ing, and _____ studies.

20. Computer-enhanced techniques are providing three-dimensional _____ of the living human brain and its _____ . Examples of such techniques are CT scans, MRI scans, and PET scans.

• *How is the brain organized and what do its higher structures do?*

Recite and Review: Pages 52−58

21. The human _____ is marked by advanced corticalization, or enlargement of the cerebral _____ , which covers the outside surface of the cerebrum.

22. The _____ cerebral hemisphere contains speech or language "centres" in most people. It also specializes in _____ , calculating, judging time and rhythm, and ordering complex movements.

23. The _____ hemisphere is largely non-verbal. It excels at spatial and perceptual skills, visualization, and recognition of _____ , faces, and melodies.

24. "Split brains" have been created by _____ the corpus callosum. This type of surgery is usually performed on _____ patients. The split-brain individual shows a remarkable degree of independence between the right and left _____ .

25. Individuals born without a _____ callosum do not show as much independence between the two hemispheres probably because other brain _____ take over some of the functions of the corpus _____ .

26. Another way to summarize specialization in the brain is to say that the _____ hemisphere is good at analysis and processing information sequentially; the _____ hemisphere processes information simultaneously and holistically.

27. The most basic functions of the lobes of the cerebral cortex are as follows: occipital lobes— _____ ; parietal lobes—bodily sensation; temporal lobes— _____ and language; frontal lobes—motor control, speech, and abstract thought.

• *Why are the brain's association areas important? What happens when they are injured?*

Recite and Review: Pages 58—60

28. Association areas receive their input from the _____ areas and are involved in transforming this information in the _____ skills expressed by the brain such as perception, language, memory, and problem-solving.

29. Damage to either Broca's area or Wernicke's area causes _____ and language problems known as aphasias.

30. Damage to Broca's area causes problems with _____ and pronunciation. Damage to Wernicke's area causes problems with the _____ of words.

• *What kinds of behaviours are controlled by the subcortex?*

Recite and Review: Pages 60—63

31. All of the brain areas below the _____ are called the subcortex.

32. The medulla contains centres essential for reflex control of _____ , breathing, and other "vegetative" functions.

33. The cerebellum maintains _____ , posture, and muscle tone.

34. The reticular formation directs sensory and motor messages, and part of it, known as the RAS, acts as an _____ system for the cerebral cortex.

35. The thalamus carries _____ information to the cortex. The hypothalamus exerts powerful control over eating, drinking, sleep cycles, body temperature, and other basic _____ and behaviours.

36. The limbic system is strongly related to _____ and motivated behaviour. It also contains distinct reward and punishment areas.

37. A part of the limbic system called the amygdala is related to an alert system that triggers a _____ response in a danger situation. An area known as the hippocampus is important for forming _____ .

- ### *Does the glandular system affect behaviour?*

Recite and Review: Pages 63—66

38. The endocrine system provides _____ communication in the body through the release of _____ into the bloodstream. Endocrine glands influence moods, behaviour, and even personality.

39. Many of the endocrine glands are influenced by the pituitary (the " _____ gland"), which is in turn influenced by the hypothalamus.

40. The pituitary supplies _____ hormone. Too little GH causes _____ ; too much causes giantism or acromegaly.

41. Body rhythms and _____ cycles are influenced by melatonin, secreted by the pineal gland.

42. The thyroid gland regulates _____ . Hyperthyroidism refers to an overactive thyroid gland; hypothyroidism to an underactive thyroid.

43. The adrenal glands supply _____ and norepinephrine to activate the body. They also regulate salt balance, responses to stress, and they are a secondary source of _____ hormones.

44. Evidence shows that part of the gender differences in mental abilities (mathematical reasoning, verbal skills, motor skills) are due to the presence of _____ hormones in male and female _____ .

- ### *In what ways do right- and left-handed individuals differ?*

Recite and Review: Psychology in Action

45. Hand dominance ranges from strongly left- to strongly right-handed, with _____ handedness and ambidexterity in between.

46. Ninety percent of the population is basically _____ , 10 percent _____ .

47. The vast majority of people are right-handed and therefore _____ brain dominant for motor skills. Ninety-seven percent of right-handed persons and 68 percent of the left-handed also produce _____ from the left hemisphere.

48. In general, the _____ are less strongly lateralized in brain function than are _____ persons.

Connections

1. _____ soma
2. _____ neurilemma
3. _____ axon collateral
4. _____ myelin
5. _____ dendrites
6. _____ axon terminals
7. _____ axon

8. _____ spinal cord
9. _____ autonomic system
10. _____ parasympathetic
11. _____ peripheral nervous system
12. _____ sympathetic branch
13. _____ brain
14. _____ somatic system

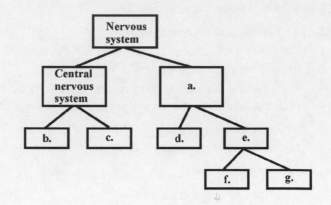

15. _____ Wernicke's area
16. _____ temporal lobe
17. _____ cerebellum
18. _____ Broca's area
19. _____ parietal lobe
20. _____ frontal lobe
21. _____ occipital lobe

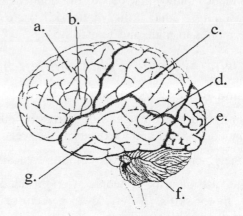

22. _____ midbrain
23. _____ reticular formation
24. _____ cerebrum
25. _____ medulla
26. _____ hypothalamus
27. _____ corpus callosum
28. _____ pituitary
29. _____ spinal cord
30. _____ thalamus

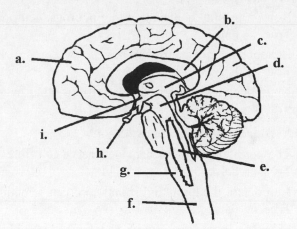

31. _____ pituitary	a.	brain waves
32. _____ pineal gland	b.	radioactive glucose
33. _____ thyroid gland	c.	testosterone
34. _____ adrenal glands	d.	surgery
35. _____ testes	e.	metabolism
36. _____ CT scan	f.	electrode
37. _____ EEG	g.	growth hormone
38. _____ ablation	h.	epinephrine
39. _____ deep lesioning	i.	computerized X-rays
40. _____ PET scan	j.	melatonin

Check Your Memory

Check Your Memory: Pages 41—45

1. The dendrites receive incoming information from the neurilemma.
   True or False

2. Human axons may be up to a metre long.
   True or False

3. The resting potential is about plus 70 millivolts.
   True or False

4. The interior of the axon becomes positive during an action potential.
   True or False

5. The action potential is an all-or-nothing event.
   True or False

6. The negative after-potential is due to an inward flow of potassium ions.
   True or False

7. Nerve impulses travel faster in axons surrounded by myelin.
   True or False

8. Neurotransmitters activate other neurons, neuropeptides activate muscles and glands.
   True or False

9. Enkephalins are neuropeptides.
   True or False

10. Neuropeptides regulate the activity of other neurons.
    True or False

Check Your Memory: Pages 45—49

11. The neurilemma helps damaged nerve cell fibres regenerate after an injury.
    True or False

12. Neurons in the brain and spinal cord can sometimes be repaired by neurogenesis.
    True or False

13. Liisa Galea's research with rodents has provided evidence that neurogenesis
    can occur under any circumstances.
    True or False

14. A new technique to repair damaged areas to the brain or the spinal cord involves injecting stem cells.
    True or False

15. The word *autonomic* means "self-limiting."
    True or False

16. The parasympathetic branch quiets the body and returns it to a lower level of arousal.
    True or False

17. The sympathetic system generally controls voluntary behaviour.
    True or False

18. Thirty-one cranial nerves leave the brain directly.
    True or False

19. "Fight-or-flight" emergency reactions are produced by the autonomic nervous system.
    True or False

20. Activity in the parasympathetic system increases heart rate and respiration.
    True or False

21. In a reflex arc, motor neurons carry messages to effector cells.
    True or False

Check Your Memory: Pages 49—52

22. Wilder Penfiled, a Canadian neurosurgeon, was able to map some brain areas in
    humans using electrical stimulation.
    True or False

23. Deep lesioning in the brain is usually done surgically.
    True or False

24. Micro-electrodes are needed in order to record from single neurons.
    True or False

25. CT scans form "maps" of brain activity.
    True or False

26. Electroencephalography records waves of electrical activity produced by the brain.
    True or False

27. Radioactive glucose is used to make PET scans.
    True or False

Check Your Memory: Pages 52—58

28. Elephants have brain-body ratios similar to those of humans.
    True or False

29. The corpus callosum connects the right and left brain hemispheres.
    True or False

30. The cerebellum makes up a large part of the cerebral cortex.
    True or False

31. Much of the cerebral cortex is made up of grey matter.
    True or False

32. Damage to the left cerebral hemisphere usually causes spatial neglect.
    True or False

33. In general, smart brains tend to be the hardest working brains.
    True or False

34. The right half of the brain mainly controls left body areas.
    True or False

35. Roger Sperry won a Nobel prize for his work on corticalization.
    True or False

36. Cutting the reticular formation produces a "split brain."
    True or False

37. Acallosal individuals will, from birth, perform as well as individuals with an
    intact corpus callosum on complex tasks.
    True or False

38. Information from the right side of vision is sent directly to the right cerebral hemisphere.
    True or False

39. The right hemisphere tends to be good at speaking, writing, and math.
    True or False

40. The left hemisphere is mainly involved with analysis.
    True or False

41. Both brain hemispheres are normally active at all times.
    True or False

42. The motor cortex is found on the occipital lobes.
    True or False

43. The somatosensory area is located on the parietal lobes.
    True or False

44. Electrically stimulating the motor cortex causes movement in various parts of the body.
    True or False

Check Your Memory: Pages 58—60

45. Large parts of the lobes of the brain are made up of association cortex.
    True or False

46. Damage to either brain hemisphere usually causes an aphasia.
    True or False

47. A person with Broca's aphasia might say "pear" when shown an apple.
    True or False

48. Damage to Wernicke's area causes the condition known as spatial neglect.
    True or False

49. Women are much more likely than men to use both cerebral hemispheres for language processing.
    True or False

Check Your Memory: Pages 60—63

50. The cerebrum makes up much of the medulla.
    True or False

51. Injury to the medulla may affect breathing.
    True or False

52. Injury to the cerebellum affects attention and wakefulness.
    True or False

53. Smell is the only major sense that does not pass through the thalamus.
    True or False

54. Stimulating various parts of the limbic system can produce rage, fear, pleasure, or arousal.
    True or False

55. The hippocampus is associated with hunger and eating.
    True or False

Check Your Memory: Pages 63—66

56. The rewarding effect of drugs comes from activating pathways of the limbic system.
    True or False

57. Androgens ("male" hormones) are related to the sex drive in both men and women.
    True or False

58. "Normal short" children grow faster when given synthetic growth hormone, but
    their final height is not taller.
    True or False

59. Activity of the pituitary is influenced by the hypothalamus.
    True or False

60. A person who is slow, sleepy, and overweight could be suffering from hypothyroidism.
    True or False

61. Virilism and premature puberty may be caused by problems with the adrenal glands.
    True or False

62. Steroid drugs may cause sexual impotence and breast enlargement in males.
    True or False

63. Injecting female rats with the female hormone estrogen will improve their spatial performance.
    True or False

Check Your Memory: Psychology in Action

64. Left-handers have an advantage in fencing, boxing, and baseball.
    True or False

65. Most left-handed persons produce speech from their right hemispheres.
    True or False

66. Left- or right-handedess is inherited from one's parents.
    True or False

67. On average, left-handed persons die at younger ages than right-handed persons do.
    True or False

Final Survey and Review

- ### *How do nerve cells operate and communicate?*

1. The brain and nervous system are made up of linked nerve cells called _____ , which pass information from one to another through _____ .

2. The basic conducting fibres of neurons are axons, but _____ (a receiving area), the _____ (the cell body and also a receiving area), and axon terminals (the branching ends of an axon) are also involved in communication.

3. The firing of an _____ _____ (nerve impulse) is basically electrical, whereas communication between neurons is chemical.

4. An action potential occurs when the resting potential is altered enough to reach the _____ for firing. At that point, _____ ions flow into the axon, through ion channels.

5. After each action potential, the neuron has a brief negative _____ . Next, _____ ions flow out of the axon, restoring the resting potential.

6. The action potential is an _____ event.

7. In chemical synapses, neurons release _____ . These cross to receptor sites on the receiving cell, causing it to be excited or inhibited. For example, the transmitter chemical _____ activates muscles.

8. Chemicals called _____ do not carry messages directly. Instead, they regulate the activity of other neurons.

9. Opiate-like neural regulators called enkephalins and _____ are released in the brain to relieve pain and stress.

- ### *What are the functions of major parts of the nervous system?*

10. _____ are made of axons and associated tissues. Neurons and nerves in the _____ nervous system can often regenerate; damage in the _____ nervous system is usually permanent.

11. The layer of fatty tissue coating the _____ is called myelin.

12. The nervous system can be divided into the _____ nervous system (the brain and _____) and the peripheral nervous system.

13. While we lose many brain cells everyday, it is now believed that new neurons grow to replace _____ of them.

14. A new method to treat some types of brain damage involves injecting _____ _____ . These immature cells will _____ _____ with existing cells in the damaged area.

15. The PNS includes the _____ (bodily) and _____ (involuntary) nervous systems.

16. The autonomic system has two divisions: the _____ (emergency, activating) branch and the _____ (sustaining, conserving) branch.

17. Thirty-one pairs of _____ nerves leave the spinal cord. Twelve pairs of _____ nerves leave the brain directly. Together, these nerves carry sensory and _____ messages between the brain and the body.

18. The simplest behaviour is a _____ , which involves a sensory neuron, a _____ neuron, and a _____ neuron.

• *How do we know how the brain works?*

19. Conventional brain research relies on _____ (separation into parts), staining, ablation, deep lesioning, electrical recording, electrical _____ , micro-electrode recording, EEG recording, and clinical studies.

20. Computer-enhanced techniques are providing three-dimensional images of the living human brain and its activities. Examples of such techniques are CT scans, _____ scans, and _____ scans, which record brain activity.

• *How is the brain organized and what do its higher structures do?*

21. The human brain is marked by advanced _____ , or enlargement of the cerebral cortex, which covers the outside surface of the _____ .

22. The right cerebral _____ contains speech or language "centres" in most people. It also specializes in writing, calculating, judging time and rhythm, and ordering complex _____ .

23. The left hemisphere is largely non-verbal. It excels at _____ and perceptual skills, visualization, and recognition of patterns, _____ , and melodies.

24. "Split brains" have been created by cutting the _____ _____ of adult patients. The split-brain individual shows a remarkable degree of independence between the right and left _____ .

25. Individuals born without a _____ _____ do not show as much independence between the two _____ probably because other _____ structures take over some of the functions.

26. Another way to summarize specialization in the brain is to say that the left hemisphere is good at _____ and processing information sequentially; the right hemisphere processes information _____ and holistically.

27. The most basic functions of the lobes of the cerebral _____ are as follows: occipital lobes—vision; parietal lobes—bodily _____ ; temporal lobes—hearing and language; frontal lobes—motor control, _____ , and abstract thought.

• *Why are the brain's association areas important? What happens when they are injured?*

28. Association areas on the cortex are neither _____ nor _____ in function. They are related to more complex skills such as _____ , memory, recognition, and problem solving.

29. Damage to either Broca's area or Wernicke's area causes speech and language problems known as _____ .

30. Damage to _____ area causes problems with speech and pronunciation. Damage to _____ area causes problems with the meaning of words.

• *What kinds of behaviours are controlled by the subcortex?*

31. All of the brain areas below the cortex are called the _____ .

32. The _____ contains centres essential for reflex control of heart rate, breathing, and other "vegetative" functions.

33. The _____ maintains coordination, posture, and muscle tone.

34. The _____ formation directs sensory and motor messages, and part of it, known as the RAS, acts as an activating system for the _____ .

35. The _____ carries sensory information to the cortex. The _____ exerts powerful control over eating, drinking, sleep cycles, body temperature, and other basic motives and behaviours.

36. The _____ system is strongly related to emotion and motivation. It also contains distinct _____ and punishment areas.

37. A part of the limbic system called the _____ is related to fear. An area known as the _____ is important for forming lasting memories.

• *Does the glandular system affect behaviour?*

38. The _____ system provides chemical communication in the body through the release of hormones into the _____ .

39. Many of the endocrine glands are influenced by the _____ (the "master gland"), which is in turn influenced by the _____ .

40. The _____ supplies growth hormone. Too little GH causes dwarfism; too much causes giantism or _____ .

41. Body rhythms and sleep cycles are influenced by _____ , secreted by the _____ gland.

42. The thyroid gland regulates metabolism. Hyperthyroidism refers to an _____ thyroid gland; hypothyroidism to an _____ thyroid.

43. The _____ glands supply epinephrine and norepinephrine to activate the body. They also regulate salt balance, responses to _____ , and they are a secondary source of sex hormones.

44. Evidence shows that part of the gender differences in _____ _____ are due to the presence of different _____ in male and female fetuses.

• *In what ways do right- and left-handed individuals differ?*

45. _____ _____ ranges from strongly left- to strongly right-handed, with mixed handedness and _____ in between.

46. _____ percent of the population is basically right-handed, _____ percent left-handed.

47. The vast majority of people are _____ and therefore _____ brain dominant for motor skills. Ninety-seven percent of right-handed persons and sixty-eight percent of the left-handed produce speech from the _____ hemisphere.

48. In general, the left-handed are less strongly _____ in brain function than are right-handed persons.

Mastery Test

1. At times of emergency, anger, or fear, what part of the nervous system becomes more active?
    a. corpus callosum of the forebrain
    b. sympathetic branch of the ANS
    c. parasympathetic branch of the PNS
    d. Broca's area

2. The highest and largest brain area in humans is the
   a. cerebrum
   b. cerebellum
   c. frontal lobes
   d. grey matter of the callosum

3. A tumor in which brain area would most likely cause blind spots in vision?
   a. occipital lobe
   b. temporal lobe
   c. somatosensory area
   d. association cortex

4. Neurotransmitters are found primarily in
   a. the spinal cord
   b. the neurilemma
   c. axon terminals
   d. motor neurons

5. Enkephalins are an example of
   a. acetylcholine blockers
   b. neuropeptides
   c. receptor sites
   d. adrenal hormones

6. Electrically stimulating a portion of which brain area would produce movements in the body?
   a. occipital lobe
   b. frontal lobe
   c. parietal lobe
   d. temporal lobe

7. When a neuron reaches its threshold, a/an _____ occurs.
   a. volume potential
   b. ion potential
   c. action potential
   d. dendrite potential

8. A person's ability to work as a commercial artist would be most impaired by damage to the
   a. left temporal lobe
   b. right cerebral hemisphere
   c. left cerebral hemisphere
   d. frontal association cortex

9. ESB will most likely produce anger if it is applied somewhere in the
   a. association cortex
   b. limbic system
   c. parasympathetic branch
   d. reticular activating system

10. Information in neurons usually flows in what order?
    a.　soma, dendrites, axon
    b.　dendrites, soma, axon
    c.　dendrites, myelin, axon terminals
    d.　axon, soma, axon terminals

11. Regulating the activity of other neurons is most characteristic of
    a.　neuropeptides
    b.　acetylcholine
    c.　reflex arcs
    d.　resting potentials

12. Nerve impulses occur when _____ rush into the axon.
    a.　sodium ions
    b.　potassium ions
    c.　negative charges
    d.　neurotransmitters

13. Attempts to repair brain injuries by injecting immature stem cells into the damaged area make use of the recently discovered existence of
    a.　myelin
    b.　neurogenesis
    c.　neuropeptides
    d.　corticalization

14. Negative after-potentials are caused by the outward flow of _____ from the axon.
    a.　negative charges
    b.　potassium ions
    c.　neurotransmitters
    d.　sodium ions

15. A person who says "bife" for bike and "seep" for sleep probably suffers from
    a.　Broca's aphasia
    b.　Wernicke's aphasia
    c.　spatial neglect
    d.　the condition known as "mindblindness"

16. Damage to which part of the limbic system would most likely impair memory?
    a.　thalamus
    b.　hypothalamus
    c.　amygdala
    d.　hippocampus

17. Changes in heart rate, blood pressure, digestion, and sweating are controlled by the
    a.　thoracic nerves
    b.　parietal lobes
    c.　somatic system

    d.   autonomic system

18. In which of the following pairs are both structures part of the forebrain?

    a.   medulla, hypothalamus

    b.   cerebrum, cerebellum

    c.   medulla, thalamus

    d.   cerebrum, thalamus

19. Which of the following is a specialized type of X-ray?

    a.   PET scan

    b.   CT scan

    c.   MRI scan

    d.   EEG scan

20. Which two problems are associated with the pituitary gland?

    a.   dwarfism, acromegaly

    b.   virilism, acromegaly

    c.   mental retardation, dwarfism

    d.   giantism, premature puberty

21. The cerebral hemispheres are interconnected by the

    a.   reticular system

    b.   cerebellum

    c.   cerebrum

    d.   corpus callosum

22. Damage to which of the following would most likely make it difficult for a person to play catch with a ball?

    a.   reticular formation

    b.   limbic system

    c.   cerebellum

    d.   association cortex

23. Speech, language, calculation, and analysis are special skills of the

    a.   right cerebral hemisphere

    b.   limbic system

    c.   left cerebral hemisphere

    d.   right somatosensory area

24. The usual flow of information in a reflex arc is

    a.   cranial nerve, connector nerve, spinal nerve

    b.   sensory neuron, connector neuron, motor neuron

    c.   effector cell, interneuron, connector neuron

    d.   sensory neuron, connector neuron, reflex neuron

25. A person will "hear" a series of sounds when which area of the cortex is electrically stimulated?

    a.   frontal lobe

    b.   parietal lobe

c. occipital lobe

d. temporal lobe

26. Which of the following pairs contains the "master gland" and its master?

    a. pineal—thalamus

    b. thyroid—RAS

    c. pituitary—hypothalamus

    d. adrenal—cortex

27. Many basic motives and emotions are influenced by the

    a. thalamus

    b. hypothalamus

    c. corpus callosum

    d. cerebellum

28. Both surgical ablation and _____ remove brain tissue.

    a. the MEG technique

    b. tomography

    c. micro-electrode sampling

    d. deep lesioning

29. Which of the following techniques requires access to the interior of the brain?

    a. micro-electrode recording

    b. EEG recordings

    c. PET scanning

    d. functional MRI

30. Which of the following statements about handedness is FALSE?

    a. Handedness is inherited from one's parents.

    b. A majority of left-handers produce speech from the left hemisphere.

    c. The left-handed are less lateralized than the right-handed.

    d. Left-handedness is an advantage in boxing and fencing.

31. Which of the following explanations is true concerning the relationship found between hormone levels and the behavioural differences between men and women?

    a. Sex differences are due to the presence of different hormones in male and female fetuses.

    b. Finding such a relationship is a guarantee that hormone levels are the cause of gender differences.

    c. These sex differences are caused by the different upbringing boys and girls receive in our society.

    d. Both A and C are two possible causes for this relationship.

32. Which famous Canadian neurosurgeon did research in the 1960s on the specialization of the cerebral cortex using electrical stimulation?

    a. Doreen Kimura

    b. Liisa Galea

    c. Wilder Penfield

    d. Donald Hebb

Solutions

Recite and Review

1. brain, neurons
2. axons, axon
3. nerve impulse
4. resting, ions, ion
5. negative, axon
6. action
7. chemical, receptor, muscles
8. regulate
9. pain
10. axons, permanent
11. myelin
12. central, brain
13. new
14. injecting, immature
15. bodily, involuntary
16. branch, branch
17. nerves, nerves
18. behaviour, motor
19. clinical
20. images, activity
21. brain, cortex
22. left, writing
23. right, patterns
24. cutting, adult, hemispheres
25. corpus, structures, callosum
26. left, right
27. vision, hearing
28. sensory, complex
29. speech
30. grammar, meaning
31. cortex
32. heart rate
33. coordination
34. activating
35. sensory, motives
36. emotion
37. fear, memories
38. chemical, hormones
39. master
40. growth, dwarfism
41. sleep
42. metabolism
43. epinephrine, sex
44. different, fetuses
45. mixed
46. right-handed, left-handed
47. left, speech
48. left-handed, right-handed

Connections

1. G
2. D
3. E
4. C
5. A
6. F
7. B
8. C or B
9. E
10. F or G
11. A
12. F
13. C or B
14. D
15. D
16. G
17. F
18. B
19. C
20. A
21. E
22. D
23. E
24. A
25. G
26. I
27. B
28. H
29. F
30. C
31. G
32. J
33. E
34. H
35. C
36. I
37. A
38. D
39. F
40. B

Check Your Memory

1. F
2. T
3. F
4. T
5. T
6. F
7. T
8. F
9. T
10. T

11. T	47. F	13. some
12. T	48. F	14. stem, cells, team, up
13. F	49. T	15. somatic, autonomic
14. T	50. F	16. sympathetic, parasympathetic
15. F	51. T	17. spinal, cranial, motor
16. T	52. F	18. reflex arc, connector, motor
17. F	53. T	19. dissection, stimulation
18. F	54. T	20. MRI, PET
19. T	55. F	21. corticalization, cerebrum
20. F	56. T	22. hemisphere, movements
21. T	57. T	23. spatial, faces
22. T	58. T	24. corpus, callosum, hemispheres
23. F	59. T	25. corpus, callosum, hemispheres, brain
24. T	60. T	
25. F	61. T	26. analysis, simultaneously
26. T	62. T	27. cortex, sensation, speech
27. T	63. F	28. sensory, motor, language
28. F	64. F	29. aphasias
29. T	65. F	30. Broca's, Wernicke's
30. F	66. F	31. subcortex
31. T	67. F	32. medulla
32. F		33. cerebellum
33. F		34. reticular, cerebral cortex
34. T		35. thalamus, hypothalamus
35. F	**Final Survey and Review**	36. limbic, reward
36. F		37. amygdala, hippocampus
37. F	1. neurons, synpases	38. endocrine, bloodstream
38. F	2. dendrites, soma	39. pituitary, hypothalamus
39. F	3. action , potential	40. pituitary, acromegaly
40. T	4. threshold, sodium	41. melatonin, pineal
41. T	5. after-potential, potassium	42. overactive, underactive
42. F	6. all-or-nothing	43. adrenal, stress
43. T	7. neurotransmitters, acetylcholine	44. mental, abilities, hormones
44. T	8. neuropeptides	45. Hand, dominance, ambidexterity
45. T	9. endorphins	46. Ninety, ten
46. F	10. Nerves, peripheral, central	47. right-handed, left, left
	11. axon	
	12. central, spinal cord	

48. lateralized

31. D (p. 65)

32. C (p. 49)

Mastery Test

1. B (p. 47)

2. A (p. 52)

3. A (p. 57)

4. C (p. 41)

5. B (p. 45)

6. B (p. 57)

7. C (p. 43)

8. B (p. 56)

9. B (p. 62)

10. B (p. 42)

11. A (p. 44)

12. A (p. 43)

13. B (p. 45)

14. B (p. 43)

15. A (p. 59)

16. D (p. 62)

17. D (p. 47)

18. D (p. 61)

19. B (p. 50)

20. A (p. 64)

21. D (p. 53)

22. C (p. 60)

23. C (p. 56)

24. B (p. 48)

25. D (p. 57)

26. C (p. 64)

27. B (p. 62)

28. D (p. 49)

29. A (p. 49)

30. A (p. 68)

Chapter 3

Human Development

Chapter Overview

Heredity affects personal characteristics, including temperament, and it organizes the human growth sequence. Environmental influences can have especially lasting effects during critical periods in development. Prenatal development is affected by diseases, drugs, radiation, and the mother's diet, health, and emotions. Early perceptual, intellectual, and emotional deprivation seriously retards development. Deliberate enrichment of the environment has a beneficial effect on early development.

Most psychologists accept that heredity and environment are inseparable and interacting forces. A child's developmental level reflects heredity, environment, and the effects of the child's own behaviour.

Human newborns have adaptive reflexes, are capable of learning, and have visual preferences, especially for familiar faces. Maturation underlies the orderly sequence of motor, cognitive, language, and emotional development.

Emotional attachment of infants to their caregivers is a critical event in social development.

Caregiving styles affect social, emotional, and intellectual development. Optimal caregiving includes proactive involvement, a good fit between the temperaments of parent and child, and responsiveness to a child's needs and signals. Three major parenting styles are authoritarian, permissive, and authoritative (effective). Effective parental discipline tends to emphasize child management techniques, rather than power assertion or withdrawal of love.

Language development is based on a biological predisposition, which is augmented by learning. Language acquisition begins with prelanguage communication between parent and child.

Jean Piaget theorized that children go through a series of cognitive stages as they develop intellectually. Learning principles provide an alternate explanation which does not assume that cognitive development occurs in stages. Lev Vygotsky's sociocultural theory says that cognitive gains occur primarily in a child's zone of proximal development. Adults who engage in the scaffolding of a child's intellectual growth also impart cultural values and beliefs to the child.

Responsibility, mutual respect, consistency, love, encouragement, and clear communication are features of effective parenting.

Learning Objectives

1. Define developmental psychology.

2. Explain the basic mechanisms of the transmission of heredity.

3. Define or describe each of the following terms:
   a. chromosome
   b. DNA
   c. gene
   d. polygenic

    e.   dominant trait (gene)

    f.   recessive trait (gene)

4.   Define the terms *senescence* and *human growth sequence.*

5.   Characterize the three types of children according to temperament.

6.   Briefly describe the impact that environment can have on development.

7.   Briefly discuss the concept of critical periods.

8.   Distinguish between congenital and genetic problems. Define the term *teratogen.*

9.   Discuss the effects of environmental influences (including drugs and tobacco) on an unborn child.

10.   Describe the symptoms of fetal alcohol syndrome.

11.   Compare, contrast, and give examples of the effects of enrichment and deprivation on development.

12.   Discuss the effects of deliberate enrichment of the environment in infancy.

13.   Explain what is meant by the nature-nurture controversy. Discuss the outcome of this debate.

14.   Define the term *developmental level* and list the three factors which combine to determine it.

15.   Name and describe four adaptive reflexes of a neonate.

16.   Describe the intellectual capabilities and the sensory preferences of a neonate.

17.   Discuss the concepts of maturation, cephalocaudal pattern, proximodistal pattern, and readiness.

18.   Describe (in general) the course of emotional development according to Bridges.

19.   Discuss the concept emotional attachment (including the concept of separation anxiety).

20.   Differentiate between the three types of attachment identified by Mary Ainsworth.

21.   Discuss the effects of daycare on a child's sense of security and attachment. Include a brief discussion of the role of play in social development.

22.   Discuss the meaning and importance of infant affectional needs.

23.   Describe the range of effects of the maternal caregiving styles.

24.   Discuss the importance of paternal influences in child development.

25.   Describe Baumrind's three major styles of parenting, including characteristics of both parents and children in each style.

26.   Give a brief description of each of the following child-rearing techniques and describe their effects on children and children's self-esteem:

    a.   power assertion

    b.   withdrawal of love

    c.   management techniques

27.   List and briefly describe five stages of language acquisition (including crying).

28.   Briefly discuss the period known as the "terrible twos."

29.   Describe the "language dance" and explain why children probably do it.

30.   Define the term *psycholinguist.* Describe the role of learning in the acquisition of language.

31. Explain how parents communicate with infants before the infants can talk. Include the ideas of signals, turn-taking, and parentese.

32. Explain how a child's intelligence and thinking differ from an adult's. Explain the concept of transformation.

33. With regard to Piaget's stages of cognitive development,
    a. explain the concepts of assimilation and accommodation
    b. list (in order) and briefly describe each stage
    c. evaluate the usefulness of Piaget's theory, including a review of current research on infant cognition

34. Briefly discuss Vygotsky's sociocultural theory, including how his theory differed from Piaget's theory. Define the terms *zone of proximal development* and *scaffolding*.

35. Define the terms *developmental milestone, developmental task* and *psychosocial dilemma*.

36. Explain, according to Erikson, how the resolution of the psychosocial dilemmas affects a person's adjustment to life.

37. State the nature of the psychosocial crisis and the nature of an adequate or inadequate outcome for each of Erikson's eight life stages. Match each crisis with the corresponding age range.

38. Describe the basic ingredients of positive parent-child interactions.

39. Discuss the elements of effective communication, including the concepts of I-messages and you-messages. Define natural and logical consequences.

Practice Quizzes

Recite and Review

• *How do heredity and environment affect development?*

Recite and Review: Pages 76−82

1. Developmental psychology is the study of progressive changes in _____ and abilities, from _____ to _____ .

2. The nature-nurture debate concerns the realtive contributions to development of heredity (_____) and environment (_____).

3. Hereditary instructions are carried by _____ (deoxyribonucleic acid) in the form of chromosomes and _____ in each cell of the body.

4. Most characteristics are polygenic (influenced by a combination of _____) and reflect the combined effects of dominant and recessive _____ .

5. Heredity organizes the general human growth sequence-the general pattern of _____ _____ from birth to death.

6. Heredity also influences differences in temperament (the physical core of _____).
    Most infants fall into one of three temperament categories: easy children, _____
    children, and slow-to-warm-up children.

7. Environment refers to all _____ conditions that affect development.

8. A variety of critical periods (times of increased _____ to environmental
    influences) exist in development.

9. Prenatal development is subject to _____ influences in the form of diseases,
    drugs, radiation, and the mother's diet, health, and emotions.

10. Prenatal damage to the fetus may cause congenital problems, or _____ _____ .
    In contrast, genetic problems are inherited from one's parents.

11. Early perceptual, intellectual, and emotional deprivation seriously retards _____ .

12. Poverty greatly increases the likelihood that children will experience various forms of _____ .

13. Research on deprivation suggests that attachment and perceptual stimulation are
    essential for _____ development.

14. Deliberate enrichment of the _____ in infancy and early childhood has
    a beneficial effect on development.

15. Ultimately, most psychologists accept that _____ and environment are
    inseparable and interacting forces.

16. A child's developmental level (current state of development) reflects heredity, environment,
    and the effects of the child's _____ _____ .

• *What can newborn babies do?*

Recite and Review: Pages 82–84

17. The human _____ (newborn) has a number of _____ reflexes, including
    the grasping, rooting, sucking, and Moro reflexes.

18. Newborns begin to _____ immediately and they imitate adults.

19. Tests in a looking chamber reveal a number of _____ preferences in the newborn. The
    neonate is drawn to complex, _____ , curved and brightly-lighted designs.

20. Infants prefer human face patterns, especially _____ _____ . In
    later infancy, interest in the unfamiliar emerges.

• *What influence does maturation have on early development?*

Recite and Review: Pages 84–87

21. Maturation of the body and nervous system underlies the orderly _____ of
    motor, cognitive, language, and emotional development.

22. While the rate of maturation varies from child to child, the _____ is nearly universal.

23. The development of _____ control (motor development) is cephalocaudal (from head
    to toe) and proximodistal (from the _____ of the body to the extremities).

24. Many early _____ are subject to the principle of readiness.

25. Emotional development begins with a capacity for _____ excitement. After
    that the first pleasant and unpleasant emotions develop.

26. Some psychologists believe that basic emotional expressions are _____ and
    that some appear as early as 2.5 months of age.

27. By age 10 months, babies display a social smile when other _____ are nearby.

• *Of what significance is a child's emotional bond with parents?*

Recite and Review: Pages 87—90

28. _____ development refers to the emergence of self-awareness and forming relationships with parents and others.
29. Emotional attachment of human infants to their _____ is a critical early event.
30. Infant attachment is reflected by _____ anxiety (distress when infants are away from parents).
31. Mary Ainsworth was a _____ psychologist who did extensive research on _____ _____ .
32. Ainsworth classified the quality of infant-mother attachment as _____ , insecure-avoidant, or insecure-ambivalent.
33. High-quality day care does not _____ children; high-quality care can, in fact, accelerate some areas of development.
34. A child's _____ development is also affected by playing with other children. For example, cooperative _____ is a major step toward participation in social life outside the family.
35. An infant's affectional _____ are every bit as important as more obvious needs for physical care.

• *How important are parenting roles?*

Recite and Review: Pages 90—93

36. Caregiving styles (patterns of parental care) have a substantial impact on emotional and intellectual _____ .
37. Maternal influences (the effects _____ have on their children) tend to centre on caregiving.
38. Optimal caregiving includes proactive maternal _____ , a good fit between the temperaments of parent and child, and responsiveness to a child's needs and _____ .
39. Paternal influences differ in their impact because _____ tend to function as a playmate for the infant.
40. Authoritarian parents enforce rigid _____ and demand strict obedience to _____ .
41. Overly permissive parents give little _____ and don't hold children accountable for their actions.
42. Authoritative (_____) parents supply firm and consistent guidance, combined with love and affection.
43. Effective child _____ is based on a consistent framework of guidelines for acceptable behaviour.
44. Good discipline tends to emphasize child management techniques (especially communication), rather than _____ assertion or withdrawal of _____ .
45. _____ techniques tend to produce the highest levels of self-esteem in children.

• *How do children acquire language?*

Recite and Review: Pages 93—96

46. Language development proceeds from control of _____ , to cooing, then babbling, the use of single words, and then to telegraphic _____ .
47. The patterns of early speech suggest a _____ predisposition to acquire language.
48. Psycholinguists (psychologists who study _____) believe that innate language predispositions are augmented by _____ .

49. Prelanguage communication between parent and child involves shared rhythms, non-verbal _____ , and turn-taking.

50. Parents help children learn language by using distinctive caretake _____ or parentese.

• *How do children learn to think?*

Recite and Review: Pages 97—102

51. The intellects of children are _____ abstract than those of adults. Jean Piaget theorized that _____ growth occurs through a combination of assimilation and accommodation.

52. Piaget also held that children go through a fixed series of cognitive _____ .

53. These are: sensorimotor (0-2), preoperational (2-7), _____ operational (7-11), and formal _____ (11-adult).

54. Learning theorists dispute the idea that cognitive development occurs in _____ . Recent studies suggest infants are capable of levels of thinking beyond that observed by _____ .

55. Young children don't seem to understand that the _____ of other people contain different information, beliefs, and thoughts than theirs do. In other words, they have a very simplified theory of _____ .

56. A one-step-ahead strategy that takes into account the child's level of _____ development helps adapt instruction to a child's needs.

57. According to the sociocultural theory of Russian scholar Lev Vygotsky, a child's interactions with others are most likely to aid _____ development if they they take place within the child's _____ of proximal _____ .

58. Adults help children learn how to think by scaffolding, or _____ , their attempts to solve problems or discover principles.

59. During their collaborations with adults, children learn important cultural _____ and values.

• *What are the typical tasks and dilemmas through the life span?*

Recite and Review: Pages 102—105

60. Psychologists are interested in _____ milestones, or prominent land-marks in personal development.

61. According to Erik Erikson, each life stage provokes a specific psychosocial _____ .

62. During childhood these are: trust versus mistrust, autonomy versus _____ and doubt, initiative versus _____ , and industry versus _____ .

63. In _____ , identity versus role confusion is the principal dilemma.

64. In young adulthood we face the dilemma of intimacy versus _____ . Later, generativity versus _____ becomes prominent.

65. Old age is a time when the dilemma of integrity versus _____ must be faced.

66. In addition, each life stage requires successful mastery of certain _____ tasks (personal changes required for optimal development).

• *How do effective parents discipline their children?*

Recite and Review: Psychology in Action

67. Responsibility, mutual _____ , consistency, love, encouragement, and clear _____ are features of effective parenting.

68. Much misbehaviour can be managed by use of I-_____ and by applying
_____ and logical consequences to children's behaviour.

Connections

1.	_____ grasping reflex	a.	rapid motor learning
2.	_____ rooting reflex	b.	DNA area
3.	_____ Moro reflex	c.	old age
4.	_____ readiness	d.	nature
5.	_____ gene	e.	palm grip
6.	_____ chromosome	f.	nurture
7.	_____ senescence	g.	startled embrace
8.	_____ heredity	h.	conception to birth
9.	_____ environment	i.	coloured body
10.	_____ prenatal period	j.	food search

11.	_____ FAS	a.	control of muscles and movement
12.	_____ Vygotsky	b.	caregiving style
13.	_____ motor development	c.	love and attention
14.	_____ super mother	d.	vowel sounds
15.	_____ critical period	e.	prenatal alcohol
16.	_____ attachment	f.	sociocultural theory
17.	_____ affectional needs	g.	vowels and consonants
18.	_____ cooing	h.	emotional bond
19.	_____ babbling	i.	caretaker speech
20.	_____ parentese	j.	environmental sensitivity

21.	_____ assimilation	a.	changing existing mental patterns
22.	_____ accommodation	b.	egocentrism
23.	_____ sensorimotor stage	c.	applying mental patterns
24.	_____ preoperational stage	d.	abstract principles
25.	_____ concrete operations	e.	social development
26.	_____ formal operations	f.	stage theory of cognitive development
27.	_____ psychosocial dilemmas	g.	Erikson
28.	_____ cooperative play	h.	conservation
29.	_____ Piaget	i.	adolescence
30.	_____ role confusion	j.	object permanence

Check Your Memory

Check Your Memory: Pages 76–82

1. Developmental psychology is the study of progressive changes in behaviour and abilities during childhood.
    True or False

2. Each cell in the human body (except sperm cells and ova) contains 23 chromosomes.
    True or False

3. The order of organic bases in DNA acts as a genetic code.
    True or False

4. Two brown-eyed parents cannot have a blue-eyed child.
    True or False

5. Identical twins have identical genes.
    True or False

6. More children have a slow-to-warm-up temperament than a difficult temperament.
    True or False

7. The critical period during which German measles can damage the fetus occurs near the end of pregnancy.
    True or False

8. Teratogens are substances capable of causing birth defects.
    True or False

9. An infant damaged by exposure to X-rays during the prenatal period suffers from a genetic problem.
    True or False

10. Many drugs can reach the fetus within the intrauterine environment.
    True or False

11. To prevent FAS, the best advice to pregnant women is to get plenty of rest, vitamins, and good nutrition.
    True or False

12. Cocaine use by a pregnant woman can injure the fetus.
    True or False

13. Poverty is associated with retarded emotional and intellectual development.
    True or False

14. In animals, enriched environments can actually increase brain size and weight.
    True or False

15. Reading daily to a child between the age of two and three will help his or her performance in the first 2 school years.
    True or False

16. There is evidence that the "Mozart effect" might just be based on the fact that college students were more alert or in a better mood after listening to music.
    True or False

Check Your Memory: Pages 82–84

17. The Moro reflex helps infants hold onto objects placed in their hands.
    True or False

18. As early as 9 weeks of age, infants can imitate actions a full day after seeing them.
    True or False

19. Three-day-old infants prefer to look at simple coloured backgrounds, rather than more complex patterns.
    True or False

20. After age 2, familiar faces begin to hold great interest for infants.
    True or False

Check Your Memory: Pages 84—87

21. Most infants learn to stand alone before they begin crawling.
    True or False

22. Motor development follows a top-down, centre-outward pattern.
    True or False

23. Toilet training should begin soon after a child is 1 year old.
    True or False

24. Anger and fear are the first two emotions to emerge in infancy.
    True or False

25. An infant's social smile appears within one month after birth.
    True or False

Check Your Memory: Pages 87—90

26. Most infants have to be 15 weeks old before they can recognize themselves on videotape.
    True or False

27. The psychologist Jean Piaget did extensive research on mother-infant attachment.
    True or False

28. Securely attached infants turn away from their mother when she returns after a period of separation.
    True or False

29. Any day care experience before the age of two will have a negative effect on a mother-child attachment.
    True or False

30. A small number of children per caregiver is desirable in day care settings.
    True or False

31. Children who spend too much time in poor quality day care tend to be insecure and aggressive.
    True or False

32. The question of when secure attachment occurs is less important than the question of whether it occurs at all.
    True or False

33. The Canadian study that observed adopted Romanian children showed that a lack of attention and affection in early life will not affect a child's capacity to develop a secure relationship with adults later on.
    True or False

34. Children typically first begin to engage in cooperative play around age 4 or 5.
    True or False

Check Your Memory: Pages 90—93

35. Early patterns of competence are well established by the time a child reaches age 3.
    True or False

36. The "zoo-keeper" mother provides poor physical, emotional, and intellectual care for her child.
    True or False

37. The goodness of fit between parents and children refers mainly to how compatible their temperaments are.
    True or False

38. Responsive parents are sensitive to a child's feelings, needs, rhythms, and signals.
    True or False

39. Fathers typically spend about half their time in caregiving and half playing with the baby.
    True or False

40. Paternal play tends to be more physically arousing for infants than maternal play is.
    True or False

41. Authoritarian parents view children as having adult-like responsibilities.
    True or False

42. Permissive parents basically give their children the message "Do it because I say so."
    True or False

43. The children of authoritarian parents tend to be independent, assertive, and inquiring.
    True or False

44. Asian cultures tend to be group-oriented and they emphasize interdependence among individuals.
    True or False

45. As a means of child discipline, power assertion refers to rejecting a child.
    True or False

46. Severely punished children tend to be defiant and aggressive.
    True or False

47. Punishment is most effective when it is given immediately after a disapproved act.
    True or False

Check Your Memory: Pages 93–96

48. The single-word stage begins at about 6 months of age.
    True or False

49. Deaf babies also show a babbling stage with hand gestures rather than verbal babbling.
    True or False

50. "That red ball mine," is an example of telegraphic speech.
    True or False

51. Noam Chomsky believes that basic language patterns are innate.
    True or False

52. The "terrible twos" refers to the two-word stage of language development.
    True or False

53. The "I'm going to get you" game is an example of prelanguage communication.
    True or False

54. Parentese is spoken in higher pitched tones with a musical inflection.
    True or False

Check Your Memory: Pages 97–102

55. According to Piaget, children first learn to make transformations at about age 3.
    True or False

56. Assimilation refers to modifying existing ideas to fit new situations or demands.
    True or False

57. Cognitive development during the sensorimotor stage is mostly non-verbal.
True or False

58. Reversibility of thoughts and the concept of conservation both appear during the concrete operational stage.
True or False

59. Three-year-old children are surprisingly good at understanding what other people are thinking.
True or False

60. An understanding of hypothetical possibilities develops during the preoperational stage.
True or False

61. Playing peekaboo is a good way to establish the permanence of objects for children in the sensorimotor stage.
True or False

62. Contrary to what Piaget observed, infants as young as 3 months of age show signs of object permanence.
True or False

63. Vygotsky's key insight was that children's thinking develops through dialogues with more capable persons.
True or False

64. Learning experiences are most helpful when they take place outside of a child's zone of proximal development.
True or False

65. Scaffolding is like setting up temporary bridges to help children move into new mental territory.
True or False

66. Vygotsky empasized that children use adults to learn about their culture and society.
True or False

Check Your Memory: Pages 102−105

67. Learning to read in childhood and establishing a vocation as an adult are typical life stages.
True or False

68. Psychosocial dilemmas occur when a person is in conflict with his or her social world.
True or False

69. Initiative versus guilt is the first psychosocial dilemma a child faces.
True or False

70. Answering the question "Who am I?" is a primary task during adolescence.
True or False

71. Generativity is expressed through taking an interest in the next generation.
True or False

Check Your Memory: Psychology in Action

72. Consistency of child discipline is more important than whether limits on children's behaviour are strict or lenient.
True or False

73. Encouragement means giving recognition for effort and improvement.
True or False

74. Logical consequences should be stated as you-messages.
True or False

Final Survey and Review

- ### *How do heredity and environment affect development?*

1. _____ psychology is the study of _____ changes in behaviour and abilities, from birth to death.

2. The nature-nurture debate concerns the relative contributions to development of _____ (nature) and _____ (nurture).

3. Hereditary instructions are carried by DNA (_____ acid) in the form of _____ ("coloured bodies") and genes in every cell.

4. Most characteristics are _____ (influenced by a combination of genes) and reflect the combined effects of dominant and _____ genes.

5. Heredity organizes the general human _____ _____ —the general pattern of physical development from birth to death.

6. Heredity also influences differences in _____ (the physical foundations of personality). Most infants fall into one of three categories: _____ children, difficult children, and _____ children.

7. _____ refers to all external conditions that affect development.

8. A variety of _____ _____ (times of increased sensitivity to environmental influences) exist in development.

9. During pregnancy, _____ development is subject to environmental influences in the form of diseases, _____ , _____ , and the mother's diet, health, and emotions.

10. Prenatal damage to the fetus may cause _____ problems, or birth defects. In contrast, _____ problems are inherited from one's parents.

11. Early perceptual and intellectual _____ seriously retards development.

12. _____ greatly increases the likelihood that children will experience various forms of deprivation.

13. Research on deprivation suggests that secure _____ and perceptual _____ are essential for normal development.

14. Deliberate _____ of the environment in infancy and early childhood has a beneficial effect on development.

15. Ultimately, most psychologists accept that heredity and environment are insep-arable and _____ forces.

16. A child's _____ _____ (current state of development) reflects heredity, environment, and the effects of the child's own behaviour.

- ### *What can newborn babies do?*

17. The human neonate (newborn) has a number of adaptive reflexes, including the _____ , rooting, _____ , and _____ reflexes.

18. Newborns begin to learn immediately and they _____ (mimic) adults.

19. Tests in a _____ _____ reveal a number of visual preferences in the newborn. The neonate is drawn to _____ , circular, curved, and brightly-lighted designs.

20. Infants prefer _____ _____ patterns, especially familiar faces. In later infancy, interest in the _____ emerges.

58

- ### *What influence does maturation have on early development?*

21. _____ of the body and _____ _____ underlies the orderly sequence of motor, cognitive, language, and emotional development.

22. While the _____ of maturation varies from child to child, the order is nearly _____ .

23. The development of muscular control (_____ development) is _____ (from head to toe) and _____ and from the centre of the body to the extremities.

24. Many early skills are subject to the principle of _____ .

25. Emotional development begins with a capacity for general _____ . After that the first _____ and _____ emotions develop.

26. Some psychologists believe that basic _____ expressions are innate and that some appear as early as 2.5 _____ of age.

27. By age 10 months, babies display a _____ smile when other people are nearby.

- ### *Of what significance is a child's emotional bond with parents?*

28. Social development refers to the emergence of self- _____ and forming _____ with parents and others.

29. Emotional _____ of human infants to their caregivers is a critical early event.

30. Infant attachment is reflected by separation _____ (distress when infants are away from parents).

31. _____ _____ was a developmental psychologist who did extensive research on _____ attachment.

32. _____ classified the quality of infant-mother attachment as secure, insecure- _____ , or insecure- _____ .

33. _____ day care does not harm children; excellent care can, in fact, _____ some areas of development.

34. A child's social development is also affected by playing with other children. For example, _____ play is a major step toward participation in social life outside the family.

35. An infant's _____ needs are every bit as important as more obvious needs for physical care.

- ### *How important are parenting styles?*

36. _____ _____ (patterns of parental care) have a substantial impact on emotional and intellectual development.

37. _____ influences (the effects mothers have on their children) tend to centre on _____

38. Optimal caregiving includes _____ maternal involvement, a good fit between the _____ of parent and child, and responsiveness to a child's needs and signals.

39. _____ influences differ in their impact because fathers tend to function as a _____ for the infant. _____ parents enforce rigid rules and demand strict obedience to authority.

40. Overly _____ parents give little guidance and don't hold children accountable for their actions.

41. _____ (effective) parents supply firm and consistent guidance, combined with love and affection.

42. Effective child discipline is based on consistent parental _____ concerning acceptable behaviour.

43. Good discipline tends to emphasize child _____ techniques (especially communication), rather than power _____ or withdrawal of love.

44. Management techniques tend to produce the highest levels of _____ in children.

• *How do children acquire language?*

45. Language development proceeds from control of crying, to _____ , then _____ , the use of single words, and then to _____ speech (two-word sentences).

46. The patterns of early speech suggest a biological _____ to acquire language.

47. _____ (psychologists who study language) believe that innate language predispositions are augmented by learning.

48. _____ communication between parent and child involves shared rhythms, non-verbal signals, and _____ -taking.

49. Parents help children learn language by using distinctive caretaker speech or _____ .

• *How do children learn to think?*

50. The intellects of children are less _____ than those of adults. Jean Piaget theorized that cognitive growth occurs through a combination of _____ and accommodation.

51. Piaget also held that children go through a fixed series of _____ stages.

52. The stages are: _____ (0-2), _____ (2-7), concrete operational (7-11), and formal operations (11-adult).

53. _____ theorists dispute the idea that cognitive development occurs in stages. Recent studies suggest infants are capable of levels of _____ beyond that observed by Piaget.

54. Young children don't seem to understand that the _____ of other people contain different information, beliefs, and thoughts than theirs do. In other words, they have a very simplified _____ of _____ .

55. A _____ strategy that takes into account the child's level of cognitive development helps adapt instruction to a child's needs.

56. According to the _____ theory of Russian scholar Lev _____ , a child's interactions with others are most likely to aid cognitive development if they they take place within the child's zone of _____ development.

57. Adults help children learn how to think by _____ , or supporting, their attempts to solve problems or discover principles.

58. During their collaborations with others, children learn important _____ beliefs and values.

• *What are the typical tasks and dilemmas through the life span?*

59. Psychologists are interested in developmental _____ , or prominent landmarks in personal development.

60. According to Erik _____ , each life stage provokes a specific _____ dilemma.

61. During childhood these are: _____ , _____ versus shame and doubt, initiative versus guilt, and _____ versus inferiority.

62. In adolescence, _____ versus _____ confusion is the principal dilemma.

63. In young adulthood we face the dilemma of _____ versus isolation. Later, _____ versus stagnation becomes prominent.

64. Old age is a time when the dilemma of _____ versus despair must be faced.

65. In addition, each life stage requires successful mastery of certain developmental _____ (personal changes required for optimal development).

- *How do effective parents discipline their children?*

66. Responsibility, mutual respect, _____ , love, _____ , and clear communication are features of effective parenting.

67. Much misbehaviour can be managed by use of I-messages and by applying natural and _____ _____ to children's behaviour.

Mastery Test

1. The universal patterns of the human growth sequence can be attributed to
   a. recessive genes
   b. environment
   c. polygenic imprinting
   d. heredity.

2. Exaggerated or musical voice inflections are characteristic of
   a. prelanguage turn-taking
   b. parentese
   c. telegraphic speech
   d. prompting and expansion

3. The emotion most clearly expressed by newborn infants is
   a. joy
   b. fear
   c. anger
   d. excitement

4. Explaining things abstractly or symbolically to a child becomes most effective during which stage of cognitive development?
   a. postconventional
   b. formal operations
   c. preoperational
   d. post-intuitive

5. An infant startled by a loud noise will typically display
   a. a Moro reflex
   b. a rooting reflex
   c. a Meltzoff reflex
   d. an imprinting reflex

6. If one identical twin has a *Y* chromosome, the other must have a
   a. recessive chromosome
   b. sex-linked trait
   c. dominant chromosome
   d. *Y* chromosome

7. Ideas about Piaget's stages and the cognitive abilities of infants are challenged by infants' reactions to
   a. hypothetical possibilities
   b. impossible events

    c.   turn-taking

    d.   separation anxiety

8.   The type of play that is observed first in most children is called

    a.   selective play

    b.   secure play

    c.   solitary play

    d.   social play

9.   The largest percentage of children display what type of temperament?

    a.   easy

    b.   difficult

    c.   slow-to-warm-up

    d.   generic

10.   Which of the following is a congenital problem?

    a.   FAS

    b.   sickle-cell anemia

    c.   hemophilia

    d.   muscular dystrophy

11.   A child might begin to question the idea that Santa Claus's sack could carry millions of toys when the child has grasped the concept of

    a.   assimilation

    b.   egocentricism

    c.   conservation

    d.   reversibility of permanence

12.   In most areas of development, heredity and environment are

    a.   independent

    b.   interacting

    c.   conflicting

    d.   responsible for temperament

13.   According to Erikson, developing a sense of integrity is a special challenge in

    a.   adolescence

    b.   young adulthood

    c.   middle adulthood

    d.   late adulthood

14.   Children who grow up in poverty run a high risk of

    a.   insecure scaffolding

    b.   hospitalism

    c.   deprivation

    d.   colostrum

15. According to Erikson, the first dilemma a newborn infant must resolve is
    a. independence versus dependence
    b. initiative versus guilt
    c. trust versus mistrust
    d. attachment versus confusion

16. By definition, a trait that is controlled by a dominant gene cannot be
    a. eugenic
    b. hereditary
    c. carried by DNA
    d. polygenic

17. _____ development proceeds head-down and centre-outward.
    a. Cognitive
    b. Motor
    c. Prelanguage
    d. Preoperational

18. You could test for _____ by videotaping a child and then letting the child see the video on television.
    a. social referencing
    b. self-awareness
    c. the quality of attachment
    d. the degree of readiness

19. After age 2, infants become much more interested in
    a. bonding
    b. non-verbal communication
    c. familiar voices
    d. unfamiliar faces

20. According to Piaget, one of the major developments during the sensorimotor stage is emergence of the concept of
    a. assimilation
    b. accommodation
    c. object permanence
    d. transformation

21. Poverty is to deprivation as early childhood stimulation is to
    a. imprinting
    b. enrichment
    c. responsiveness
    d. assimilation

22. Which principle is most relevant to the timing of toilet training?
    a. readiness
    b. critical periods
    c. non-verbal signals

d.   assimilation

23. High self-esteem is most often a product of what style of child discipline?

    a.   power assertion

    b.   child management

    c.   withdrawal of love

    d.   the natural consequences method

24. Consonants first enter a child's language when the child begins

    a.   babbling

    b.   cooing

    c.   the single word stage

    d.   turn-taking

25. Physically arousing play is typically an element of

    a.   the zoo-keeper mother's caregiving style

    b.   paternal influences

    c.   proactive maternal involvement

    d.   secure attachment

26. Insecure attachment is revealed by

    a.   separation anxiety

    b.   seeking to be near the mother after separation

    c.   turning away from the mother after separation

    d.   social referencing

27. A healthy balance between the rights of parents and their children is characteristic of

    a.   authoritarian parenting

    b.   permissive parenting

    c.   authoritative parenting

    d.   consistent parenting

28. Studies of infant imitation

    a.   are conducted in a looking chamber

    b.   confirm that infants mimic adult facial gestures

    c.   show that self-awareness precedes imitation

    d.   are used to assess the quality of infant attachment

29. Threatening, accusing, bossing, and lecturing children is most characteristic of

    a.   PET

    b.   you-messages

    c.   applying natural consequences

    d.   management techniques

30. Three-year-old Sheila is unable to fully understand what other people think and feel, because at her age she has a very limited

    a.   attachment to others

    b.   theory of mind

c. sensorimotor capacity

d. zone of proximal development

31. According to Vygotsky, children learn important cultural beliefs and values when adults provide _____ to help them gain new ideas and skills.

    a. scaffolding

    b. proactive nurturance

    c. imprinting stimuli

    d. parentese

32. One thing that all forms of effective child discipline have in common is that they

    a. are consistent

    b. make use of punishment

    c. involve temporary withdrawal of love

    d. emphasizes you-messages

33. A *major* problem with using the "Mozart effect" as a basis for promoting intellectual development in babies is that the original research was done on

    a. laboratory animals

    b. mentally retarded infants

    c. children in the concrete operations stage

    d. college students

34. This Canadian psychologist became one of the most influential developmental psychologists due to her work on parent and child attachment.

    a. Jean Piaget

    b. Noam Chomsky

    c. Mary Ainsworth

    d. Kristin Nantais

35. You are looking for day care for your two-year-old son. What day care option should you immediately scratch off your list?

    a. A private home care where one woman takes care of 4 children and offers stimulating activities.

    b. An established day care centre where 3 trained caregivers take care of 30 children between the ages of 3 months and 5 years.

    c. A new day care centre with 6 trained caregivers and 36 children between the ages of 2 and 5 years.

    d. An established day care centre that offers small group size with one caregiver and educational activities.

Solutions

Recite and Review

1. behaviour, birth, death
2. nature, nurture
3. DNA, genes
4. genes, genes
5. physical, development
6. personality, difficult
7. external
8. sensitivity
9. environmental
10. birth, defects
11. development
12. deprivation
13. normal
14. environment
15. heredity
16. own, behaviour
17. neonate, adaptive
18. learn
19. visual, circular
20. famliar, faces
21. sequence
22. order
23. muscular, centre
24. skills
25. general
26. innate
27. people
28. Social
29. caregivers
30. separation
31. developmental, infant-mother, attachment
32. secure
33. harm
34. social, play
35. needs
36. development
37. mothers
38. involvement, preferences
39. fathers
40. rules, authority
41. guidance
42. effective
43. discipline
44. power, love
45. Management
46. crying, speech
47. biological
48. language, learning
49. signals
50. speech
51. less, intellectual
52. stages
53. concrete, operations
54. stages, Piaget
55. minds, mind
56. cognitive
57. cognitive, zone, development
58. supporting
59. beliefs
60. developmental
61. dilemma
62. shame, guilt, inferiority
63. adolescence
64. isolation, stagnation
65. despair
66. developmental
67. respect, communication
68. messages, natural

Connections

1. E
2. J
3. G
4. A
5. B
6. I
7. C
8. D
9. F
10. H
11. E
12. F
13. A
14. B
15. J
16. H
17. C
18. D
19. G
20. I
21. C
22. A
23. J
24. B
25. H
26. D
27. G
28. E
29. F
30. I

Check Your Memory

1. F
2. F
3. T
4. F
5. T
6. T
7. F
8. T
9. F
10. T
11. F
12. T
13. T
14. T
15. T
16. T
17. F
18. F
19. F
20. F
21. F
22. T
23. F
24. F
25. F
26. F
27. F
28. F
29. F
30. T
31. T
32. T
33. F
34. T
35. T
36. F
37. T
38. T
39. F
40. T
41. T
42. F
43. F
44. T
45. F
46. T
47. T
48. F
49. T
50. F
51. T
52. F
53. T
54. T
55. F
56. F
57. T
58. T
59. F
60. F
61. T
62. T
63. T
64. F
65. T
66. T
67. F
68. T
69. F
70. T
71. T
72. T
73. T
74. F

Final Survey and Review

1. Developmental, progressive
2. heredity, environment
3. deoxyribonucleic, chromosomes
4. polygenic, recessive
5. growth, sequence
6. temperament, easy, slow-to-warm-up
7. Environment
8. critical, periods
9. prenatal, drugs, radiation
10. congenital, genetic
11. deprivation
12. Poverty
13. attachment, stimulation
14. enrichment
15. interacting
16. developmental, level
17. grasping, sucking, Moro
18. imitate
19. looking, chamber, complex
20. human, face, unfamiliar
21. Maturation, nervous, system
22. rate, universal
23. motor, cephalocaudal, proximodistal
24. readiness
25. excitement, pleasant, unpleasant
26. emotional, months
27. social
28. awareness, relationships

29. attachement
30. anxiety
31. Mary, Ainsworth, mother-infant
32. Ainsworth, avoidant, ambivalent
33. High-quality, accelerate
34. cooperative
35. affectional
36. Caregiving, styles
37. Maternal, caregiving
38. proactive, temperaments
39. Paternal, playmate, Authoritarian
40. permissive
41. Authoritative
42. guidance
43. management, assertion
44. self-esteem
45. cooing, babbling, telegraphic
46. predisposition
47. Psycholinguists
48. Prelanguage, turn
49. parentese
50. abstract, assimilation
51. cognitive
52. sensorimotor, preoperational
53. Learning, thinking
54. minds, theory, mind
55. one-step-ahead
56. sociocultural, Vygotsky, proximal
57. scaffolding
58. cultural
59. milestones
60. Erikson, psychosexual
61. trust, autonomy, industry

62. identity, role
63. intimacy, generativity
64. integrity
65. tasks
66. consistency, encouragement
67. logical, consequences

Mastery Test

1. D (p. 77)
2. B (p. 95)
3. D (p. 86)
4. B (p. 99)
5. A (p. 82)
6. D (p. 78)
7. B (p. 101)
8. C (p. 89)
9. A (p. 78)
10. A (p. 79)
11. C (p. 99)
12. B (p. 81)
13. D (p. 105)
14. C (p. 80)
15. C (p. 104)
16. D (p. 76)
17. B (p. 84)
18. B (p. 87)
19. D (p. 84)
20. C (p. 98)
21. B (p. 80)
22. A (p. 85)
23. B (p. 92)
24. A (p. 93)

25. B (p. 91)
26. C (p. 88)
27. C (p. 91)
28. B (p. 82)
29. B (p. 108)
30. B (p. 98)
31. A (p. 102)
32. A (p. 106)
33. D (p. 80)
34. C (p. 88)
35. B (p. 89)

Chapter 4

Sensation and Perception

Chapter Overview

Sensory systems collect, select, transduce, analyze, and code information from the environment and send it to the brain.

Vision and visual problems can be partly understood by viewing the eyes as optical systems. However, the visual system also analyzes light stimuli to identify patterns and basic visual features. Colour sensations are explained by the trichromatic theory (in the retina) and the opponent-process theory (for the rest of the visual system).

The inner ear is a sensory mechanism for transducing sound waves in the air into nerve impulses. The frequency and place theories of hearing explain how sound information is coded.

Olfaction is based on receptors that respond to gaseous molecules in the air. The lock-and-key theory and the locations of olfactory receptors activated by different scents explain how various odours are coded. Taste is another chemical sense. A lock-and-key match between dissolved molecules and taste receptors also explains many taste sensations.

The somesthetic, or bodily, senses include the skin senses, the kinesthetic senses, and the vestibular senses.

Our awareness of sensory information is altered by sensory adaptation, selective attention, and sensory gating.

Perception involves organizing sensations into meaningful patterns. Visual perceptions are stabilized by size, shape, and brightness constancies. The most basic perceptual pattern (in vision) is figure-ground organization. Sensations tend to be organized on the basis of nearness, similarity, continuity, closure, contiguity, and common region.

Depth perception depends on accommodation, convergence, retinal disparity, and various pictorial cues. The pictorial cues include linear perspective, relative size, light and shadow, overlap, texture gradients, aerial haze, and relative motion.

Learning, in the form of perceptual habits, influences perceptions. Perceptions are also greatly affected by attention, motives, values, and expectations (perceptual sets).

Parapsychology is the study of purported psi phenomena, including clairvoyance, telepathy, precognition, and psychokinesis. The bulk of the evidence to date is against the existence of extrasensory perception. Stage ESP is based on deception and tricks.

Because perceptions are reconstructions of events, eyewitness testimony can be unreliable. Perceptual accuracy can be improved by reality testing, dishabituation, actively paying attention, breaking perceptual habits, using broad frames of reference, and being aware of perceptual sets.

Learning Objectives

1. Explain how our senses act as a data reduction system. Include the concepts of *perceptual features* and *feature detectors*.

2. Explain how sensory receptors act as biological transducers.

3. Explain the concept of sensory localization.

4. Define the terms *sensation* and *perception.*

5. Describe hue, saturation, and brightness in terms of their representation in the visual spectrum of electromagnetic radiation.

6. Briefly describe the functions of the lens, the photoreceptors, and the retina. Explain how the eye focuses and describe the process of accommodation.

7. Describe the following four conditions:
   a. hyperopia
   b. myopia
   c. astigmatism
   d. presbyopia

8. Describe the functions of the rods and cones, including the fovea and visual acuity.

9. Discuss the following theories of colour vision:
   a. trichromatic theory
   b. opponent-process theory

10. Describe colour blindness and colour weakness.

11. Briefly describe the process of dark adaptation including the function of rhodopsin in night vision and night blindness.

12. Explain the stimulus for hearing.

13. Describe the location and explain the function(s) of the following parts of the ear:
   a. pinna
   b. eardrum (tympanic membrane)
   c. auditory ossicles
   d. oval window
   e. cochlea
   f. hair cells
   g. stereocilia
   h. organ of Corti

14. Describe the frequency theory and the place theory of hearing.

15. List and describe the three general types of deafness and include a description of cochlear implants.

16. Describe the factors that determine whether hearing loss will occur from stimulation deafness.

17. Describe the sense of smell including:
   a. its nature and how it works
   b. a description of the condition called *anosmia*
   c. a description of the lock and key theory

18. Describe the sense of taste including:
   a. its nature and how it works
   b. the five basic taste sensations

    c.   the tastes to which humans are most and least sensitive

    d.   the location and function of the taste buds

19.   List the three somesthetic senses and be able to describe the function of each.

20.   List and be able to recognize the five different sensations produced by the skin receptors.

21.   Describe the concepts *warning pain* and *reminding pain*.

22.   List and discuss the three reasons why many sensory events never reach conscious awareness.

23.   Discuss how sensory gating affects pain.

24.   Describe the following perceptual constancies:

    a.   size

    b.   shape

    c.   brightness

25.   Give examples of the following as they relate to organizing perceptions:

    a.   figure-ground

    b.   nearness

    c.   similarity

    d.   continuity

    e.   closure

    f.   contiguity

    g.   common region

26.   Explain what a perceptual hypothesis is and give an example of an ambiguous stimulus.

27.   Define depth perception and describe the visual cliff research.

28.   Describe the following cues for depth perception and indicate in each case whether the cue is monocular or binocular:

    a.   accommodation

    b.   convergence

    c.   retinal disparity (include the term stereoscopic vision)

29.   Describe the following two-dimensional, monocular, pictorial depth cues:

    a.   linear perspective

    b.   relative size

    c.   height in the picture plane

    d.   light and shadow

    e.   overlap

    f.   texture gradients

    g.   aerial perspective

    h.   relative motion (motion parallax)

30.   Describe the phenomenon of the moon illusion. Include in your explanation the apparent distance hypothesis.

31. Define the terms *perceptual learning* and *perceptual habit,* and explain how the latter allows learning to affect perception. Include the Ames room as an example.

32. Describe research which demonstrates the brain's sensitivity to perceptual features in the environment.

33. Differentiate between an illusion and a hallucination.

34. Describe the Müller-Lyer illusion and explain how perceptual habits may account for this illusion.

35. Explain what bottom-up and top-down processing are.

36. Explain how perceptual expectancies may influence perception. Include the concept of perceptual sets.

37. Define extrasensory perception and the term *parapsychology*.

38. Describe the following purported psychic abilities:
    a. clairvoyance
    b. telepathy
    c. precognition
    d. psychokinesis

39. Describe the research with Zener cards, and explain why most psychologists remain skeptical about psi abilities.

40. Describe the best conclusion to make about psi events.

41. Explain why most eyewitness testimony is inaccurate, including the concept of weapon focus.

42. Explain what the term *reality testing* means.

43. Explain Maslow's concept of perceptual awareness and discuss how attention affects perception.

44. List seven ways to become a better "eyewitness" to life.

Practice Quizzes

Recite and Review

• *In general, how do sensory systems function?*

Recite and Review: Pages 116–117

1. Sensory organs transduce physical energies into _____ impulses.

2. The senses act as _____ reduction systems that select, _____ , and filter sensory information.

3. A good example of sensory analysis is the identification of basic _____ features in a stimulus pattern.

4. In fact, many sensory systems act as feature _____ .

5. Phosphenes and visual pop-out are examples of feature detection and _____ coding in action.

6. Sensory response can be partially understood in terms of _____ localization in the brain. That is, the area of the brain _____ ultimately determines which type of sensory experience we have.

• *How is vision accomplished?*

Recite and Review: Pages 117−125

7. The _____ spectrum consists of electromagnetic radiation in a narrow range.

8. The electromagnetic spectrum ranges from violet, with a _____ of 400 nanometres, to red with a _____ of 700 nanometres.

9. Hue refers to a colour's name, which corresponds to its _____ . Saturated or "pure" colours come from a _____ band of wavelengths. Brightness corresponds to the amplitude of light waves.

10. The eye is in some ways like a camera. At its back lies an array of photoreceptors, called _____ and _____ , that make up a light-sensitive layer called the retina.

11. Vision is focused by the _____ of the cornea and lens and by changes in the _____ of the lens, called accommodation.

12. Four common visual defects, correctable with glasses, are myopia (_____), hyperopia (farsightedness), presbyopia (loss of _____), and astigmatism (in which portions of vision are out of focus).

13. In the retina, the _____ specialize in night vision, black and white reception, and motion detection.

14. The _____ , found exclusively in the fovea and otherwise toward the middle of the eye, specialize in _____ vision, acuity (perception of fine detail), and daylight vision.

15. The _____ supply much of our peripheral vision. Loss of peripheral vision is called tunnel vision.

16. The rods and cones differ in colour _____ . Yellow-green is brightest for cones; blue-green for the rods (although they will see it as colourless).

17. The hypothesis that _____ separate visual systems exist, one for movement (vision-for-action) and one to perceive (_____), is supported by a specific case study (the Scottish woman who suffered from carbon monoxide intoxication).

18. In the _____ , colour vision is explained by the trichromatic theory. The theory says that three types of _____ exist, each most sensitive to either red, green, or blue.

19. Three types of light-sensitive visual pigments are found in the _____ , each pigment is most sensitive to either red, green, or blue light.

20. Beyond the retina, the visual system analyzes colours into _____ messages. According to the opponent-process theory, colour information can be coded as either red or green, yellow or blue, and _____ _____ _____ messages.

21. _____ colour blindness is rare, but 8 percent of males and 1 percent of females are red-green colour blind or colour weak.

22. The Ishihara test is used to detect _____ _____ .

23. Dark adaptation, an _____ in sensitivity to light, is caused by increased concentrations of visual pigments in the _____ and the _____ .

24. Most dark adaptation is the result of increased rhodopsin concentrations in the _____ . Vitamin A deficiencies may cause _____ blindness by impairing the production of rhodopsin.

• *What are the mechanisms of hearing?*

Recite and Review: Pages 126–129

25. Sound waves are the stimulus for hearing. Sound travels as waves of compression (_____) and rarefaction (_____) in the air.

26. The _____ of a sound corresponds to the frequency of sound waves. Loudness corresponds to the amplitude (_____) of sound waves.

27. Sound waves are transduced by the _____ , auditory ossicles, oval window, cochlea, and ultimately, the _____ cells in the organ of Corti.

28. The frequency theory says that the _____ of nerve impulses in the auditory nerves matches the _____ of incoming sounds (up to 4000 hertz).

29. Place theory says that _____ tones register near the base of the cochlea and _____ tones near its tip.

30. Three basic types of deafness are _____ deafness, conduction deafness, and stimulation deafness.

31. Conduction deafness can often be overcome with a hearing aid. _____ deafness can sometimes be alleviated by cochlear implants.

32. Stimulation deafness can be prevented by avoiding excessive exposure to _____ sounds. Sounds above 120 decibels pose an immediate danger to hearing. Two warning signs of stimulation deafness are temporary threshold _____ and tinnitus.

• *How do the chemical senses operate?*

Recite and Review: Pages 129–131

33. Olfaction (_____) and gustation (_____) are chemical senses responsive to airborne or liquefied molecules.

34. The lock and key theory partially explains smell. In addition, the _____ of the olfactory receptors in the nose helps identify various scents.

35. The top outside edges of the tongue are responsive to sweet, salty, sour, and _____ tastes. It is suspected that a fifth taste quality called *umami* also exists.

36. Taste also appears to be based in part on lock-and-key _____ of molecule shapes.

• *What are the somesthetic senses and why are they important?*

Recite and Review: Pages 131–134

37. The somesthetic senses include the _____ senses, vestibular senses, and kinesthetic senses (receptors that detect muscle and joint positioning).

38. The skin senses include touch, _____ , pain, cold, and warmth. Sensitivity to each is related to the _____ of receptors found in an area of skin.

39. Distinctions can be made between warning system pain, and _____ system pain.

40. Pain can be reduced by _____ anxiety and redirecting attention to stimuli other than the pain stimulus.

41. Feeling that you have control over a stimulus tends to _____ the amount of pain you experience.

42. Various forms of motion sickness are related to messages received from the vestibular system, which senses gravity and _____ movement.

43. The otolith organs detect the pull of _____ and rapid head movements.

44. The movement of _____ within the semicircular canals, and the movement of the _____ within each ampulla, detects head movement and positioning.

45. According to sensory conflict theory, motion sickness is caused by a _____ of visual, kinesthetic, and vestibular sensations. Motion sickness can be avoided by minimizing sensory conflict.

- ### *Why are we more aware of some sensations than others?*

Recite and Review: Pages 134–137

46. Incoming sensations are affected by sensory adaptation (a _____ in the number of nerve impulses sent).

47. Selective attention (selection and diversion of messages in the brain) and sensory _____ (blocking or alteration of messages flowing toward the brain) also alter sensations.

48. Selective gating of pain messages apparently takes place in the _____ _____ . Gate control theory proposes an explanation for many pain phenomena.

- ### *How do perceptual constancies affect our perception?*

Recite and Review: Pages 137–138

49. In vision, the retinal _____ changes from moment to moment, but the external world appears stable and undistorted because of _____ constancies.

50. In size and shape _____ , the perceived sizes and shapes of objects remain the same even though their retinal images change size and shape. The apparent brightness of objects remains stable (a property called brightness constancy) because each reflects a _____ proportion of light.

51. Perceptual constancies are partly native (_____) and partly empirical (_____).

- ### *What basic principles do we use to group sensations into meaningful patterns?*

Recite and Review: Pages 139–141

52. The most basic organization of sensations is a division into figure and ground (_____ and _____). Reversible figures, however, allow figure-ground organization to be reversed.

53. A number of factors, identified by the Gestalt psychologists, contribute to the _____ , continuity, closure, contiguity, _____ region, and combinations of the preceding.

54. Stimuli near one another tend to be perceptually _____ together. So, too, do stimuli that are similar in _____ . Continuity refers to the fact that perceptions tend to be organized as simple, uninterrupted patterns.

55. Closure is the tendency to _____ a broken or incomplete pattern. Contiguity refers to nearness in _____ and space. Stimuli that fall in a defined area, or common region, also tend to be grouped together.

56. A perceptual organization may be thought of as an _____ held until evidence contradicts it. Camouflage patterns disrupt perceptual _____ , especially figure-ground perceptions.

57. Perceptual organization shifts for ambiguous _____ , which may have more than one interpretation. An example is Necker's _____ . Impossible figures resist stable organization altogether.

- ### *How is it possible to see depth and judge distance?*

Recite and Review: Pages 142–147

58. _____ perception is the ability to perceive three-dimensional space and judge distances.

59. Depth perception is present in basic form soon after _____ as shown by testing with the visual cliff and other methods. As soon as infants become active _____ they refuse to cross the visual cliff.

60. Depth perception depends on the muscular cues of accommodation (bending of the _____) and convergence (inward movement of the _____).

61. A number of pictorial _____ , which will work in _____ paintings, drawings, and photographs, also underlie normal depth perception.

62. Some pictorial cues are: linear perspective (the apparent convergence of _____ _____), relative size (more distant objects appear _____), height in the _____ plane, light and shadow (shadings of light), and overlap or interposition (one object overlaps another).

63. Additional pictorial cues include: texture gradients (textures become _____ in the distance), aerial haze (loss of colour and detail at large distances), and relative _____ or _____ parallax (differences in the apparent movement of objects when a viewer is moving).

64. All the pictorial cues are monocular depth cues (only _____ _____ is needed to make use of them).

65. The moon illusion refers to the fact that the moon appears _____ near the horizon than it does when overhead.

66. The moon illusion appears to be explained by the apparent _____ hypothesis, which emphasizes the greater number of depth cues present when the moon is on the _____ .

• *How is perception altered by learning, expectations, and motives?*

Recite and Review: Pages 147—153

67. Perception is the process of assembling sensations into _____ that provide a usable mental _____ of the world.

68. Organizing and interpreting sensations is greatly influenced by learned perceptual _____ . An example is the Ames room, which looks rectangular but is actually distorted so that objects in the room appear to change _____ .

69. Sensitivity to perceptual _____ is also partly learned. Studies of inverted vision show that even the most basic organization is subject to a degree of change.

70. Illusions are often related to perceptual _____ . One of the most familiar of all illusions, the Müller-Lyer illusion, seems to be related to perceptual learning based on experience with box-shaped _____ and rooms.

71. Linear perspective and _____ invariance relationships contribute to the Müller-Lyer illusion.

72. Personal motives and _____ _____ stimuli often alter perceptions by changing the evaluation of what is seen or by altering attention to specific details.

73. Perceptions may be based on _____ or bottom-up processing of information.

74. Bottom-up processing, perceptions begin with the organization of low-level _____ . In top-down processing, previous knowledge is used to rapidly _____ sensory information.

75. Attention, prior experience, suggestion, and motives combine in various ways to create perceptual sets, or _____ . A perceptual set is a readiness to perceive in a particular way, induced by strong expectations.

- ### *Is extrasensory perception possible?*

Recite and Review: Pages 154—156

76. Parapsychology is the study of purported _____ phenomena, including clairvoyance (perceiving events at a distance), _____ ("mind reading"), precognition (perceiving future events), and psychokinesis (mentally influencing inanimate objects).

77. Clairvoyance, telepathy, and precognition are purported types of extrasensory _____ .

78. Research in parapsychology remains controversial owing to a variety of problems. _____ and after-the-fact reinterpretation are problems with "natural" ESP episodes. Many studies of ESP overlook the impact of statistically unusual outcomes that are no more than runs of _____ .

79. The bulk of the evidence to date is _____ the existence of ESP. Very few positive results in ESP research have been replicated (_____) by independent scientists.

80. Stage ESP is based on _____ and tricks.

- ### *What can be done to enhance perceptual accuracy?*

Recite and Review: Psychology in Action

81. Perceptions are a reconstruction of events. This is one reason why eyewitness testimony is surprisingly _____ .

82. In many crimes, eyewitness accuracy is further damaged by weapon _____ . Similar factors, such as observer stress, brief exposure times, cross-racial inaccuracies, and the wording of questions can _____ eyewitness accuracy.

83. An underlying difficulty of perceptual accuracy comes from the innate ability of our _____ system to habituate (_____ _____).

84. Perceptual accuracy is enhanced by reality _____ , dishabituation, and conscious efforts to pay _____ .

85. It is also valuable to break perceptual habits, to _____ frames of reference, to beware of perceptual sets, and to be aware of the ways in which motives and emotions influence perceptions.

Connections

1. _____ ciliary muscle
2. _____ iris
3. _____ cornea
4. _____ blind spot
5. _____ lens
6. _____ fovea
7. _____ retinal veins
8. _____ optic nerve
9. _____ aqueous humor
10. _____ pupil
11. _____ retina

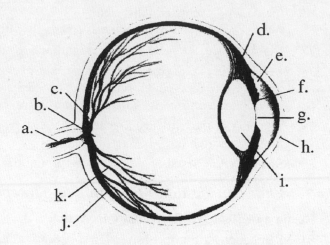

12. _____ vestibular system
13. _____ cochlea
14. _____ round window
15. _____ auditory canal
16. _____ stapes
17. _____ auditory nerve
18. _____ incus
19. _____ oval window
20. _____ tympanic membrane
21. _____ malleus

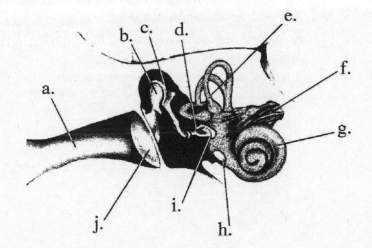

22. _____ texture gradients
23. _____ stereoscopic vision
24. _____ convergence
25. _____ continuity
26. _____ light and shadow
27. _____ common region
28. _____ relative size
29. _____ closure
30. _____ overlap
31. _____ retinal disparity
32. _____ linear perspective
33. _____ nearness
34. _____ similarity

35. _____ reversible figure
36. _____ visual cliff
37. _____ binocular muscle cue
38. _____ mismatch
39. _____ Ponzo illusion
40. _____ Zulus
41. _____ top-down
42. _____ perceptual awareness
43. _____ Zener card
44. _____ ESP capacity

a. convergence
b. stereoscopic vision
c. run of luck
d. moon illusion
e. clairvoyance test
f. diminished Müller-Lyer illusion
g. infant depth perception
h. figure-ground
i. reality testing
j. perceptual expectancy

Check Your Memory

Check Your Memory: Pages 116–117

1. The electromagnetic spectrum includes ultraviolet light and radio waves.
   True or False

2. Each sensory organ is sensitive to a select range of physical energies.
   True or False

3. The artificial vision system described in the text is based on electrodes implanted in the retina.
   True or False

4. The retina responds to pressure, as well as light.
   True or False

Check Your Memory: Pages 117—125

5. A nanometre is one-millionth of a metre.
   True or False

6. The lens of the eye is found in the back of the eyeball.
   True or False

7. Farsightedness is corrected with a convex lens.
   True or False

8. The myopic eye is longer than normal.
   True or False

9. There are more rods than cones in the eyes.
   True or False

10. The blind spot is the point where the optic nerve leaves the eye.
    True or False

11. Vision rated at 20/200 is better than average.
    True or False

12. Poor acuity can limit someone's capacity to think of a solution.
    True or False

13. Blue emergency lights and taxiway lights are used because at night they are more visible to the cones.
    True or False

14. The trichromatic theory of colour vision says that colour is produced by three
    types of cones: blue, green, red.
    True or False

15. According to the opponent-process theory it is impossible to have a reddish green or yellowish blue.
    True or False

16. Yellow-blue colour weakness is very rare.
    True or False

17. In Canada, stoplights are always on the bottom of traffic signals.
    True or False

18. Colour perception in infants is fully developed around 12 months of age.
    True or False

19. Complete dark adaptation takes about 12 minutes.
    True or False

20. Dark adaptation can be preserved by working in an area lit with red light.
    True or False

Check Your Memory: Pages 126—129

21. Sound cannot travel in a vacuum.
    True or False

22. No cases have yet been found of individuals with a pitch perception disorder specific to music.
    True or False

23. The visible, external portion of the ear is the malleus.
    True or False

24. The hair cells are part of the organ of Corti.
    True or False

25. Damage to the ossicles of the ear could produce conduction deafness.
    True or False

26. Hunter's notch occurs when the auditory ossicles are damaged by the sound of gunfire.
    True or False

27. Cochlear implants stimulate the auditory nerve directly.
    True or False

28. A 40 decibel sound could be described as quiet.
    True or False

29. A 100 decibel sound can damage hearing in less than 8 hours.
    True or False

Check Your Memory: Pages 129—131

30. At least 1,000 different types of olfactory receptors exist.
    True or False

31. Etherish odours smell like garlic.
    True or False

32. Flavours are greatly influenced by odour, as well as taste.
    True or False

33. Taste buds are mainly found on the tongue.
    True or False

34. *Umami* is a pleasant "brothy" taste.
    True or False

Check Your Memory: Pages 131—134

35. Vibration is one of the five basic skin sensations.
    True or False

36. Areas of the skin that have high concentrations of pain receptors are no more sensitive to pain than other areas of the body.
    True or False

37. Small nerve fibres generally carry warning-system pain messages.
    True or False

38. High levels of anxiety tend to amplify the amount of pain a person experiences.
    True or False

39. As a means of reducing pain, hot-water bottles are an example of counterirritation.
    True or False

40. The semicircular canals are especially sensitive to the pull of gravity.
    True or False

41. The vestibular system responds to movement when you are sleeping.
    True or False

42. Motion sickness is believed to be related to the body's reactions to being poisoned.
    True or False

Check Your Memory: Pages 134—137

43. If you wear a ring, you are rarely aware of it because of sensory gating.
    True or False

44. The "seat-of-your pants" phenomenon is related to selective attention.
    True or False

45. Attention is related to contrast or changes in stimulation.
    True or False

46. Mild electrical stimulation of the skin can block reminding system pain.
    True or False

47. Mild electrical stimulation of the skin causes a release of endorphins in free nerve endings.
    True or False

Check Your Memory: Pages 137—138

48. Perception involves selecting, organizing, and integrating sensory information.
    True or False

49. Some perceptual abilities must be learned after sight is restored to the previously blind.
    True or False

50. Newborn babies show some evidence of size constancy.
    True or False

51. Houses and cars look like toys from a low-flying airplane because of shape constancy.
    True or False

52. Brightness constancy does not apply to objects illuminated by different amounts of light.
    True or False

Check Your Memory: Pages 139—141

53. Basic figure-ground organization is learned at about age 2.
    True or False

54. Contiguity refers to our tendency to see lines as continuous.
    True or False

55. Necker's cube and the "three-pronged widget" are impossible figures.
    True or False

Check Your Memory: Pages 142—147

56. Depth perception is partly learned and partly innate.
    True or False

57. Human depth perception typically emerges at about 4 months of age.
    True or False

58. Accommodation and convergence are muscular depth cues.
    True or False

59. Accommodation acts as a depth cue primarily for distances greater than 1.2 metres from the eyes.
    True or False

60. Convergence acts as a depth cue primarily for distances less than 1.2 metres from the eyes.
    True or False

61. With one eye closed, the pictorial depth cues no longer provide information about depth and distance.
    True or False

62. Changing the image size of an object implies that its distance from the viewer has changed, too.
    True or False

63. In a drawing, the closer an object is to the horizon line, the nearer it appears to be to the viewer.
    True or False

64. Aerial perspective is most powerful when the air is exceptionally clear.
    True or False

65. When an observer is moving forward, objects beyond the observer's point of fixation appear to move forward too.
    True or False

66. The moon's image is magnified by the dense atmosphere near the horizon.
    True or False

67. More depth cues are present when the moon is viewed near the horizon.
    True or False

Check Your Memory: Pages 147—153

68. The Ames room is primarily used to test the effects of inverted vision.
    True or False

69. Cats who grow up surrounded by horizontal stripes are unusually sensitive to vertical stripes when they reach maturity.
    True or False

70. Hearing voices when no one is speaking is an example of a perceptual illusion.
    True or False

71. According to Richard Gregory, the arrowhead-tipped line in the Müller-Lyer illusion looks like the outside corner of a building.
    True or False

72. Zulus rarely see round shapes and therefore fail to experience the Müller-Lyer illusion.
    True or False

73. Analyzing information into small features and then building a recognizable pattern is called top-up processing.
    True or False

74. Perceptual sets are frequently created by suggestion.
    True or False

75. Labels and categories have been shown to have little real effect on perceptions.
    True or False

Check Your Memory: Pages 154—156

76. Uri Geller was one of the first researchers in parapsychology to use the Zener cards.
    True or False

77. Psychokinesis is classified as a psi event, but not a form of ESP.
    True or False

78. Prophetic dreams are regarded as a form of precognition.
    True or False

79. Strange coincidences are strong evidence for the existence of ESP.
    True or False

80. The Zener cards eliminated the possibility of fraud and "leakage" of information in ESP experiments.
    True or False

81. "Psi missing" is perhaps the best current evidence for ESP.
    True or False

82. Belief in psi events has declined among parapsychologists in recent years.
    True or False

Check Your Memory: Psychology in Action

83. In many ways we see what we believe, as well as believe what we see.
    True or False

84. The more confident an eyewitness is about the accuracy of his or her testimony,
    the more likely it is to be accurate.
    True or False

85. The testimony of crime victims is generally more accurate than the testimony of bystanders.
    True or False

86. Police officers and other trained observers are more accurate eyewitnesses than the average person.
    True or False

87. Reality testing is the process Abraham Maslow described as a "surrender" to experience.
    True or False

88. Perceptually, Zen masters have been shown to habituate more rapidly than the average person.
    True or False

Final Survey and Review

• *In general, how do sensory systems function?*

1. Sensory organs _____ physical energies into nerve impulses.

2. The senses act as data _____ systems that select, analyze, and
    _____ sensory information.

3. A good example of _____ _____ is the identification of basic
    perceptual features in a stimulus pattern.

4. In fact, many sensory systems act as _____ detectors.

5. _____ and visual pop-out are examples of feature detection and
    sensory _____ in action.

6. Sensory response can be partially understood in terms of sensory _____ in the brain. That is, the
    _____ of the brain activated ultimately determines which type of sensory experience we have.

• *How is vision accomplished?*

7. The visible spectrum consists of _____ radiation in a narrow range.

8. The visible spectrum ranges from violet, with a wavelength of _____ _____ ,
    to red with a wavelength of _____ _____ .

9. _____ refers to a colour's name, which corresponds to its wavelength.
    Saturated or "pure" colours come from a narrow band of wavelengths. Brightness
    corresponds to the _____ of light waves.

10. The eye is in some ways like a camera. At its back lies an array of _____ , called rods
    and cones, that make up a light-sensitive layer called the _____ .

11. Vision is focused by the shape of the _____ and lens and by changes in
    the shape of the lens, called _____ .

12. Four common visual defects, correctable with glasses, are _____ (nearsightedness), hyperopia (farsightedness), presbyopia (loss of accommodation), and _____ (in which portions of vision are out of focus).

13. In the retina, the rods specialize in night vision, black and white reception, and _____ detection.

14. The cones, found exclusively in the _____ and otherwise toward the middle of the eye, specialize in colour vision, _____ (perception of fine detail), and daylight vision.

15. The rods supply much of our _____ vision. Loss of _____ vision is called tunnel vision.

16. The rods and cones differ in colour sensitivity. _____ -green is brightest for cones; _____ -green for the rods (although they will see it as colourless).

17. The hypothesis that two separate _____ systems exist, one for movement (_____) and one to perceive (_____), is supported by a specific _____ study (the Scottish woman who suffered from carbon monoxide intoxication).

18. In the retina, colour vision is explained by the _____ theory. The theory says that three types of cones exist, each most sensitive to either red, green, or blue.

19. Three types of light-sensitive visual _____ are found in the cones, each is most sensitive to either red, green, or blue light.

20. Beyond the retina, the visual system analyzes colours into either-or messages. According to the _____ theory, colour information can be coded as either _____ _____ _____ , yellow or blue, and black or white messages.

21. Total colour blindness is rare, but 8 percent of males and 1 percent of females are _____ colour blind or colour weak.

22. The _____ test is used to detect colour blindness.

23. Dark adaptation, an increase in sensitivity to light, is caused by increased concentrations of _____ _____ in the rods and the cones.

24. Most dark adaptation is the result of increased _____ concentrations in the rods. Vitamin _____ deficiencies may cause night blindness.

- ## *What are the mechanisms of hearing?*

25. Sound waves are the stimulus for hearing. Sound travels as waves of _____ (peaks) and _____ (valleys) in the air.

26. The pitch of a sound corresponds to the _____ of sound waves. Loudness corresponds to the _____ (height) of sound waves.

27. Sound waves are transduced by the eardrum, auditory _____ , oval window, cochlea, and ultimately, the hair cells in the organ of _____ .

28. The frequency theory says that the frequency of nerve impulses in the _____ _____ matches the frequency of incoming sounds (up to 4000 hertz).

29. Place theory says that high tones register near the _____ of the cochlea and low tones near its _____ .

30. Three basic types of deafness are nerve deafness, conduction deafness, and _____ deafness.

31. Conduction deafness can often be overcome with a hearing aid. Nerve deafness can sometimes be alleviated by _____ implants.

32. Stimulation deafness can be prevented by avoiding excessive exposure to loud sounds. Sounds above _____ _____ pose an immediate danger to hearing. Two warning signs of stimulation deafness are temporary threshold shift and a ringing in the ears, called _____ .

• *How do the chemical senses operate?*

33. _____ (smell) and _____ (taste) are chemical senses responsive to airborne or liquefied molecules.

34. The _____ _____ _____ theory partially explains smell. In addition, the location of the olfactory receptors in the nose helps identify various scents.

35. The top outside edges of the tongue are responsive to _____ , _____ , _____ , and bitter tastes. It is suspected that a fifth taste quality called _____ also exists.

36. Taste also appears to be based in part on lock-and-key coding of _____ shapes.

• *What are the somesthetic senses and why are they important?*

37. The somesthetic senses include the skin senses, vestibular senses, and _____ senses (receptors that detect muscle and joint positioning).

38. The skin senses include touch, pressure, _____ , cold, and warmth. Sensitivity to each is related to the number of _____ found in an area of skin.

39. Distinctions can be made between _____ system pain, and _____ system pain.

40. Pain can be reduced by lowering anxiety and redirecting _____ to stimuli other than the pain stimulus.

41. Feeling that you have _____ over a stimulus tends to reduce the amount of pain you experience.

42. Various forms of motion sickness are related to messages received from the _____ system, which senses gravity and head movement.

43. The _____ organs detect the pull of gravity and rapid head movements.

44. The movement of fluid within the _____ canals, and the movement of the crista within each _____ , detects head movement and positioning.

45. According to _____ _____ theory, motion sickness is caused by a mismatch of visual, kinesthetic, and vestibular sensations. Motion sickness can be avoided by minimizing sensory conflict.

• *Why are we more aware of some sensations than others?*

46. Incoming sensations are affected by sensory _____ (a decrease in the number of nerve impulses sent).

47. Selective _____ (selection and diversion of messages in the brain) and sensory gating (blocking or alteration of messages flowing toward the brain) also alter sensations.

48. Selective gating of pain messages apparently takes place in the spinal cord. _____ _____ theory proposes an explanation for many pain phenomena.

• *How do perceptual constancies affect our perceptions?*

49. In vision, the _____ image changes from moment to moment, but the external world appears stable and undistorted because of perceptual _____ .

50. In size and shape constancy, the perceived sizes and shapes of objects remain the same even though their retinal images change size and shape. The apparent _____ of objects remains stable (a property called brightness constancy) because each reflects a constant _____ of _____ .

51. Perceptual constancies are partly _____ (inborn) and partly _____ (learned).

- ## *What basic principles do we use to group sensations into meaningful patterns?*

52. The most basic organization of sensations is a division into _____ and
_____ (object and background).

53. A number of factors, identified by the _____ psychologists, contribute to the
organization of sensations. These are _____ , similarity, continuity, _____ ,
contiguity, common region, and combinations of the preceding.

54. Stimuli near one another tend to be perceptually grouped together. So, too, do stimuli that are
similar in appearance. _____ refers to the fact that perceptions tend to be organized
as simple, uninterrupted patterns.

55. _____ refers to nearness in time and space. Stimuli that fall in a defined area,
or common region, also tend to be grouped together.

56. A perceptual organization may be thought of as an hypothesis held until evidence contradicts it.
_____ patterns disrupt perceptual organization, especially figure-ground perceptions.

57. Perceptual organization shifts for _____ stimuli, which may have more than one interpretation.
An example is _____ cube. Impossible _____ resist stable organization altogether.

- ## *How is it possible to see depth and judge distance?*

58. Depth perception is the ability to perceive _____ space and judge distances.

59. Depth perception is present in basic form soon after birth as shown by testing with the
_____ _____ and other methods. As soon as infants become active crawlers
they refuse to cross the deep side of the _____ _____ .

60. Depth perception depends on the muscular cues of _____ (bending of the lens)
and _____ (inward movement of the eyes).

61. A number of _____ cues, which will work in flat paintings, drawings, and
photographs, also underlie normal depth perception.

62. Some of these cues are: _____ _____ (the apparent convergence of parallel lines),
relative size (more distant objects appear smaller), height in the picture plane, light and shadow
(shadings of light), and overlap or _____ (one object overlaps another).

63. Additional pictorial cues include: texture _____ (textures become finer in the distance), aerial
haze (loss of colour and detail at large distances), and relative motion or motion _____
(differences in the apparent movement of objects when a viewer is moving).

64. All the pictorial cues are _____ depth cues (only one eye is needed to make use of them).

65. The moon illusion refers to the fact that the moon appears larger near the _____

66. The moon illusion appears to be explained by the _____ _____
hypothesis, which emphasizes the greater number of _____ _____
present when the moon is on the horizon.

- ## *How is perception altered by learning, expectations, and motives?*

67. Perception is the process of assembling _____ into patterns that provide a
usable _____ _____ of the world.

68. Organizing and interpreting sensations is greatly influenced by learned _____
_____ . An example is the _____ room, which looks rectangular but is
actually distorted so that objects in the room appear to change size.

69. Sensitivity to perceptual features is also partly learned. Studies of _____ vision show that even the most basic organization is subject to a degree of change.

70. Illusions are often related to perceptual habits. One of the most familiar of all illusions, the _____ illusion, involves two equal-length lines tipped with arrowheads and V's. This illusion seems to be related to perceptual learning based on experience with box-shaped buildings and rooms.

71. Linear perspective and size-distance _____ relationships contribute to the Müller-Lyer illusion.

72. Personal _____ and emotionally significant stimuli often alter perceptions by changing the evaluation of what is seen or by altering attention to specific details.

73. Perceptions may be based on top-down or bottom-up _____ of information.

74. _____ perceptions begin with the organization of low-level features. In _____ processing, previous knowledge is used to rapidly organize sensory information.

75. Attention, prior experience, suggestion, and motives combine in various ways to create _____ _____ , or expectancies. A _____ _____ is a readiness to perceive in a particular way, induced by strong expectations.

• *Is extrasensory perception possible?*

76. _____ is the study of purported psi phenomena, including clairvoyance (perceiving events at a distance), telepathy ("mind reading"), _____ (perceiving future events), and psychokinesis (mentally influencing inanimate objects).

77. Clairvoyance, telepathy, and precognition are purported types of _____ perception.

78. Research in parapsychology remains controversial owing to a variety of problems. Coincidence and after-the-fact _____ are problems with "natural" ESP episodes.

79. Many studies of ESP overlook the impact of _____ unusual outcomes that are no more than runs of luck.

80. The bulk of the evidence to date is against the existence of ESP. Very few positive results in ESP research have been _____ (repeated) by independent scientists.

81. _____ ESP is based on deception and tricks.

• *What can be done to enhance perceptual accuracy?*

82. Perception is an active _____ of events. This is one reason why eyewitness testimony is surprisingly inaccurate.

83. In many crimes, eyewitness accuracy is further damaged by _____ focus. Similar factors, such as observer _____ , brief exposure times, cross-racial inaccuracies, and the wording of questions can lower eyewitness accuracy.

84. An underlying difficulty of perceptual accuracy comes from the innate ability of our perceptual system to _____ (_____ _____).

85. Perceptual accuracy is enhanced by reality testing, _____ , and conscious efforts to pay attention.

86. It is also valuable to break _____ _____ , to broaden frames of reference, to beware of perceptual sets, and to be aware of the ways in which motives and emotions influence perceptions.

Mastery Test

1. Sensory conflict theory attributes motion sickness to mismatches between what three systems?
   a. olfaction, kinesthesis, and audition
   b. vision, kinesthesis, and the vestibular system
   c. kinesthesis, audition, and the somesthetic system
   d. vision, gustation, and the skin senses

2. Which of the following types of colour blindness is most common?
   a. yellow-blue, male
   b. yellow-blue, female
   c. red-green, female
   d. red-green, male

3. Which of the following does not belong with the others?
   a. Pacinian corpuscle
   b. Merkle's disk
   c. organ of Corti
   d. free nerve endings

4. Which theory of colour vision best explains the fact that we do not see yellowish blue?
   a. trichromatic
   b. chromatic gating
   c. Ishihara hypothesis
   d. opponent process

5. Dark adaptation is closely related to concentrations of _____ in the _____.
   a. retinal, aqueous humor
   b. photopsin, cones
   c. rhodopsin, rods
   d. photons, optic nerve

6. Sensory analysis tends to extract perceptual _____ from stimulus patterns.
   a. thresholds
   b. features
   c. transducers
   d. amplitudes

7. Which pair of terms is most closely related?
   a. hyperopia—colour blindness
   b. astigmatism—presbyopia
   c. myopia—astigmatism
   d. hyperopia—presbyopia

8. The painkilling effects of acupuncture are partly explained by _____ theory.
   a. lock-and-key
   b. gate control
   c. opponent-process

    d.   frequency

9.   According to the _____ theory of hearing, low tones cause the greatest movement near the _____ of the cochlea.

    a.   place, outer tip

    b.   frequency, outer tip

    c.   place, base

    d.   frequency, base

10.   Which of the following best represents the concept of a transducer?

    a.   Translating English into Spanish.

    b.   Copying a computer file from one floppy disk to another.

    c.   Speaking into a telephone receiver.

    d.   Turning water into ice.

11.   Rods and cones are to vision as _____ are to hearing.

    a.   auditory ossicles

    b.   vibrations

    c.   pinnas

    d.   hair cells

12.   You lose the ability to smell floral odours. This is called _____ and it is compatible with the _____ theory of olfaction.

    a.   anosmia, lock-and-key

    b.   anhedonia, place

    c.   tinnitus, gate-control

    d.   sensory adaptation, molecular

13.   The main problem with current artificial vision systems is

    a.   the retina's lack of an absolute threshold

    b.   the danger of damaging the eyes while producing phosphenes

    c.   their inability to transduce letters

    d.   the rejection of implanted electrodes

14.   Which two dimensions of colour are related to the wavelength of electromagnetic energy?

    a.   hue and saturation

    b.   saturation and brightness

    c.   brightness and hue

    d.   brightness and amplitude

15.   The existence of the blind spot is explained by a lack of

    a.   rhodopsin

    b.   peripheral vision

    c.   photoreceptors

    d.   activity in the fovea

16.   In vision, a loss of accommodation is most associated with aging of the

    a.   iris

    b.   fovea

    c.   lens

    d.   cornea

17. Visual acuity and colour vision are provided by the _____ found in large numbers in the _____ of the eye.

    a.   cones, fovea

    b.   cones, periphery

    c.   rods, fovea

    d.   rods, periphery

18. The Ames room creates a conflict between

    a.   horizontal features and vertical features

    b.   attention and habituation

    c.   top-down and bottom-up processing

    d.   shape constancy and size constancy

19. Weapon focus tends to lower eyewitness accuracy because it affects

    a.   selective attention

    b.   the adaptation level

    c.   perceptions of contiguity

    d.   dishabituation

20. The fact that Canadian tourists in London tend to look in the wrong direction before stepping into crosswalks is based on

    a.   sensory localization

    b.   perceptual habits

    c.   sensory gating

    d.   unconscious transference

21. Size constancy

    a.   emerges at about 4 months of age

    b.   is affected by experience with seeing objects of various sizes

    c.   requires that objects be illuminated by light of the same intensity

    d.   all of the preceding

22. Which of the following cues would be of greatest help to a person trying to thread a needle?

    a.   light and shadow

    b.   texture gradients

    c.   linear perspective

    d.   overlap

23. Size-distance invariances contribute to which of the following?

    a.   Müller-Lyer illusion

    b.   the stroboscopic illusion

    c.   perceptual hallucinations

    d.   changes in perceptual sets

24. The visual cliff is used primarily to test infant
    a. size constancy
    b. figure-ground perception
    c. depth perception
    d. adaptation to spatial distortions

25. Which of the following organizational principles is based on nearness in time and space?
    a. continuity
    b. closure
    c. contiguity
    d. size constancy

26. Which of the following is both a muscular and a monocular depth cue?
    a. convergence
    b. relative motion
    c. aerial perspective
    d. accommodation

27. A previously blind person has just had her sight restored. Which of the following perceptual experiences is she most likely to have?
    a. perceptual set
    b. size constancy
    c. linear perspective
    d. figure-ground

28. An artist manages to portray a face with just a few unconnected lines. Apparently the artist has capitalized on
    a. closure
    b. contiguity
    c. the reversible figure effect
    d. the principle of camouflage

29. The most basic source of stereoscopic vision is
    a. accommodation
    b. retinal disparity
    c. convergence
    d. stroboscopic motion

30. Necker's cube is a good example of
    a. an ambiguous stimulus
    b. an impossible figure
    c. camouflage
    d. a binocular depth cue

31. Skeptics regard the decline effect as evidence that _____ occurred in an ESP test.
    a. replication
    b. cheating
    c. a run of luck

d.   leakage

32. Which of the following is a binocular depth cue?

    a.   accommodation

    b.   convergence

    c.   linear perspective

    d.   motion parallax

33. Ambiguous stimuli allow us to hold more than one perceptual

    a.   gradient

    b.   parallax

    c.   constancy

    d.   hypothesis

34. Increased perceptual awareness is especially associated with

    a.   dishabituation

    b.   unconscious transference

    c.   high levels of stress

    d.   stimulus repetition without variation

35. According to researchers, which is the first colour that infants are able to perceive?

    a.   red

    b.   green

    c.   yellow

    d.   blue

36. If you lost your sense of touch you would probably (as shown by the case study of Ginette Lizotte of Quebec)

    a.   not be able to walk because of lack of balance.

    b.   be incapable of using any of your senses since they are all linked.

    c.   not know how or whether you are moving without seeing where your body is.

    d.   have constant physical pain.

Solutions

Recite and Review

1. nerve
2. data , analyze
3. perceptual
4. detectors
5. sensory
6. sensory, activated
7. visible
8. wavelength, wavelength
9. wavelength, narrow
10. rods , cones
11. shape , shape
12. nearsightedness, accommodation
13. rods
14. cones, colour
15. rods
16. sensitivity
17. two, vision-for-perception
18. retina, cones
19. cones
20. either-or, black, or, white
21. Total
22. colour, blindness
23. increase, rods , cones
24. rods, night
25. peaks, valleys
26. pitch, height
27. eardrum, hair
28. frequency, frequency
29. high, low
30. nerve
31. Nerve
32. loud, shifts

33. smell, taste
34. location
35. bitter
36. coding
37. skin
38. pressure, number
39. reminding
40. lowering
41. reduce
42. head
43. gravity
44. fluid, crista
45. mismatch
46. reduction (or decrease)
47. gating
48. spinal, cord
49. image, perceptual
50. constancy, constant
51. inborn, learned
52. object, background
53. organization, common
54. grouped, appearnce
55. complete, time
56. hypothesis, organization
57. stimuli, cube
58. Depth
59. birth, crawlers
60. lens, eyes
61. cues, flat
62. parallel, lines, smaller, picture
63. finer, motion, motion
64. one, eye
65. larger
66. distance, horizon
67. patterns, model
68. habits, size

69. features
70. habits, buildings
71. size-distance
72. emotional, significant
73. top-down
74. features, organize
75. expectancies
76. psi, telepathy
77. perception
78. Coincidence, luck
79. against, repeated
80. deception
81. inaccurate
82. focus, lower
83. perceptual, respond, less
84. testing, attention
85. broaden

Connections

1. D
2. F
3. H
4. B
5. I
6. C
7. K
8. A
9. E
10. G
11. J
12. E
13. G
14. H
15. A
16. D

17. F
18. C
19. I
20. J
21. B
22. M
23. G
24. F
25. C
26. L
27. E
28. J
29. D
30. K
31. H
32. I
33. A
34. B
35. H
36. G
37. A
38. B
39. D
40. F
41. J
42. I
43. E
44. C

Check Your Memory

1. T
2. T
3. F
4. T
5. F
6. F
7. T
8. T
9. T
10. T
11. F
12. T
13. F
14. T
15. T
16. T
17. F
18. F
19. F
20. T
21. T
22. F
23. F
24. T
25. T
26. F
27. T
28. T
29. T
30. T
31. F
32. T
33. T
34. T
35. F
36. F
37. F
38. T
39. T
40. F
41. T
42. T
43. F
44. T
45. T
46. T
47. F
48. T
49. T
50. T
51. F
52. T
53. F
54. F
55. F
56. T
57. T
58. T
59. F
60. F
61. F
62. T
63. F
64. F
65. T
66. F
67. T
68. F
69. F
70. F
71. T
72. F
73. F
74. T
75. F
76. F
77. T

78. T
79. F
80. F
81. F
82. T
83. T
84. F
85. F
86. F
87. F
88. F

Final Survey and Review

1. transduce
2. reduction, filter
3. sensory, analysis
4. feature
5. Phosphenes, coding
6. localization, area
7. electromagnetic
8. 400, nanometres, 700, nanometres
9. Hue, amplitude
10. photoreceptors, retina
11. cornea, accommodation
12. myopia, astigmatism
13. motion
14. fovea, acuity
15. peripheral, peripheral
16. Yellow, blue
17. visual, vision-for-action, vision-for-perception, case
18. trichormatic
19. pigments
20. opponent-process, red, or, green
21. red-green

22. Ishihara
23. visual, pigments
24. rhodopsin, A
25. compression, rarefaction
26. frequency, amplitude
27. ossicles, Corti
28. auditory, nerves
29. base, tip
30. stimulation
31. cochlear
32. 120, decibels, tinnitus
33. Olfaction, gustation
34. lock, and, key
35. sweet, salty, sour, umami
36. molecule
37. kinesthetic
38. pain, receptors
39. warning, reminding
40. attention
41. control
42. vestibular
43. otolith
44. semicircular, ampulla
45. sensory, conflict
46. adaptation
47. attention
48. Gate, control
49. retinal, constancies
50. brightness, propertion, light
51. native, empirical
52. figure, ground
53. Gestalt, nearness, closure
54. Closure
55. Contiguity
56. Camouflage
57. ambiguous, Necker's, figures

58. three-dimensional
59. visual, cliff, visual, cliff
60. accommodation, convergence
61. pictorial
62. linear, perspective, interposition
63. gradients, parallax
64. monocular
65. horizon
66. apparent, distance, depth, cues
67. sensations, mental, model
68. perceptual, habits, Ames
69. inverted
70. Müller-Lyer
71. invariance
72. motives
73. processing
74. Bottom-up, top-down
75. perceptual, sets, perceptual, set
76. Parapsychology, precognition
77. extrasensory
78. reinterpretation
79. statistically
80. replicated
81. Stage
82. reconstruction
83. weapon, stress
84. habituate, respond, less
85. dishabituation
86. perceptual, habits

Mastery Test

1. B (p. 134)
2. D (p. 123)
3. C (p. 126)
4. D (p. 122)

5. C (p. 123)

6. B (p. 149)

7. D (p. 118)

8. B (p. 136)

9. A (p. 126)

10. C (p. 116)

11. D (p. 126)

12. A (p. 129)

13. D (p. 117)

14. A (p. 117)

15. C (p. 120)

16. C (p. 119)

17. A (p. 120)

18. D (p. 137)

19. A (p. 157)

20. B (p. 148)

21. B (p. 137)

22. D (p. 145)

23. A (p. 150)

24. C (p. 142)

25. C (p. 139)

26. D (p. 142)

27. D (p. 139)

28. A (p. 139)

29. B (p. 143)

30. A (p. 140)

31. C (p. 155)

32. B (p. 142)

33. D (p. 140)

34. A (p. 159)

35. A (p. 123)

36. C (p. 131)

Chapter 5

States of Consciousness

Chapter Overview

Consciousness consists of everything you are aware of at a given instant. Altered states of consciousness (ASCs) differ significantly from normal waking consciousness. Many conditions produce ASCs, which frequently have culturally defined meanings.

Sleep is an innate biological rhythm characterized by changes in consciousness and brain activity. Brain-wave patterns and sleep behaviours define four stages of sleep. The two most basic forms of sleep are rapid eye movement (REM) sleep and non-rapid eye movement (NREM) sleep. Dreams and nightmares occur primarily in REM sleep. Sleepwalking, sleeptalking, and night terrors are NREM events. Insomnia and other sleep disturbances are common, but generally treatable. Dreaming is emotionally restorative and it may help form adaptive memories. The psychodynamic view portrays dreams as a form of wish fulfillment; the activation-synthesis hypothesis says that dreaming is a physiological process with little meaning.

Hypnosis is characterized by narrowed attention and increased openness to suggestion. People vary in hypnotic susceptibility. Most hypnotic phenomena are related to the basic suggestion effect. Hypnosis can relieve pain and it has other useful effects, but it is not magic. Stage hypnotists simulate hypnosis in order to entertain.

Meditation can be used to alter consciousness, promote relaxation, and reduce stress. Two particular benefits of meditation are its ability to interrupt anxious thoughts and its ability to elicit the relaxation response. Sensory deprivation refers to any major reduction in external stimulation. Sensory deprivation also produces deep relaxation and a variety of perceptual effects. It can be used to help people enhance creative thinking and to change bad habits.

Psychoactive drugs are substances that alter consciousness. Most can be placed on a scale ranging from stimulation to depression, although some drugs are better classified as hallucinogens. The potential for abuse is high for drugs that lead to physical dependence, but psychological dependence can also be a serious problem. Drug abuse is often a symptom, rather than a cause, of personal maladjustment. It is supported by the immediate pleasure but delayed consequences associated with many psychoactive drugs and by cultural values that encourage drug abuse.

Various strategies, ranging from literal to highly symbolic, can be used to reveal the meanings of dreams. Dreaming—especially lucid dreaming—can be a source of creativity and it may be used for problem solving and personal growth.

Learning Objectives

1. Define consciousness and explain what waking consciousness is.

2. Define and describe an altered state of consciousness. Include a description of the meaning and uses of altered states of consciousness in other cultures.

3. Describe the limitations of sleep learning.

4. Define the terms *biological rhythm* and *circadian rhythm* and explain their relationship to sleep.

5. Define and describe the term *microsleep.*

6. Describe the general effects of 2 to 3 days of sleep deprivation. Name and describe the condition that occurs when a person is deprived of sleep for a longer period of time.

7. State how long the average sleep-waking cycle is. Explain how we tie our sleep rhythms to a 24 hour day.

8. Describe the normal range of sleep needs. Describe how the aging process affects sleep.

9. State the average ratio of time awake to time asleep.

10. Describe how the brain's systems and chemistry promote sleep.

11. Briefly describe each of the four stages of sleep. Include a description of the brain waves associated with each and those associated with wakefulness.

12. Describe the cyclical nature of the sleep stages.

13. Name and differentiate the two basic states of sleep. State the average amount of time spent in each one and explain how the relative amounts of each can be influenced.

14. State how many times per night most people dream and how long the dreams usually last.

15. List the physiological changes that occur during REM sleep including a description of REM behaviour disorder.

16. Define insomnia. Describe the effects of nonprescription and prescription drugs on insomnia.

17. Describe the characteristics and treatment of the three types of insomnia: drug dependency, temporary, and chronic insomnia.

18. List and briefly describe six behavioural remedies that can be used to combat insomnia.

19. Characterize the following major sleep disturbances of NREM sleep.
    a.   somnambulism
    b.   sleeptalking
    c.   night terrors (include a differentiation between night terrors and nightmares)

20. List and briefly describe the twelve sleep disorders that are found in the DSM-IV. (See Table 5.1.)

21. Explain the concepts of REM rebound and REM myth. Describe the relationship between alcoholism and REM rebound.

22. Describe the probable functions of REM sleep.

23. Explain Calvin Hall's view of dreams.

24. Explain how Freud viewed dreams, and present the evidence against his view.

25. Describe the activation-synthesis hypothesis concerning dreaming.

26. Give the general definition of hypnosis and then describe how it is that the general definition is not accepted by all psychologists.

27. Briefly trace the history of hypnosis from Mesmer through its use today.

28. State the proportion of people who can be hypnotized.

29. Explain how a person's hypnotic susceptibility can be determined. Include a brief description of the dimensions of the Stanford Hypnotic Susceptibility Scale.

30. List the four common factors in all hypnotic techniques. Explain why all hypnosis may really be self-hypnosis.

31. Explain what the basic suggestion effect is.

32. Explain how hypnosis can affect:
    a. strength
    b. memory
    c. amnesia
    d. pain relief
    e. age regression
    f. sensory changes

33. List three areas in which hypnosis appears to have its greatest value, and then state a general conclusion concerning the effectiveness of hypnosis.

34. Using the five characteristics of the stage setting outlined in the chapter, explain how a stage hypnotist gets people to perform the way they do in front of an audience.

35. Name and describe the two major forms of meditation.

36. Describe the relaxation response.

37. Describe what is known about the effects of meditation.

38. Explain what sensory deprivation is. Include a discussion of the positive and negative effects of this procedure.

39. Define the term *psychoactive drug*.

40. Differentiate physical dependence from psychological dependence.

41. Describe the following frequently abused drugs in terms of their effects, possible medical uses, side effects or long term symptoms, organic damage potential, and potential for physical and/or psychological dependence.
    a. amphetamines (include the term amphetamine psychosis)
    b. cocaine (include the three signs of abuse)
    c. MDMA ("ecstasy")
    d. caffeine (include the term *caffeinism*)
    e. nicotine
    f. barbiturates
    g. tranquilizers
    h. alcohol
    i. hallucinogens (including marijuana)

42. Compare the efficacy of quitting smoking "cold turkey" versus cutting down or smoking low-tar cigarettes. (Also see the Using Psychology highlight.)

43. Explain what a drug interaction is.

44. Define the term binge drinking. List and explain the three steps in the development of a drinking problem.

45. Generally describe the treatment process for alcoholism. Name the form of therapy that has probably been the most successful.

46. Explain why drug abuse is such a common problem.

47. List and describe the four processes identified by Freud, which disguise the hidden meaning of dreams.

48. Contrast Hall's and Cartwright's views of dream interpretation.

49. List the eight steps for remembering dreams.

50. Explain how Perls viewed dreams and how he suggested that people interpret them.

51. Describe how one could use dreams to aid in problem solving. Include a description of lucid dreams and how they have been used in the problem solving process.

Practice Quizzes

Recite and Review

* *What is an altered state of consciousness?*

Recite and Review: Page 166

1. States of _____ that differ from normal, alert, _____ consciousness are called altered states of consciousness (ASCs).
2. ASCs involved distinct shifts in the quality and _____ of mental activity.
3. Altered states are especially associated with _____ and _____ , hypnosis, meditation, _____ deprivation, and psychoactive drugs.
4. Cultural conditioning greatly affects what altered states a person recognizes, seeks, considers _____ and attains.

* *What are the effects of sleep loss or changes in sleep patterns?*

Recite and Review: Pages 166–169

5. Sleep is an innate biological _____ essential for _____ .
6. Our circadian rhythm works on a _____ hour cycle and is controlled by an internal _____ clock.
7. Higher animals and people deprived of sleep experience _____ microsleeps.
8. Moderate sleep loss mainly affects alertness and self-motivated performance on _____ or boring tasks.
9. Extended sleep _____ can (somewhat rarely) produce a _____ sleep-deprivation psychosis, marked by confusion, delusions, and possibly hallucinations.
10. Sleep patterns show some flexibility, but 7 to 8 hours remains average. The unscheduled human sleep-waking cycle averages _____ hours, but cycles of _____ and _____ tailor it to 24-hour days.

101

11. The amount of daily sleep _____ steadily from birth to old age and switches from multiple sleep-wake cycles to once-a-day sleep periods.

12. Once-a-day sleep patterns, with a 2-to-1 ratio of _____ and _____ , are most efficient for most people.

• *Are there different stages of sleep?*

Recite and Review: Pages 169−172

13. Sleepiness is associated with the accumulation of a sleep hormone in the _____ and spinal cord.

14. Sleep depends on where your body is in its biological _____ rhythm. This system is found in the brain.

15. Sleep occurs in _____ stages defined by changes in behaviour and brain _____ recorded with an electroencephalograph (EEG).

16. Stage 1, _____ sleep, has small irregular brain waves. In stage 2, _____ spindles appear. _____ Waves appear in stage 3. Stage 4, or deep sleep, is marked by almost pure delta waves.

17. Sleepers _____ between stages 1 and 4 (passing through stages 2 and 3) several times each night.

18. There are two basic sleep states, rapid eye _____ (REM) sleep and non-REM (NREM) sleep.

19. REM sleep is much more strongly associated with _____ than non-REM sleep is.

20. _____ and REMs occur mainly during stage 1 sleep but usually not during the first stage 1 period.

21. Dreaming is accompanied by sexual and _____ arousal but relaxation of the skeletal _____ . People who move about violently while asleep may suffer from _____ behaviour disorder.

• *What are the causes of sleep disorders and unusual sleep events?*

Recite and Review: Pages 173−176

22. Insomnia, which is difficulty in getting to sleep or staying asleep, may be _____ or chronic.

23. When insomnia is treated with drugs, sleep quality is often _____ and drug-dependency _____ may develop.

24. The amino acid tryptophan, found in bread, pasta, and other foods, helps promote _____ .

25. Behavioural approaches to managing insomnia, such as relaxation, sleep restriction, _____ control, and paradoxical _____ are quite effective.

26. _____ (somnambulism) and sleeptalking occur during NREM sleep in stages 3 and 4.

27. Night terrors occur in _____ sleep, whereas nightmares occur in _____ sleep.

28. Nightmares can be eliminated by the method called imagery _____ .

29. Sleep _____ is believed to be one cause of sudden _____ death syndrome (SIDS).

• *Do dreams have meaning?*

Recite and Review: Pages 176−178

30. People deprived of dream sleep show a _____ rebound when allowed to sleep without interruption. However, total sleep loss seems to be more important than loss of a single sleep _____ .

31. One of the more important functions of REM sleep appears to be the processing of adaptive _____ .

32. Calvin Hall found that most dream content is about _____ settings, people, and actions. Dreams more often involve negative _____ than positive _____ .

33. The Freudian, or psychodynamic, view is that dreams express unconscious _____ , frequently hidden by dream symbols.

34. Allan Hobson and Robert McCarley's _____ -synthesis model portrays dreaming as a physiological process. The brain, they say, creates dreams to explain _____ and motor messages that occur during REM sleep.

• *How is hypnosis done, and what are its limitations?*

Recite and Review: Pages 178—182

35. Hypnosis is an altered state characterized by narrowed attention and _____ suggestibility.

36. The term _____ was first used by James Braid, an English doctor.

37. People vary in hypnotic susceptibility; _____ out of 10 can be hypnotized, as revealed by scores on the Stanford Hypnotic Susceptibility _____ .

38. The core of hypnosis is the _____ suggestion effect—a tendency to carry out suggested actions as if they wcrc involuntary.

39. Hypnosis appears capable of producing relaxation, controlling _____ , and altering perceptions.

40. Stage hypnotism takes advantage of typical stage behaviour, _____ suggestibility, responsive subjects, disinhibition, and _____ to simulate hypnosis.

• *What is meditation? Does it have any benefits?*

Recite and Review: Pages 182—184

41. Meditation refers to mental exercises that are used to alter _____ .

42. In receptive meditation, attention is _____ to include an awareness of one's entire moment-by-moment experience.

43. In concentrative meditation, attention is focused on a _____ object or thought.

44. Two major benefits of meditation are its ability to interrupt anxious thoughts and its ability to elicit the relaxation response (the pattern of changes that occur in the body at times of deep _____).

45. Sensory deprivation takes place when there is a major reduction in the amount or variety of sensory _____ available to a person.

46. Prolonged sensory deprivation is stressful and disruptive, leading to _____ distortions.

47. Brief or mild sensory deprivation can enhance sensory sensitivity and induce deep _____ .

48. Sensory deprivation also appears to aid the breaking of long-standing _____ and promotes creative thinking. This effect is the basis for Restricted Environmental Stimulation Therapy (REST).

• *What are the effects of the more commonly used psychoactive drugs?*

Recite and Review: Pages 185—199

49. A psychoactive drug is a substance that alters human _____ .

50. Most psychoactive drugs can be placed on a scale ranging from stimulation to _____ . Some, however, are best described as hallucinogens (drugs that alter _____ impressions).

51. Drugs may cause a physical dependence (_____) or a psychological dependence, or both.

52. The physically addicting drugs are heroin, morphine, codeine, methadone, barbiturates, alcohol, amphetamines, tobacco, and cocaine. All psychoactive drugs can lead to _____ dependence.

53. Stimulant drugs are easily abused because of the period of _____ that often follows stimulation. The greatest risks are associated with amphetamines, cocaine, and nicotine, but even _____ can be a problem.

54. "Designer drugs," such as MDMA, are chemical _____ of other drugs. Their long-term _____ effects are not known.

55. _____ includes the added risk of lung cancer, heart disease, and other health problems.

56. Barbiturates are _____ drugs whose overdose level is close to the intoxication dosage, making them dangerous drugs. Mixing barbiturates and alcohol may result in a fatal _____ interaction (in which the joint effect of two drugs exceeds the effects of adding one drug's effects to the other's).

57. Benzodiazepine tranquilizers, such as _____ , are used to lower anxiety. When abused, they have a strong _____ potential.

58. Alcohol is the most heavily abused drug in common use today. The development of a drinking problem is usually marked by an _____ phase of increasing consumption, a crucial phase, in which a _____ drink can set off a chain reaction, and a chronic phase, in which a person lives to drink and drinks to live.

59. Marijuana is a hallucinogen subject to a _____ dependence. Studies have linked chronic marijuana use with memory impairment, lung cancer, reproductive problems, immune system disorders, and other health problems.

60. Drug abuse is related to personal and social maladjustment, attempts to cope, and the _____ reinforcing qualities of psychoactive drugs.

• *How are dreams used to promote personal understanding?*

Recite and Review: Psychology in Action

61. Freud held that the meaning of dreams is _____ by four dream _____ he called condensation, displacement, symbolization, and secondary elaboration.

62. Calvin Hall emphasizes the setting, cast, _____ , and emotions of a dream.

63. Rosalind Cartwright's view of dreams as feeling statements and Fritz Perls's technique of _____ for dream characters and objects are also helpful.

64. Dreams may be used for _____ problem solving, especially when dream control is achieved through lucid dreaming (a dream in which the dreamer feels capable of normal thought and action).

Connections

1.	_____ Biological clock	a.	over 9 hours
2.	_____ Randy Gardner	b.	infancy
3.	_____ long sleepers	c.	reflex muscle contraction
4.	_____ sleep patterns	d.	awake, alert
5.	_____ short sleep cycles	e.	circadian rhythm
6.	_____ beta waves	f.	interrupted breathing
7.	_____ alpha waves	g.	relaxed
8.	_____ hypnic jerk	h.	sleep deprivation
9.	_____ apnea	i.	sexual arousal
10.	_____ REM sleep	j.	2 to 1 ratio

11.	_____ REST	a.	violent actions
12.	_____ hypersomnia	b.	fatal to infants
13.	_____ REM behaviour disorder	c.	unconscious meanings
14.	_____ narcolepsy	d.	sensory deprivation
15.	_____ SIDS	e.	designer drug
16.	_____ tryptophan	f.	sudden daytime REM sleep
17.	_____ dream symbols	g.	relaxation
18.	_____ auto suggestion	h.	self-hypnosis
19.	_____ MDMA	i.	sleep inducing foods
20.	_____ flotation tank	j.	excessive sleepiness

21.	_____ drug tolerance	a.	cocaine rush
22.	_____ amphetamine	b.	cancer agent
23.	_____ dopamine	c.	reduced response
24.	_____ nicotine	d.	sedative
25.	_____ carcinogen	e.	hallucinogen
26.	_____ barbiturate	f.	detoxification
27.	_____ AAA	g.	loss of pleasure
28.	_____ alcohol treatment	h.	stimulant
29.	_____ THC	i.	self-help group
30.	_____ anhedonia	j.	insecticide

Check Your Memory

Check Your Memory: Page 166

1. The quality and pattern of mental activity changes during an ASC.
    True or False

2. All people experience at least some ASCs
   True or False

3. Both sensory overload and monotonous stimulation can produce ASCs.
   True or False

4. Almost every known religion has accepted some ASCs as desirable.
   True or False

Check Your Memory: Pages 166—169

5. Through sleep learning it is possible to master a foreign language.
   True or False

6. A total inability to sleep results in death.
   True or False

7. Even after extended sleep loss, most symptoms are removed by a single night's sleep.
   True or False

8. Hallucinations and delusions are the most common reaction to extended sleep deprivation.
   True or False

9. Without scheduled light and dark periods, human sleep rhythms would drift into unusual patterns.
   True or False

10. Very short sleep-waking cycles are actually more efficient than the standard 24-hour day.
    True or False

11. Statistics Canada found that 50 percent of Canadians get less than 6.5 hours of sleep per night.
    True or False

12. Short sleepers are defined as those who average less than 5 hours of sleep per night.
    True or False

13. Shortened sleep cycles, such as 3 hours of sleep to 6 hours awake, are more
    efficient than sleeping once a day.
    True or False

Check Your Memory: Pages 169—172

14. Sleep is promoted by a chemical that accumulates in the bloodstream.
    True or False

15. Body temperature drops as a person falls asleep.
    True or False

16. A hypnic jerk is a sign of serious problems.
    True or False

17. Delta waves typically first appear in stage 2 sleep.
    True or False

18. About 45 percent of awakenings during REM periods produce reports of dreams.
    True or False

19. REM sleep occurs mainly in stages 3 and 4.
    True or False

20. REM sleep increases when a person is subjected to daytime stress.
    True or False

21. The average dream only lasts 3 to 4 minutes.
    True or False

22. Most people change positions in bed during REM sleep.
    True or False

23. REM sleep patterns could one day help doctors identify which patients will develop a more severe form of Alzheimer's disease.
    True or False

24. REM behaviour disorder causes people to briefly fall asleep and become paralyzed during the day.
    True or False

Check Your Memory: Pages 173–176

25. Bread, pasta, pretzels, cookies, and cereals all contain melatonin.
    True or False

26. Caffeine, alcohol, and tobacco can all contribute to insomnia.
    True or False

27. The two most effective behavioural treatments for insomnia are sleep restriction and stimulus control.
    True or False

28. Sleepwalking occurs during NREM periods, sleeptalking during REM periods.
    True or False

29. People who have NREM night terrors usually can remember very little afterward.
    True or False

30. Imagery rehearsal is an effective way to treat recurrent nightmares.
    True or False

31. REM sleep appears to help the brain process memories formed during the day.
    True or False

32. Alcoholics who quit drinking often experience a REM rebound.
    True or False

33. Newborn babies spend 8 or 9 hours a day in REM sleep.
    True or False

Check Your Memory: Pages 176–178

34. The favourite dream setting is outdoors.
    True or False

35. Pleasant emotions are more common in dreams than unpleasant emotions.
    True or False

36. According to Freud, dreams represent thoughts and wishes expressed as images.
    True or False

37. The activation-synthesis hypothesis emphasizes the unconscious meanings of dream symbols.
    True or False

Check Your Memory: Pages 178–182

38. The Greek word hypnos means "magnetism."
    True or False

39. Only about 4 people out of 10 can be hypnotized.
    True or False

40. The "finger-lock" is an example of animal magnetism.
    True or False

41. Physical strength cannot be increased with hypnosis.
    True or False

42. Hypnosis is better at changing subjective experiences than behaviours.
    True or False

43. Stage hypnotists look for responsive volunteers who will cooperate and not spoil the show.
    True or False

Check Your Memory: Pages 182—184

44. Receptive meditation is typically harder to do than concentrative meditation.
    True or False

45. A mantra is used as a focus for attention during receptive meditation.
    True or False

46. Herbert Benson states that the physical benefits of meditation are based on evoking the body's relaxation response.
    True or False

47. The harder you try to meditate the more likely you are to succeed.
    True or False

48. Sensory deprivation is almost always unpleasant, and it usually causes distorted perceptions.
    True or False

49. Prolonged sensory deprivation produces deep relaxation.
    True or False

50. REST is a form of brainwashing used during the Vietnam War.
    True or False

Check Your Memory: Pages 185—199

51. Abuse of any psychoactive drug can produce physical dependence.
    True or False

52. Amphetamines are used to treat narcolepsy.
    True or False

53. Amphetamine is more rapidly metabolized by the body than cocaine is.
    True or False

54. MDMA is chemically similar to amphetamine.
    True or False

55. Disregarding consequences is a sign of cocaine abuse.
    True or False

56. Caffeine can increase the risk of miscarriage during pregnancy.
    True or False

57. Twenty-five cigarettes could be fatal for a non-smoker.
    True or False

58. Regular use of nicotine leads to drug tolerance, and often to physical addiction.
    True or False

59. Every cigarette reduces a smoker's life expectancy by 7 minutes.
    True or False

60. In order to stop smoking, tapering off is generally more successful than quitting abruptly.
    True or False

61. One of the most effective ways to stop smoking is to schedule the number of cigarettes smoked each day.
True or False

62. There have been no known deaths caused by barbiturate overdoses.
True or False

63. It is legal and safe to drive as long as blood alcohol level does not exceed .8.
True or False

64. Drinking alone is a serious sign of alcohol abuse.
True or False

65. To pace alcohol intake, you should limit drinking primarily to the first hour of a social event or party.
True or False

66. Over 80 percent of fraternity and sorority members have engaged in binge drinking.
True or False

67. Hallucinogens generally affect brain transmitter systems.
True or False

68. THC receptors are found in large numbers in the cerebellum of the brain.
True or False

69. The debate on the legalization of marijuana for medical use is supported by known scientific facts about the effects of this drug on the reduction of pain.
True or False

70. Drug abuse is frequently part of general pattern of personal maladjustment
True or False

71. The negative consequences of drug use typically follow long after the drug has been taken.
True or False

Check Your Memory: Psychology in Action

72. Displacement refers to representing two or more people with a single dream image.
True or False

73. Secondary elaboration is the tendency to make a dream more logical when remembering it.
True or False

74. According to Calvin Hall, the overall emotional tone of a dream is the key to its meaning.
True or False

75. Alcohol decreases REM sleep.
True or False

76. It is basically impossible to solve daytime problems in dreams.
True or False

77. Lucid dreams either occur or they don't; there is no way to increase their frequency.
True or False

78. Lucid dreaming has been used in the treatment of nightmares.
True or False

Final Survey and Review

- *What is an altered state of consciousness?*

1. States of awareness that differ from normal, alert, waking _____ are called altered states of _____ (ASCs).
2. ASCs involve distinct shifts in the quality and pattern of _____ _____ .
3. Altered states are especially associated with sleep and dreaming, _____ , meditation, sensory _____ , and psychoactive drugs.
4. _____ conditioning greatly affects what altered states a person recognizes, seeks, considers normal, and attains.

- *What are the effects of sleep loss or changes in sleep patterns?*

5. Sleep is an _____ _____ rhythm essential for survival.
6. Our circadian _____ works on a 24-hour cycle and is controlled by an internal _____ _____ .
7. Higher animals and people deprived of sleep experience involuntary _____ (a brief shift to sleep patterns in the brain).
8. Moderate sleep loss mainly affects _____ and self-motivated performance on routine or boring tasks.
9. Extended sleep loss can (somewhat rarely) produce a temporary sleep-deprivation _____ , marked by confusion, _____ , and possibly hallucinations.
10. Sleep patterns show some flexibility, but 7 to 8 hours remains average. The unscheduled human _____ _____ averages 25 hours, but cycles of light and dark tailor it to 24-hour days.
11. The amount of daily sleep decreases steadily from birth to _____ and switches from _____ sleep-wake cycles to once-a-day sleep periods.
12. Once-a-day sleep patterns, with a _____ ratio of sleep and waking, are most efficient for most people.

- *Are there different stages of sleep?*

13. Sleepiness is associated with the accumulation of a sleep _____ in the brain and _____ .
14. Sleep depends on where your body is in its _____ circadian rhythm. This system is found in the _____ .
15. Sleep occurs in 4 stages defined by changes in behaviour and brain waves recorded with an _____ (EEG).
16. Stage 1, light sleep, has small irregular brain waves. In stage 2, sleep _____ appear. Delta waves appear in stage 3. Stage 4, or deep sleep, is marked by almost pure _____ _____ .
17. Sleepers alternate between stages _____ and _____ (passing through stages _____ and _____) several times each night.
18. There are two basic sleep states, _____ _____ movement (REM) sleep and non-REM (NREM) sleep.
19. _____ sleep is much more strongly associated with dreaming than _____ sleep is.
20. Dreams and REMs occur mainly during _____ sleep, but usually not during the first _____ period.

21. Dreaming is accompanied by sexual and emotional _____ but _____ of the skeletal muscles. People who move about violently while asleep may suffer from REM behaviour _____ .

• *What are the causes of sleep disorders and unusual sleep events?*

22. Insomnia, which is difficulty in getting to sleep or staying asleep, may be temporary or _____ .

23. When insomnia is treated with drugs, sleep quality is often lowered and drug-_____ insomnia may develop.

24. The amino acid _____ , found in bread, pasta, and other foods, helps promote sleep.

25. Behavioural approaches to managing insomnia, such as relaxation, sleep _____ , stimulus control, and _____ intention are quite effective.

26. Sleepwalking (_____) and sleeptalking occur during _____ sleep in stages 3 and 4.

27. Night terrors occur in _____ sleep, whereas nightmares occur in _____ sleep.

28. Nightmares can be eliminated by the method called _____ _____ .

29. Sleep _____ is believed to be _____ cause of sudden infant death syndrome (SIDS).

• *Do dreams have meanings?*

30. People deprived of dream sleep show a REM _____ when allowed to sleep without interruption. However, _____ sleep loss seems to be more important than loss of a single sleep stage.

31. One of the more important functions of _____ _____ appears to be the processing of adaptive memories.

32. Calvin _____ found that most dream content is about familiar settings, people, and actions. Dreams more often involve _____ emotions than _____ emotions.

33. The Freudian, or _____ , view is that dreams express unconscious wishes, frequently hidden by dream _____ .

34. Allan Hobson and Robert McCarley's activation- _____ model portrays dreaming as a physiological process. The brain, they say, creates dreams to explain sensory and _____ messages that occur during REM sleep.

• *How is hypnosis done, and what are its limitations?*

35. Hypnosis is an altered state characterized by narrowed attention and increased _____ .

36. The term hypnosis was first used by James _____ , an English doctor.

37. People vary in hypnotic susceptibility; 8 out of 10 can be hypnotized, as revealed by scores on the _____ Hypnotic Susceptibility Scale.

38. The core of hypnosis is the basic _____ effect—a tendency to carry out suggested actions as if they were _____ .

39. Hypnosis appears capable of producing _____ , controlling pain, and altering perceptions.

40. _____ _____ takes advantage of typical stage behaviour, waking suggestibility, responsive subjects, disinhibition, and deception to _____ hypnosis.

• *What is meditation? Does it have any benefits?*

41. _____ refers to mental exercises that are used to alter consciousness.

42. In _____ meditation, attention is broadened to include an awareness of one's entire moment-by-moment experience.

43. In _____ meditation, attention is focused on a single object or thought.

44. Two major benefits of meditation are its ability to interrupt anxious thoughts and its ability to elicit the _____ _____ (the pattern of changes that occur in the body at times of deep relaxation).

45. Sensory deprivation takes place when there is a major reduction in the amount or variety of _____ _____ available to a person.

46. _____ sensory deprivation is stressful and disruptive, leading to perceptual distortions.

47. Brief or mild sensory _____ can induce deep _____ .

48. Sensory deprivation also appears to aid the breaking of long-standing habits and promotes creative thinking. This effect is the basis for _____ _____ Stimulation Therapy (REST).

• *What are the effects of the more commonly used psychoactive drugs?*

49. A psychoactive drug is a substance that affects the brain in ways that alter _____ .

50. Most psychoactive drugs can be placed on a scale ranging from _____ to _____ . Some, however, are best described as _____ (drugs that alter sensory impressions).

51. Drugs may cause a physical _____ (addiction) or a psychological _____ , or both.

52. The _____ _____ drugs are heroin, morphine, codeine, methadone, barbiturates, alcohol, amphetamines, tobacco, and cocaine. All psychoactive drugs can lead to psychological dependence.

53. Stimulant drugs are easily abused because of the period of depression that often follows stimulation. The greatest risks are associated with amphetamines, _____ , and nicotine, but even caffeine can be a problem.

54. " _____ drugs," such as MDMA, are chemical variations of other drugs. Their long-term health effects are not known.

55. Nicotine (smoking) includes the added risk of _____ _____ , heart disease, and other health problems.

56. Barbiturates are depressant drugs whose overdose level is close to the intoxication dosage, making them dangerous drugs. Mixing barbiturates and _____ may result in a fatal drug _____ (in which the joint effect of two drugs exceeds the effects of adding one drug's effects to the other's).

57. _____ tranquilizers, such as Valium, are used to lower anxiety. When abused, they have a strong addictive potential.

58. _____ is the most heavily abused drug in common use today. The development of a drinking problem is usually marked by an initial phase of increasing consumption, a _____ phase, in which a single drink can set off a chain reaction, and a chronic phase, in which a person lives to drink and drinks to live.

59. Marijuana is a _____ subject to a psychological dependence. Studies have linked chronic marijuana use with memory impairment, _____ cancer, reproductive problems, immune system disorders, and other health problems.

60. Drug abuse is related to personal and social _____ , attempts to cope, and the immediate reinforcing qualities of psychoactive drugs.

• *How are dreams used to promote personal understanding?*

61. Freud held that the meaning of dreams is hidden by the dream processes he called _____ , displacement, symbolization, and _____ elaboration.

62. Calvin Hall emphasizes the _____ , _____ , plot, and emotions of a dream.

63. Rosalind Cartwright's view of dreams as _____ statements and Fritz Perl's technique of speaking for dream _____ and _____ are also helpful.

64. Dreams may be used for creative problem solving, especially when dream control is achieved through _____ dreaming (a dream in which the dreamer feels capable of normal thought and action).

Mastery Test

1. Delirium, ecstasy, and daydreaming all have in common the fact that they are
   a. forms of normal waking consciousness
   b. caused by sensory deprivation
   c. perceived as subjectively real
   d. ASCs

2. Alcoholics who quit drinking and people who have been prevented from dreaming typically experience
   a. sleep apnea
   b. REM rebound
   c. cataplexy
   d. sleep-deprivation psychosis

3. Which of the following does not belong with the others?
   a. nicotine
   b. caffeine
   c. cocaine
   d. codeine

4. Sleep spindles usually first appear in stage _____, whereas delta waves first appear in stage _____.
   a. 1, 2
   b. 2, 3
   c. 3, 4
   d. 1, 4

5. Which of the following is NOT one of the dream processes described by Freud?
   a. condensation
   b. illumination
   c. displacement
   d. symbolization

6. Which of the following most clearly occurs under hypnosis?
   a. unusual strength
   b. memory enhancement
   c. pain relief
   d. age regression

7. Alcohol, amphetamines, cocaine, and marijuana have in common the fact that they are all
   a. physically addicting
   b. psychoactive
   c. stimulants
   d. hallucinogens

113

8.   Emotional arousal, blood pressure changes, and sexual arousal all primarily occur during
   a.   REM sleep
   b.   NREM sleep
   c.   Delta sleep
   d.   stage 4 sleep

9.   The REST technique makes use of
   a.   sensory deprivation
   b.   hypodynamic imagery
   c.   hallucinogens
   d.   a CPAP mask

10.   Mesmerism, hypnosis, hypnotic susceptibility scales, and stage hypnotism all rely in part on
   a.   disinhibition
   b.   rapid eye movements
   c.   suggestibility
   d.   imagery rehearsal

11.   Shortened sleep-waking cycles overlook the fact that sleep
   a.   must match a 3 to 1 ratio of time awake and time asleep
   b.   is an innate biological rhythm
   c.   is caused by a sleep-promoting substance in the blood
   d.   cycles cannot be altered by external factors

12.   Morning drinking appears during the _____ phase in the development of a drinking problem.
   a.   initial
   b.   crucial
   c.   chronic
   d.   rebound

13.   Which of the following statements about sleep is true?
   a.   Learning math or a foreign language can be accomplished during sleep.
   b.   Some people can learn to do without sleep.
   c.   Calvin Hall had hallucinations during a sleep deprivation experiment.
   d.   Randy Gardner slept for 14 hours after ending his sleep deprivation.

14.   Amphetamine is very similar in effects to
   a.   narcotics and tranquilizers
   b.   methaqualone
   c.   codeine
   d.   cocaine

15.   Microsleeps would most likely occur
   a.   in stage 4 sleep
   b.   in a 3 to 1 ratio to microawakenings
   c.   in conjunction with delusions and hallucinations
   d.   during sleep deprivation

16. Adolescents who abuse drugs tend to be
    a.   suffering from brain dysfunctions
    b.   high in self-esteem but unrealistic about consequences
    c.   maladjusted and impulsive
    d.   similar in most respects to non-abusers

17. Sleepwalking, sleeptalking, and severe nightmares all have in common the fact that they
    a.   are REM events
    b.   are NREM events
    c.   are sleep disorders
    d.   can be controlled with imagery rehearsal

18. In its milder forms, sensory deprivation sometimes produces
    a.   cataplectic images
    b.   deep relaxation
    c.   tryptophanic images
    d.   REM symbolizations

19. The basic suggestion effect is closely related to
    a.   hypnosis
    b.   sensory enhancement after sensory deprivation
    c.   hypersomnia
    d.   the frequency of dreaming during REM sleep

20. A person who feels awake and capable of normal action while sleeping has experienced
    a.   lucid dreaming
    b.   the basic suggestion effect
    c.   sleep drunkeness
    d.   REM rebound

21. Which of the following is a hallucinogen?
    a.   LSD
    b.   THC
    c.   hashish
    d.   all of the preceding

22. The two most basic states of sleep are
    a.   stage 1 sleep and stage 4 sleep
    b.   REM sleep and NREM sleep
    c.   Alpha sleep and Delta sleep
    d.   Alpha sleep and hypnic sleep

23. A mantra would most commonly be used in
    a.   Perls' method of dream interpretation
    b.   sensory deprivation research
    c.   inducing hypnosis
    d.   concentrative meditation

24. Learning to use a computer would most likely be slowed if you were _____ each night.
    a. deprived of a half hour of NREM sleep
    b. allowed to engage in extra REM sleep
    c. prevented from dreaming
    d. awakened three times at random
25. By definition, compulsive drug use involves
    a. dependence
    b. experimentation
    c. repeated overdoses
    d. anhedonia
26. A particularly dangerous drug interaction occurs when _____ and _____ are combined.
    a. alcohol, amphetamine
    b. barbiturates, nicotine
    c. alcohol, barbiturates
    d. amphetamine, codeine
27. Narcolepsy is an example of
    a. a night terror
    b. a sleep disorder
    c. a tranquilizer
    d. an addictive drug
28. Sleep restriction and stimulus control techniques would most likely be used to treat
    a. insomnia
    b. narcolepsy
    c. sleepwalking
    d. REM behaviour disorder
29. In addition to the nicotine they contain, cigarettes release
    a. dopamine
    b. tryptophan
    c. noradrenaline
    d. carcinogens
30. Disguised dream symbols are to psychodynamic dream theory as sensory and motor messages are to
    a. the Freudian theory of dreams
    b. the activation-synthesis hypothesis
    c. Fritz Perls' methods of dream interpretation
    d. paradoxical intention
31. Which of the following groups of people will need more sleep as they age?
    a. elderlies
    b. infants
    c. adolescents
    d. none of the above

32. How can one explain the finding that less medicare money is spent on people who practice transcendental meditation (TM)?

    a. They are in better health because of the effects of meditation.

    b. Their practice of meditation and their lifestyle give them better health.

    c. It is untrue, there is no link between meditation and the amount of medicare money spent on those who practice meditation.

    d. Both a and b could be true but remains uncertain due to the fact that the evidence comes from correlational studies and that some design errors exist in TM studies.

33. According to a 1999 statistic from the Canadian Centre on Substance Abuse, how many Canadians die from smoking?

    a. 1 in 100

    b. 1 in 50

    c. 1 in 6

    d. 1 in 200

Solutions

Recite and Review

1. awareness, waking
2. pattern
3. sleep, dreaming, sensory
4. normal,
5. rhythm, survival
6. 24, biological
7. involuntary
8. routine
9. loss, temporary
10. 25, light, dark
11. decreases
12. waking, sleep
13. brain
14. circadian
15. 4, waves
16. light, sleep, Delta
17. alternate
18. movement
19. dreaming
20. Dreaming
21. emotional, muscles, REM
22. temporary
23. lowered, insomnia
24. sleep
25. stimulus, intention
26. Sleepwalking
27. NREM, REM
28. rehearsal
29. apnea, infant
30. REM, stage
31. memories
32. familiar, emotions, emotions
33. wishes
34. activation, sensory
35. increased
36. hypnosis
37. 8, Scale
38. basic
39. pain
40. waking, deception
41. consciousness
42. widened
43. single
44. relaxation
45. stimulation
46. perceptual
47. relaxation
48. habits
49. consciousness
50. depression, sensory
51. addiction
52. psychological
53. depression, caffeine
54. variations, health
55. Nicotine
56. depressant, drug
57. valium, addictive
58. initial, single
59. psychological
60. immediate
61. hidden, processes
62. plot
63. speaking
64. creative

Connections

1. E
2. H
3. A
4. J
5. B
6. D
7. G
8. C
9. F
10. I
11. D
12. J
13. A
14. F
15. B
16. I
17. C
18. H
19. C
20. G
21. C
22. H
23. A
24. J
25. B
26. D
27. I
28. F
29. E
30. G

Check Your Memory

1. T
2. T
3. T
4. T

5. F	41. T	77. F
6. T	42. T	78. T
7. T	43. T	
8. F	44. T	
9. T	45. F	

Final Survey and Review

10. F	46. T	1. consciousness, consciousness
11. F	47. F	2. mental, activity
12. T	48. F	3. hypnosis, deprivation
13. F	49. F	4. Cultural
14. F	50. F	5. innate, biological
15. T	51. F	6. rhythm, biological, clock
16. F	52. T	7. microsleeps
17. F	53. F	8. alertness
18. F	54. T	9. psychosis, delusions
19. F	55. T	10. sleep-walking, cycle
20. T	56. T	11. old age, multiple
21. F	57. T	12. 2-to-1
22. F	58. T	13. hormone, spinal cord
23. T	59. T	14. biological, brain
24. F	60. T	15. electroencephalograph
25. F	61. T	16. spindles, delta, waves
26. T	62. F	17. 1, 4, 2, 3
27. T	63. F	18. rapid, eye
28. F	64. T	19. REM, non-REM
29. T	65. T	20. stage 1, stage 1
30. T	66. T	21. arousal, relaxation, disorder
31. T	67. T	22. chronic
32. T	68. F	23. dependency
33. T	69. F	24. tryptophan
34. F	70. F	25. restriction, paradoxical
35. F	71. T	26. somnambulism, NREM
36. T	72. F	27. NREM, REM
37. F	73. T	28. imagery, rehearsal
38. F	74. F	29. apnea, one
39. F	75. T	30. rebound, total
40. F	76. F	31. REM, sleep

32. Hall, negative, positive
33. psychodynamic, symbols
34. synthesis, motor
35. suggestibility
36. Braid
37. Stanford
38. suggestion, involuntary
39. relaxation
40. Stage, hypnotism, simulate
41. Meditation
42. receptive
43. concentrative
44. relaxation, response
45. sensory, stimulation
46. Prolonged
47. deprivation, relaxation
48. Restricted, Environmental
49. consciousness
50. stimulation, depression, hallucinogens
51. dependence, dependence
52. physically, addicting
53. cocaine
54. Designer
55. lung, cancer
56. alcohol, interaction
57. Benzodiazepine
58. Alcohol, crucial
59. hallucinogen, lung
60. maladjustment
61. condensation, secondary
62. setting, cast
63. feeling, characters, objects
64. lucid

Mastery Test

1. D (p. 166)
2. B (p. 177)
3. D (p. 188)
4. B (p. 170)
5. B (p. 200)
6. C (p. 181)
7. B (p. 192)
8. A (p. 172)
9. A (p. 183)
10. C (p. 179)
11. B (p. 175)
12. A (p. 193)
13. D (p. 168)
14. D (p. 188)
15. D (p. 167)
16. C (p. 198)
17. C (p. 175)
18. B (p. 183)
19. A (p. 180)
20. A (p. 202)
21. D (p. 186)
22. B (p. 171)
23. D (p. 182)
24. C (p. 177)
25. A (p. 185)
26. C (p. 193)
27. B (p. 173)
28. A (p. 174)
29. D (p. 190)
30. B (p. 177)
31. D (p. 169)
32. D (p. 184)

33. C (p. 191)

Chapter 6

Conditioning and Learning

Chapter Overview

Learning is a relatively permanent change in behaviour due to experience. Two basic forms of learning are classical conditioning and operant conditioning.

Classical conditioning is also called respondent or Pavlovian conditioning. Classical conditioning occurs when a neutral stimulus is associated with an unconditioned stimulus (which reliably elicits an unconditioned response). After many pairings of the NS and the US, the NS becomes a conditioned stimulus that elicits a conditioned response. Learning is reinforced during acquisition of a response. Withdrawing reinforcement leads to extinction (although some spontaneous recovery of conditioning may occur). It is apparent that stimulus generalization has occurred when a stimulus similar to the CS also elicits a learned response. In stimulus discrimination, people or animals learn to respond differently to two similar stimuli. Conditioning often involves simple reflex responses, but emotional conditioning is also possible. Aversive responses to food and the development of tolerance to drugs are also due to classical conditioning.

In operant conditioning (or instrumental learning), the consequences that follow a response alter the probability that it will be made again. Positive and negative reinforcers increase responding; punishment suppresses responding; non-reinforcement leads to extinction. Various types of reinforcers and different patterns of giving reinforcers greatly affect operant learning. Informational feedback (knowledge of results) also facilitates learning and performance. Antecedent stimuli (those that precede a response) influence operant learning, through stimulus generalization, discrimination, and stimulus control.

Learning, even simple conditioning, is based on acquiring information. Higher level cognitive learning involves memory, thinking, problem solving, and language. At a simpler level, cognitive maps, latent learning, and discovery learning show that learning is based on acquiring information. Learning also occurs through observation and imitating models. Observational learning imparts large amounts of information that would be hard to acquire in other ways.

Operant principles can be applied to manage one's own behaviour and to break bad habits. A mixture of operant principles and cognitive learning underlies self-regulated learning—a collection of techniques to improve learning in school.

Learning Objectives

1. Define learning.

2. Define reinforcement and explain its role in conditioning. (See also Table 6.1.)

3. Differentiate between antecedents and consequences and explain how they are related to classical and operant conditioning. (See also Table 6.1.)

4. Give a brief history of classical conditioning.

5. Describe the following terms as they apply to classical conditioning:

   a.   neutral stimulus (NS)

b. conditioned stimulus (CS)

c. unconditioned stimulus (US)

d. unconditioned response (UR)

e. conditioned response (CR)

6. Describe and give an example of classical conditioning using the abbreviations US, UR, CS, and CR.

7. Explain how reinforcement occurs during the acquisition of a classically conditioned response. Include an explanation of higher order conditioning.

8. Explain classical conditioning in terms of the informational view.

9. Describe and give examples of the following concepts as they relate to classical conditioning:

a. extinction

b. spontaneous recovery

c. stimulus generalization

d. stimulus discrimination

10. Describe the relationship between classical conditioning and reflex responses.

11. Explain what a conditioned emotional response (CER) is and how it is acquired. Include definitions of the terms *phobia* and *desensitization*.

12. Explain the concept and the importance of vicarious classical conditioning.

13. Describe how conditioned taste aversions develop.

14. Explain how classical conditioning is involved in drug tolerance and drug cravings.

15. State the basic principle of operant conditioning.

16. Contrast operant conditioning with classical conditioning. Include a brief comparison of the differences between what is meant by the terms *reward* and *reinforcement*. (See also Table 6.2.)

17. Explain operant conditioning in terms of the informational view. Explain what response-contingent reinforcement is.

18. Describe how Skinner's vision of behavioural engineering has been put into practice.

19. Describe how the delay of reinforcement can influence the effectiveness of the reinforcement.

20. Describe response chaining and explain how it can counteract the effects of delaying reinforcement.

21. Explain why superstitious behaviour develops and why it persists.

22. Explain how shaping occurs. Include a definition of the term *successive approximations*.

23. Explain how extinction and spontaneous recovery occur in operant conditioning.

24. Describe how negative attention seeking demonstrates reinforcement and extinction in operant conditioning. (See also Table 6.3.)

25. Compare and contrast positive reinforcement, negative reinforcement, punishment, and response cost punishment and give an example of each.

26. Differentiate primary reinforcers from secondary reinforcers and list four examples of each kind.

27. Discuss two ways in which a secondary reinforcer becomes reinforcing.

28. Discuss the major advantages and disadvantages of primary reinforcers and secondary reinforcers (tokens, for instance), and describe how tokens have been used to help "special" groups of people.

29. Define social reinforcers. Name two key elements that underlie learning and explain how they function together in learning situations.

30. Define feedback, indicate three factors which increase its effectiveness, and explain its importance in learning.

31. Describe the following kinds of instruction and discuss their application in learning and teaching: programmed, computer-assisted, and interactive videodisc.

32. Compare and contrast the effects of continuous and partial reinforcement.

33. Describe, give an example of, and explain the effects of the following schedules of partial reinforcement:
    a. fixed ratio (FR)
    b. variable ratio (VR)
    c. fixed interval (FI)
    d. variable interval (VI)

34. Explain the concept of stimulus control.

35. Describe the processes of generalization and discrimination as they relate to operant conditioning.

36. Explain how punishers can be defined by their effects on behaviour.

37. List and discuss three factors which influence the effectiveness of punishment.

38. Differentiate the effects of severe punishment from mild punishment.

39. List the three basic tools available to control simple learning.

40. Discuss how and why reinforcement should be used with punishment in order to change an undesirable behaviour.

41. List six guidelines which should be followed when using punishment.

42. List and discuss three problems associated with punishment.

43. Define cognitive learning.

44. Describe the concepts of a cognitive map and latent learning.

45. Explain the difference between discovery learning and rote learning. Describe the behaviour of the students who used each approach in the Wertheimer study.

46. Discuss the factors which determine whether observational learning (modelling) will occur.

47. Describe the experiment with children and the Bo-Bo doll that demonstrates the powerful effect of modelling on behaviour.

48. Explain why what a parent does is more important than what a parent says.

49. Briefly describe the general conclusion that can be drawn from studies on the effects of TV violence on children. Explain why it would be an exaggeration to say that TV violence *causes* aggression.

50. Describe the procedures and results of Williams' natural experiment with TV.

51. List and briefly describe the seven steps in a behavioural self-management program. Explain how the Premack principle may apply.

52. Describe how self-recording can aid a self-management program.

53. Describe five ways to break a bad habit.

54. Briefly describe eight strategies that can be used to achieve self-regulated learning.

Practice Quizzes

Recite and Review

• *What is learning?*

Recite and Review: Pages 209–210

1. Learning is a relatively permanent change in _____ due to experience. To understand learning we must study antecendents (events that _____ responses) and consequences (events that _____ responses).

2. Classical, or respondent, _____ and instrumental, or operant, _____ are two basic types of learning.

3. In classical conditioning, a previously neutral _____ is associated with a stimulus that elicits a response. In operant conditioning, the pattern of voluntary _____ is altered by consequences.

4. Both types of conditioning depend on reinforcement. In classical conditioning, learning is _____ when a US follows the NS or CS. _____ reinforcement is based on the consequences that follow a response.

• *How does classical conditioning occur?*

Recite and Review: Pages 210–214

5. Classical conditioning, studied by Ivan Pavlov, occurs when a _____ stimulus (NS) is associated with an unconditioned stimulus (US). The US triggers a reflex called the unconditioned _____ (UR).

6. If the NS is consistently paired with the US, it becomes a conditioned _____ (CS) capable of producing a response by itself. This response is a conditioned (_____) response (CR).

7. During acquisition of classical conditioning, the conditioned stimulus must be consistently followed by the unconditioned _____ .

8. Higher-order conditioning occurs when a well-learned conditioned stimulus is used as if it were an unconditioned _____ , bringing about further learning.

9. When the CS is repeatedly presented alone, extinction takes place. That is, _____ is weakened or inhibited.

10. After extinction seems to be complete, a rest period may lead to the temporary reappearance of a conditioned _____ . This is called spontaneous recovery.

11. Through stimulus generalization, stimuli _____ to the conditioned stimulus will also produce a response.

12. Generalization gives way to _____ discrimination when an organism learns to respond to one stimulus, but not to similar stimuli.

13. From an informational view, conditioning creates expectancies (or expectations about events), which alter _____ patterns.

14. In classical conditioning, the CS creates an expectancy that the US will _____ it.

• *Does conditioning affect emotions?*

Recite and Review: Pages 214—216

15. Conditioning applies to visceral or emotional responses as well as simple _____ . As a result, _____ emotional responses (CERs) also occur.

16. Irrational fears called phobias may be CERs that are extended to a variety of situations by _____ generalization.

17. The conditioning of emotional responses can occur vicariously (_____) as well as directly. Vicarious classical conditioning occurs when we _____ another person's emotional responses to a stimulus.

18. Conditioned taste aversions develop when a _____ food is associated with an _____ reaction or _____ .

19. Drug tolerance comes from the body compensating (physiological responses) for the _____ of the drug. The process of injecting, _____ cues, and the paraphernalia used to prepare the drug will all become _____ with the compensatory physiological responses by _____ conditioning.

• *How does operant conditioning occur?*

Recite and Review: Pages 216—221

20. Operant conditioning (or instrumental _____) occurs when a voluntary action is followed by a reinforcer.

21. Reinforcement in operant conditioning _____ the frequency or probability of a response. This result is based on what Edward L. Thorndike called the law of _____ .

22. An operant reinforcer is any event that follows a _____ and _____ its probability.

23. Learning in operant conditioning is based on the expectation that a response will have a specific _____ .

24. To be effective, operant _____ must be _____ contingent.

25. Delay of reinforcement reduces its effectiveness, but long _____ of responses may be built up so that a _____ reinforcer maintains many responses.

26. Superstitious behaviours (unnecessary responses) often become part of _____ chains because they appear to be associated with reinforcement.

27. In a process called shaping, complex _____ responses can be taught by reinforcing successive approximations (ever closer matches) to a final desired response.

28. If an operant response is not reinforced, it may extinguish (disappear). But after extinction seems complete, it may temporarily reappear (spontaneous _____).

29. In positive reinforcement, _____ or a pleasant event follows a response. In negative reinforcement, a response that _____ discomfort becomes more likely to occur again.

30. Punishment _____ responding. Punishment occurs when a response is followed by the onset of an aversive event or by the removal of a positive event (response _____).

- ## *Are there different kinds of operant reinforcement?*

Recite and Review: Pages 222–226

31. Primary reinforcers are "natural," physiologically-based rewards. Intra-cranial stimulation of "_____ centres" in the _____ can also serve as a primary reinforcer.

32. Secondary reinforcers are _____ . They typically gain their reinforcing value by association with primary reinforcers or because they can be _____ for primary reinforcers. Tokens and money gain their reinforcing value in this way.

33. Human behaviour is often influenced by social reinforcers, which are based on learned desires for attention and _____ from others.

34. Feedback, or knowledge of _____ , aids learning and improves performance.

35. Programmed instruction breaks learning into a series of small steps and provides immediate _____ .

36. Computer-assisted _____ (CAI) does the same, but has the added advantage of providing alternate exercises and information when needed.

37. Four variations of CAI are drill and _____ , instructional games, educational simulations, and interactive videodisc instruction.

- ## *How are we influenced by patterns of reward?*

Recite and Review: Pages 226–230

38. Reward or reinforcement may be given continuously (after every _____), or on a schedule of _____ reinforcement. The study of schedules of reinforcement was begun by B. F. Skinner.

39. Partial reinforcement produces greater resistance to extinction. This is the partial reinforcement _____ .

40. The four most basic schedules of reinforcement are _____ ratio (FR), variable ratio (VR), _____ interval (FI), and variable interval (VI).

41. FR and VR schedules produce _____ rates of responding. An FI schedule produces moderate rates of responding with alternating periods of activity and inactivity. VI schedules produce _____ , steady rates of responding and strong resistance to extinction.

42. Stimuli that _____ a reinforced response tend to control the response on future occasions (stimulus control).

43. Two aspects of stimulus control are generalization and _____ .

44. In generalization, an operant response tends to occur when stimuli _____ to those preceding reinforcement are present.

45. In discrimination, responses are _____ in the presence of discriminative stimuli associated with reinforcement and _____ in the presence of stimuli associated with non-reinforcement.

- ## *What does punishment do to behaviour?*

Recite and Review: Pages 230–233

46. A punisher is any consequence that _____ the frequency of a target behaviour.

47. Punishment is most effective when it is _____ , consistent, and intense.

48. Mild punishment tends only to temporarily _____ responses that are also reinforced or were acquired by reinforcement.

49. The undesirable side effects of punishment include the conditioning of fear; the learning of _____ and avoidance responses; and the encouragement of aggression.

50. Reinforcement and non-reinforcement are a better way to change behaviour than punishment. When punishment is used, it should be _____ and combined with reinforcement of desired _____ .

• *What is cognitive learning?*

Recite and Review: Pages 234−235

51. Cognitive learning involves higher mental processes, such as understanding, knowing, or anticipating. Evidence of cognitive learning is provided by cognitive _____ (internal representations of spatial relationships) and latent (hidden) _____ .

52. Discovery learning emphasizes insight and _____ , in contrast to rote learning.

• *Does learning occur by imitation?*

Recite and Review: Pages 236−238

53. Much human learning is achieved through _____ , or modelling. Observational learning is influenced by the personal characteristics of the _____ and the success or failure of the _____ behaviour.

54. Television characters can act as powerful _____ for observational learning. Televised violence increases the likelihood of aggression by viewers.

• *How does conditioning apply to practical problems?*

Recite and Review: Psychology in Action

55. Operant principles can be readily applied to manage behaviour in everyday settings. Self-management of behaviour is based on self-reinforcement, self-recording, _____ , and behavioural contracting.

56. Prepotent, or frequent, high-probability _____ , can be used to reinforce low-frequency responses. This is known as the Premack _____ .

57. Attempts to break bad habits are aided by reinforcing alternate _____ , by extinction, breaking _____ chains, and _____ cues or antecedents.

58. In school, self-regulated _____ typically involves all of the following: setting learning _____ , planning learning strategies, using self-instruction, monitoring progress, evaluating yourself, reinforcing _____ , and taking corrective action when required.

Connections

1. _____ reflex response
2. _____ operant conditioning
3. _____ antecedents
4. _____ meat powder
5. _____ bell
6. _____ salivation
7. _____ consequences
8. _____ CS used as US
9. _____ extinction
10. _____ acquisition

a. before responses
b. Pavlov's CS
c. after responses
d. higher-order conditioning
e. contraction of the pupil
f. US missing
g. reinforcement period
h. UR
i. Pavlov's US
j. learning consequences

11. _____ phobia
12. _____ desensitization
13. _____ Skinner
14. _____ shaping
15. _____ negative reinforcement
16. _____ punishment
17. _____ tokens
18. _____ approval
19. _____ partial reinforcement
20. _____ stimulus control

a. conditioned emotional response (CER)
b. conditioning chamber
c. increased responding
d. decreased responding
e. social reinforcer
f. Chimp-O-Mat
g. approximations
h. resistance to extinction
i. antecedent stimuli
j. extinction of fear

21. _____ punishment
22. _____ expectancies
23. _____ knowledge of results (KR)
24. _____ computer-assisted instruction (CAI)
25. _____ discovery learning
26. _____ modelling
27. _____ self-instruction
28. _____ fixed ratio
29. _____ spontaneous recovery
30. _____ fixed interval

a. number of responses per reinforcer
b. reinforcement schedule
c. incomplete extinction
d. escape and avoidance
e. informational view
f. educational simulations
g. feedback
h. insight
i. self-regulated learning
j. imitation

Check Your Memory

Check Your Memory: Pages 209–210

1. Learning to press the buttons on a vending machine is based on operant conditioning.
   True or False

2. In classical conditioning, the consequences that follow responses become associated with one another.
   True or False

3. Getting compliments from friends could serve as reinforcement for operant learning.
   True or False

Check Your Memory: Pages 210—214

4. Ivan Pavlov studied digestion and operant conditioning in dogs.
   True or False

5. Pavlov used meat powder to reinforce salivation.
   True or False

6. During successful conditioning, the NS becomes a CS.
   True or False

7. During acquisition, the CS is presented repeatedly without the US.
   True or False

8. The optimal delay between the CS and the US is 5 to 15 seconds.
   True or False

9. Spontaneous recovery occurs when a CS becomes strong enough to be used like a US.
   True or False

10. Discriminations are learned when generalized responses to stimuli similar to the CS are extinguished.
    True or False

Check Your Memory: Pages 214—216

11. Narrowing of the pupils in response to bright lights is learned in early infancy.
    True or False

12. Emotional conditioning involves autonomic nervous system responses.
    True or False

13. Stimulus generalization helps convert some CERs into phobias.
    True or False

14. Pleasant music can be used as a UR to create a CER.
    True or False

15. To learn a CER vicariously, you would observe the actions of another person and try to imitate them.
    True or False

16. A drug user may suffer a fatal overdose when taking drugs in an unfamiliar setting.
    True or False

Check Your Memory: Pages 216—221

17. In operant conditioning, learners actively emit responses.
    True or False

18. Rewards are the same as reinforcers.
    Truc or False

19. The Skinner box is primarily used to study classical conditioning.
    True or False

20. Reinforcement in operant conditioning alters how frequently involuntary responses are elicited.
    True or False

21. Operant reinforcers are most effective when they are response-contingent.
    True or False

22. Rent reductions were the final reinforcers in the Experimental Living Project.
    True or False

23. Operant learning is most effective if you wait a minute or two after the response is over before reinforcing it.
    True or False

24. Response chains allow delayed reinforcers to support learning.
    True or False

25. Superstitious responses appear to be associated with reinforcement, but they are not.
    True or False

26. Teaching a pigeon to play Ping-Pong would most likely make use of the principle of response cost.
    True or False

27. Children who misbehave may be reinforced by attention from parents.
    True or False

28. Negative reinforcement is a type of punishment that is used to strengthen learning.
    True or False

29. Both response cost and negative reinforcement decrease responding.
    True or False

Check Your Memory: Pages 222−225

30. Food, water, grades, and sex are primary reinforcers.
    True or False

31. Intra-cranial stimulation (ICS) is a good example of a secondary reinforcer.
    True or False

32. Social reinforcers are secondary reinforcers.
    True or False

33. Attention and approval can be used to shape another person's behaviour.
    True or False

34. The effects of primary reinforcers may quickly decline as the person becomes satiated.
    True or False

35. The Chimp-O-Mat accepted primary reinforcers and dispensed secondary reinforcers.
    True or False

36. Computer-assisted instruction (CAI) gives frequent, immediate, and detailed feedback.
    True or False

37. In sports, feedback is most effective when a skilled coach directs attention to important details.
    True or False

38. The final level of skill and knowledge is almost always higher following CAI than it is with conventional methods.
    True or False

Check Your Memory: Pages 226−229

39. Continuous reinforcement means that reinforcers are given continuously, regardless of whether or not responses are made.
    True or False

40. A FR-3 schedule means that each correct response produces 3 reinforcers.
   True or False

41. The time interval in FI schedules is measured from the last reinforced response.
   True or False

42. In business, commissions and profit sharing are examples of FI reinforcement.
   True or False

43. Antecedent stimuli tend to control when and where previously rewarded responses will occur.
   True or False

44. Stimulus generalization is the primary method used to train dogs to detect contraband.
   True or False

Check Your Memory: Pages 230—233

45. Like reinforcement, punishment should be response-contingent.
   True or False

46. Punishment is most effective if it is unpredictable.
   True or False

47. Speeding tickets are an example of response cost (removal of a positive reinforcer).
   True or False

48. Mild punishment causes reinforced responses to extinguish more rapidly.
   True or False

49. Generally, punishment should be the last resort for altering behaviour.
   True or False

50. An apparatus known as a shuttle box is used to study escape and avoidance learning.
   True or False

51. For humans, avoidance learning is reinforced by a sense of relief.
   True or False

52. Punishment frequently leads to increases in aggression by the person who is punished.
   True or False

Check Your Memory: Pages 234—235

53. Cognitive learning involves thinking, memory, and problem solving.
   True or False

54. Animals learning their way through a maze memorize the correct order of right and left turns to make.
   True or False

55. Typically, reinforcement must be provided in order to make latent learning visible.
   True or False

56. In many situations, discovery learning produces better understanding of problems.
   True or False

Check Your Memory: Pages 236—238

57. Modelling is another term for discovery learning.
   True or False

58. After a new response is acquired through modelling, normal reinforcement determines if it will be repeated.
   True or False

59. Children imitate aggressive acts performed by other people, but they are not likely to imitate cartoon characters.
    True or False

60. Violence on television causes children to be more violent.
    True or False

Check Your Memory: Psychology in Action

61. Choosing reinforcers is the first step in behavioural self-management.
    True or False

62. Self-recording can be an effective way to change behaviour, even without using specific reinforcers.
    True or False

63. When trying to break a habit, it is best to follow the same chain of events that leads to the undesired behaviour.
    True or False

64. To use extinction to break a bad habit, you should remove, avoid, or delay the reinforcement that is supporting the habit.
    True or False

65. In a behavioural contract, you spell out what response chains you are going to extinguish.
    True or False

66. Self-regulated learners actively seek feedback in both formal and informal ways.
    True or False

Final Survey and Review

• *What is learning?*

1. Learning is a relatively permanent change in behaviour due to experience. To understand learning we must study _____ (events that precede responses) and _____ (events that follow responses).

2. Classical, or _____ , conditioning and instrumental, or _____ , conditioning are two basic types of learning.

3. In classical conditioning, a previously _____ stimulus is associated with another stimulus that elicits a response. In operant conditioning, the pattern of voluntary responses is altered by _____ .

4. Both types of conditioning depend on _____ . In classical conditioning, learning is reinforced when a _____ follows the NS or CS. Operant reinforcement is based on the consequences that follow a response.

• *How does classical conditioning occur?*

5. Classical conditioning, studied by _____ _____ , occurs when a neutral stimulus (NS) is associated with an _____ stimulus (US). The US triggers a _____ called the unconditioned response (UR).

6. If the NS is consistently paired with the US, it becomes a _____ stimulus (CS) capable of producing a response by itself. This response is a _____ (learned) response (CR).

7. During acquisition of classical conditioning, the conditioned stimulus must be consistently followed by the _____ _____ .

8. _____ conditioning occurs when a well-learned conditioned stimulus is used as if it were an unconditioned stimulus, bringing about further learning.

9. When the CS is repeatedly presented alone, _____ takes place (learning is weakened or inhibited). .

10. After extinction seems to be complete, a rest period may lead to the temporary reappearance of a conditioned response. This is called _____ _____ .

11. Through stimulus _____ , stimuli similar to the conditioned stimulus will also produce a response.

12. Generalization gives way to stimulus _____ when an organism learns to respond to one stimulus, but not to similar stimuli.

13. From an _____ view, conditioning creates expectancies (or expectations about events), which alter response patterns.

14. In classical conditioning, the _____ creates an expectancy that the _____ will follow it.

● *Does conditioning affect emotions?*

15. Conditioning applies to visceral or emotional responses as well as simple reflexes. As a result, conditioned _____ _____ (CERs) also occur.

16. Irrational fears called _____ may be CERs that are extended to a variety of situations by stimulus _____ .

17. The conditioning of emotional responses can occur secondhand as well as directly. _____ classical conditioning occurs when we observe another person's emotional responses to a stimulus.

18. Conditioned taste _____ develop when a novel food is associated with an unpleasant reaction or _____ .

19. Drug tolerance comes from the body _____ (physiological responses) for the effects of a drug. The process of injecting, environmental cues, and paraphernalia used to prepare the drug will be _____ to the _____ responses by classical conditioning.

● *How does operant conditioning occur?*

20. Operant conditioning (or _____ learning) occurs when a voluntary action is followed by a reinforcer.

21. Reinforcement in operant conditioning increases the frequency or _____ of a response. This result is based on what Edward L. _____ called the law of effect.

22. An operant reinforcer is any event that follows a _____ and _____ its probability.

23. Learning in operant conditioning is based on the _____ that a response will have a specific effect.

24. To be effective, operant reinforcers must be response _____ .

25. Delay of reinforcement _____ its effectiveness, but long chains of responses may be built up so that a single _____ maintains many responses.

26. _____ behaviours (unnecessary responses) often become part of response chains because they appear to be associated with reinforcement.

27. In a process called _____ , complex operant responses can be taught by reinforcing successive _____ (ever closer matches) to a final desired response.

28. If an operant response is not reinforced, it may _____ (disappear). But after extinction seems complete, it may temporarily reappear (_____ recovery).

29. In _____ reinforcement, reward or a pleasant event follows a response. In _____ reinforcement, a response that ends discomfort becomes more likely to occur again.

30. Punishment decreases responding. Punishment occurs when a response is followed by the onset of an _____ event or by the removal of a _____ event (response cost).

• *Are there different kinds of operant reinforcement?*

31. _____ reinforcers are "natural," physiologically-based rewards. Intra-cranial _____ of "pleasure centres" in the brain can also serve as a reinforcers of this type.

32. _____ reinforcers are learned. They typically gain their reinforcing value by association with _____ reinforcers or because they can be exchanged for _____ reinforcers. Tokens and money gain their reinforcing value in this way.

33. Human behaviour is often influenced by _____ reinforcers, which are based on learned desires for attention and approval from others.

34. Feedback, or _____ of results, aids learning and improves performance.

35. Programmed _____ breaks learning into a series of small steps and provides immediate feedback.

36. _____ _____ (CAI) does the same, but has the added advantage of providing alternate exercises and information when needed.

37. Four variations of _____ are drill and practice, instructional games, educational simulations, and interactive videodisc instruction.

• *How are we influenced by patterns of reward?*

38. Reward or reinforcement may be given continuously (after every response), or on a _____ of partial reinforcement like those studied by B. F. _____ .

39. Partial reinforcement produces greater resistance to _____ . This is the _____ reinforcement effect.

40. The four most basic schedules of reinforcement are fixed and variable _____ (FR and VR) and fixed and variable _____ (FI and VI).

41. _____ and _____ schedules produce high rates of responding. An _____ schedule produces moderate rates of responding with alternating periods of activity and inactivity. VI schedules produce slow, steady rates of responding and strong resistance to _____ .

42. Stimuli that precede a reinforced response tend to control the response on future occasions. This is called _____ _____ .

43. Two aspects of stimulus control are _____ and discrimination.

44. In _____ , an operant response tends to occur when stimuli similar to those preceding reinforcement are present.

45. In _____ , responses are given in the presence of stimuli associated with reinforcement and withheld in the presence of stimuli associated with non-reinforcement.

• *What does punishment do to behaviour?*

46. A _____ is any consequence that lowers the frequency of a target behaviour.

47. Punishment is most effective when it is immediate, _____ , and intense.

48. Mild punishment tends only to temporarily suppress responses that are also _____ in some way.

49. The undesirable side effects of punishment include the conditioning of fear; the learning of escape and _____ responses; and the encouragement of _____ against others.

50. _____ and _____ are a better way to change behaviour than punishment.

• *What is cognitive learning?*

51. Cognitive learning involves higher mental processes, such as understanding, knowing, or anticipating. Evidence of cognitive learning is provided by _____ _____ (internal representations of spatial relationships) and _____ (hidden) learning.

52. Discovery learning emphasizes insight and understanding, in contrast to _____ learning.

• *Does learning occur by imitation?*

53. Much human learning is achieved through observation, or _____ . _____ learning is influenced by the personal characteristics of the model and the success or failure of the model's behaviour.

54. Television characters can act as powerful models for _____ learning. Televised violence increases the likelihood of aggression by viewers.

• *How does conditioning apply to practical problems?*

55. Operant principles can be readily applied to manage behaviour in everyday settings. Self-management of behaviour is based on self-reinforcement, self-recording, feedback, and behavioural _____ .

56. Prepotent, or frequent, high-probability responses, can be used to _____ low-frequency responses. This is known as the _____ principle.

57. Attempts to break bad habits are aided by reinforcing _____ responses, by extinction, breaking response _____ , and removing cues or _____ .

58. In school, self-regulated learning typically involves all of the following: setting learning goals, planning learning _____ , using self-instruction, monitoring progress, evaluating yourself, _____ successes, and taking corrective action when required.

Mastery Test

1. Tokens are a good example of
   a. secondary reinforcers
   b. the effects of ICS on behaviour
   c. non-contingent reinforcers
   d. generalized reinforcers

2. The principle of feedback is of particular importance to
   a. CERs
   b. ICS
   c. CAI
   d. higher-order conditioning

3. As a coffee lover, you have become very efficient at carrying out the steps necessary to make a cup of espresso. Your learning is an example of
   a. response chaining
   b. spontaneous recovery
   c. vicarious reinforcement

      d.   secondary reinforcement

4.   To teach a pet dog to use a new dog door, it would be helpful to use

      a.   the Premack principle

      b.   shaping

      c.   respondent conditioning

      d.   delayed reinforcement

5.   To test for the presence of classical conditioning you would omit the

      a.   CS

      b.   US

      c.   CR

      d.   S+

6.   Which of the following does not belong with the others?

      a.   Thorndike

      b.   Skinner

      c.   Pavlov

      d.   instrumental learning

7.   To teach a child to say "Please" when she asks for things, you should make getting the requested item

      a.   the CS

      b.   a token

      c.   a negative reinforcer

      d.   response-contingent

8.   Money is to secondary reinforcer as food is to

      a.   ICS

      b.   prepotent responses

      c.   primary reinforcer

      d.   negative reinforcer

9.   Whether a model is reinforced has a great impact on

      a.   discovery learning

      b.   latent learning

      c.   observational learning

      d.   self-regulated learning

10.   One thing that classical and operant conditioning have in common is that both

      a.   were discovered by Pavlov

      b.   involve an expectation

      c.   are affected by the consequences of making a response

      d.   permanently change behaviour

11.   To shape the behaviour of a teacher in one of your classes you would probably have to rely on

      a.   tokens

      b.   primary reinforcers

      c.   negative attention seeking

    d.   social reinforcers

12. The concept that best explains persistence at gambling is
    a.   partial reinforcement
    b.   continuous reinforcement
    c.   fixed interval reinforcement
    d.   fixed ratio reinforcement

13. Which of the following is NOT a common side effect of mild punishment?
    a.   escape learning
    b.   avoidance learning
    c.   aggression
    d.   accelerated extinction

14. With respect to televised violence it can be said that TV violence
    a.   causes viewers to be more aggressive
    b.   makes aggression more likely
    c.   has no effect on the majority of viewers
    d.   vicariously lowers aggressive urges

15. Which of the following types of learning is most related to the consequences of making a response?
    a.   Pavlovian conditioning
    b.   classical conditioning
    c.   operant conditioning
    d.   respondent conditioning

16. Which combination would most likely make a CER into a phobia?
    a.   CER-discrimination
    b.   CER-desensitization
    c.   CER-response cost
    d.   CER-generalization

17. Active, goal-oriented learning in school is called _____ learning.
    a.   two-factor
    b.   respondent
    c.   vicarious
    d.   self-regulated

18. A loud, unexpected sound causes a startle reflex; thus, a loud sound could be used as a _____ in conditioning.
    a.   NS
    b.   CR
    c.   UR
    d.   US

19. Antecedents are to _____ as consequences are to _____.
    a.   discriminative stimuli, reinforcers
    b.   shaping, response chaining

    c.   conditioned stimuli, cognitive maps

    d.   punishment, negative reinforcement

20. The use of self-recording to change personal behaviour is closely related to the principle of

    a.   response chaining

    b.   feedback

    c.   two-factor reinforcement

    d.   stimulus control

21. _____ typically only temporarily suppresses reinforced responses.

    a.   Negative reinforcement

    b.   Extinction

    c.   Mild punishment

    d.   Stimulus generalization

22. In general, the highest rates of responding are associated with

    a.   delayed reinforcement

    b.   variable reinforcement

    c.   interval reinforcement

    d.   fixed ratio reinforcement

23. A child who has learned, through classical conditioning, to fear sitting in a dentist's chair becomes frightened when he is placed in a barber's chair. This illustrates the concept of

    a.   stimulus generalization

    b.   spontaneous recovery

    c.   higher-order discrimination

    d.   vicarious conditioning

24. The informational view of learning places emphasis on the creation of mental

    a.   expectancies

    b.   reinforcement schedules

    c.   contracts

    d.   antecedents

25. For some adults, blushing when embarrassed or ashamed is probably a _____ first formed in childhood.

    a.   conditioned stimulus

    b.   CAI

    c.   discriminative stimulus

    d.   CER

26. Learning to obey traffic signals is related to the phenomenon called

    a.   stimulus control

    b.   spontaneous recovery

    c.   avoidance learning

    d.   modelling

27. To be most effective, punishment should be combined with
    a. response costs
    b. aversive stimuli
    c. delayed feedback
    d. reinforcement

28. Involuntary responses are to _____ conditioning as voluntary responses are to _____ conditioning.
    a. classical, respondent
    b. classical, operant
    c. operant, classical
    d. operant, instrumental

29. Negative attention seeking by children demonstrates the impact of _____ on behaviour.
    a. operant extinction
    b. social reinforcers
    c. response costs
    d. prepotent responses

30. Which consequence increases the probability that a response will be repeated?
    a. punishment
    b. response cost
    c. non-reinforcement
    d. negative reinforcement

31. The conditioning of taste aversions usually involves what kind of conditioned stimulus?
    a. oddly coloured food
    b. unfamiliar and rarely eaten food
    c. both familiar and novel food
    d. it's not the food but the context you are in (e.g. who you are with) that will produce the aversion.

Solutions

Recite and Review

1. behaviour, precede, follow
2. conditioning, conditioning
3. stimulus, responses
4. reinforced, Operant
5. neutral, response
6. stimulus, learned
7. stimulus
8. stimulus
9. conditioning
10. response
11. similar
12. stimulus
13. response
14. follow
15. reflexes, conditioned
16. stimulus
17. secondhand, observe
18. novel, unpleasant, UR
19. effects, environmental, associated, classical
20. learning
21. increases, effect
22. response, increases
23. effect
24. reinforcement, response
25. chains, single
26. response
27. operant
28. recovery
29. reward, ends
30. decreases, cost
31. pleasure, brain

32. learned, exchanged
33. approval
34. results
35. feedback
36. instruction
37. practice
38. response, partial
39. effect
40. fixed, fixed
41. high, slow
42. precede
43. discrimination
44. similar
45. given, withheld
46. decreases
47. immediate
48. suppress
49. escape
50. mild, responses
51. maps, learning
52. understanding
53. imitation, model, model's
54. models
55. feedback
56. responses, principle
57. responses, response, removing
58. learning, goals, successes

Connections

1. E
2. J
3. A
4. I
5. B
6. H

7. C
8. D
9. F
10. G
11. A
12. J
13. B
14. G
15. C
16. D
17. F
18. E
19. H
20. I
21. D
22. E
23. G
24. F
25. H
26. J
27. I
28. A
29. C
30. B

Check Your Memory

1. T
2. F
3. T
4. F
5. T
6. T
7. F
8. F
9. F

10. T	45. T	11. generalization
11. F	46. F	12. discrimination
12. T	47. T	13. informational
13. T	48. F	14. CS, US
14. F	49. T	15. emotional, responses
15. F	50. T	16. phobias, generalization
16. T	51. T	17. vicarious
17. T	52. T	18. aversions, unconditioned response (UR)
18. F	53. T	
19. F	54. F	19. compensating, associated, compensatory or physiological
20. F	55. T	
21. T	56. T	20. instrumental
22. T	57. F	21. probability, Thorndike
23. F	58. T	22. response, increases
24. T	59. F	23. expectation
25. T	60. F	24. contingent
26. F	61. F	25. decreases, reinforcer
27. T	62. T	26. Superstitious
28. F	63. F	27. shaping, approximations
29. F	64. T	28. extinguish, spontaneous
30. F	65. F	29. positive, negative
31. F	66. T	30. aversive, positive
32. T		31. Primary, stimulation
33. T		32. Secondary, primary, primary
34. T		33. social
35. F		34. knowledge
36. T		35. instruction
37. T		36. Computer-assisted, Instruction
38. F		37. CAI
39. F		38. schedule, Skinner
40. F		39. extinction, partial
41. T		40. ratio, interval
42. F		41. FR, VR, FI, extinction
43. T		42. stimulus, control
44. F		43. generalization
		44. generalization

Final Survey and Review

1. antecedents, consequences
2. respondent, operant
3. neutral, consequences
4. reinforcement, US
5. Ivan, Pavlov, unconditioned, reflex
6. conditioned, conditioned
7. unconditioned, stimulus
8. Higher-order
9. extinction
10. spontaneous, recovery

45. discrimination

46. punisher

47. consistent

48. reinforced

49. avoidance, aggression

50. Reinforcement, non-reinforcement

51. cognitive, maps, latent

52. rote

53. modelling, Observational

54. observational

55. contracting

56. reinforce, Premack

57. alternate, chains, antecedents

58. strategies, reinforcing

18. D (p. 211)

19. A (p. 229)

20. B (p. 239)

21. C (p. 231)

22. D (p. 227)

23. A (p. 213)

24. A (p. 212)

25. D (p. 214)

26. A (p. 228)

27. D (p. 232)

28. B (p. 217)

29. B (p. 223)

30. D (p. 220)

31. B (p. 215)

Mastery Test

1. A (p. 222)

2. C (p. 224)

3. A (p. 214)

4. B (p. 219)

5. B (p. 212)

6. C (p. 216)

7. D (p. 218)

8. C (p. 222)

9. C (p. 236)

10. B (p. 217)

11. D (p. 223)

12. A (p. 226)

13. D (p. 231)

14. B (p. 237)

15. C (p. 216)

16. D (p. 214)

17. D (p. 241)

Chapter 7

Memory

Chapter Overview

Memory systems encode and store information for later retrieval. A popular model divides memory into three systems: sensory memory, short-term memory (STM), and long-term memory (LTM). Sensory memory stores exact copies of sensory information for very brief periods. STM is limited to about 7 bits of information, but chunking and recoding allow more information to be stored. LTM has nearly unlimited storage. Short-term memories last only a short time; long-term memories are relatively permanent. Long-term memories can be further divided into declarative memories (which may be semantic or episodic) and procedural memories.

Explicit memories are revealed by recall, recognition, and relearning tasks. Implicit memories are revealed by priming. Eidetic imagery (photographic memory) is fairly common in children, but rare among adults. Many people have internal memory images and some have exceptional memory based on internal imagery. Exceptional memory capacity is based on both learned strategies and natural abilities.

Forgetting is most rapid immediately after learning. Some "forgetting" is based on a failure to encode information. Short-term forgetting is partly explained by the decay (weakening) of memory traces. Some long-term forgetting may also occur this way. Some forgetting is related to a lack of memory cues. Much forgetting is related to interference among memories. Clinical psychologists believe that memories are sometimes repressed (unconsciously held out of awareness). Some also believe that repressed childhood memories of abuse can be "recovered." However, there is often no way to separate true memories from fantasies.

In the brain, memory traces (engrams) must be consolidated before they become relatively permanent. The hippocampus is a structure involved in memory consolidation. Information appears to be stored in the brain through changes in nerve cells.

Memory can be improved by the use of mnemonic systems and by attention to factors that affect memory, such as overlearning, serial position, organization, and the like.

Learning Objectives

1. Define *memory*.

2. Explain the three processes of memory.

3. Explain sensory memory. Include an explanation of how icons and echoes function in this memory system.

4. Explain how information is transferred from sensory memory to short-term memory.

5. Describe short-term memory in terms of capacity, how information is encoded, permanence, and susceptibility to interference.

6. Describe long-term memory in terms of permanence, capacity, and the basis on which information is stored. Include a brief description of dual memory.

7. Explain the "magic number" seven. Describe chunking and the two types of rehearsal and explain how they help memory.

8. Discuss the permanence of memory including the work of Penfield and the Loftuses.

9. Explain how memories are constructed. Include the concepts of constructive processing and pseudo-memories.

10. Discuss the effects of hypnosis on memory.

11. Briefly describe how long-term memories are organized, including the network model.

12. Differentiate procedural (skill) memory from declarative (fact) memory.

13. Differentiate the two kinds of fact memory—semantic memory and episodic memory.

14. Explain the tip-of-the-tongue phenomenon (including the feeling of knowing).

15. Describe and give an example of each of the following ways of measuring memory:
    a. recall (include the serial position effect)
    b. recognition (compare to recall and include the concept of distractors)
    c. relearning (include the concept of savings scores)

16. Distinguish between explicit and implicit memories. Include a discussion of priming.

17. Describe the concept of internal imagery and explain how it differs from eidetic imagery and exceptional memory.

18. Describe eidetic imagery and its effects on long-term memory.

19. Describe exceptional memory, including the concepts of learned strategies, the characteristics of exceptional memorizers, and mnemonics.

20. Explain Ebbinghaus's curve of forgetting.

21. Discuss the following explanations of forgetting:
    a. encoding failure
    b. decay of memory traces
    c. disuse (also giving three reasons to question this explanation)
    d. cue-dependent forgetting
    e. state-dependent learning
    f. interference (also list and explain the two types of interference as well as how they are investigated in the laboratory)
    g. positive and negative transfer
    h. repression (and differentiate it from suppression)

22. Discuss the validity of recovered memories; include arguments from each side of the debate.

23. Define *flashbulb memories, retrograde amnesia,* and *anterograde amnesia.*

24. Describe the role of consolidation in memory, including the effects of ECS.

25. Describe the effects of stimulants and alcohol on memory.

26. Name the structure in the brain that is responsible for switching information from STM to LTM. Include a discussion of the engram and the relationship between learning and transmitter chemicals.

27. Describe each of the following in terms of how it can improve or be detrimental to memory:
    a. knowledge of results
    b. recitation
    c. rehearsal
    d. selection
    e. organization
    f. whole versus part learning
    g. serial position effect
    h. cues
    i. overlearning
    j. spaced practice
    k. sleep
    l. hunger
    m. extending how long you remember
    n. review
    o. strategies to aid recall

28. Briefly discuss the four steps in a cognitive interview.

29. Define and explain the role of mnemonic systems in storing and retrieving information.

Practice Quizzes

Recite and Review

- *Is there more than one type of memory?*

Recite and Review: Pages 248–250

1. Memory is an active _____ . _____ is first encoded (changed into the form in which it will be retained).

2. Next it is _____ in memory. Later it must be retrieved to be put to use.

3. Humans appear to have _____ interrelated memory systems. These are sensory memory, _____ memory (STM), and _____ memory (LTM).

4. Sensory memory holds an _____ copy of what is seen or heard, in the form of an icon (_____) or echo (sound sensation).

5. Short-term memories tend to be stored as _____ . Long-term memories are stored on the basis of _____ , or importance.

6. STM acts as a _____ storehouse for small amounts of information. It provides a working memory where thinking, mental arithmetic, and the like take place. LTM acts as a _____ storehouse for meaningful information.

7. Sensory memory is exact, but very brief, lasting only a few _____ or less. Through selective attention, some information is transferred to _____ .

• *What are the features of each type of memory?*

Recite and Review: Pages 251—254

8. The digit-span test reveals that STM has an average upper limit of about 7 _____ of information. However, this can be extended by chunking, or recoding information into _____ units or groups.

9. Short-term memories are brief and very sensitive to _____ , or interference; however, they can be prolonged by maintenance rehearsal (silent _____).

10. Elaborative rehearsal, which emphasizes meaning, helps transfer information from _____ to LTM. Elaborative rehearsal links new information with existing _____ .

11. LTM seems to have an almost unlimited storage capacity. However, LTM is subject to constructive processing, or ongoing revision and _____ . As a result, people often have pseudo-memories (_____ memories) that they believe are true.

12. LTM is highly _____ to allow retrieval of needed information. The pattern, or structure, of memory networks is the subject of current memory research. Network _____ portray LTM as a system of linked ideas.

• *Is there more than one type of long-term memory?*

Recite and Review: Pages 254—256

13. Within long-term memory, declarative memories for _____ seem to differ from procedural memories for _____ .

14. _____ memories may be further categorized as semantic memories or episodic memories.

15. Semantic memories consist of basic factual knowledge that is almost immune to _____ .

16. Episodic memories record _____ experiences that are associated with specific times and places.

• *How is memory measured?*

Recite and Review: Pages 257—259

17. The tip-of-the-tongue _____ shows that memory is not an all-or-nothing event. Memories may be revealed by _____ , recognition, or relearning.

18. In recall, memory proceeds without specific cues, as in an _____ exam. Recall of listed information often reveals a serial position effect (_____ items on the list are most subject to errors).

19. A common test of _____ is the multiple-choice question. _____ is very sensitive to the kinds of distractors (wrong choices) used.

20. In relearning, "forgotten" material is learned again, and memory is indicated by a _____ score.

21. Recall, recognition, and relearning mainly measure explicit _____ that we are aware of having. Other techniques, such as priming, are necessary to reveal implicit _____ , which are unconscious.

22. _____ can facilitate the retrieval of an implicit memory by making use of _____ to trigger hidden memories.

- ## *What are "photographic" memories?*

Recite and Review: Pages 259–262

23. Eidetic imagery (photographic memory) occurs when a person is able to project an _____ onto an external surface. Such images allow brief, nearly complete recall by some children.

24. Eidetic imagery is rarely found in _____ . However, many adults have internal images, which can be very vivid and a basis for remembering.

25. Exceptional memory can be learned by finding ways to directly store information in _____ . Learning has no effect on the limits of _____ . Some people may have naturally superior memory abilities that exceed what can be achieved through learning.

- ## *What causes forgetting?*

Recite and Review: Pages 262–266

26. Forgetting and memory were extensively studied by Herman Ebbinghaus, whose _____ of forgetting shows that forgetting is typically most rapid immediately _____ learning.

27. Ebbinghaus used nonsense syllables to study memory. The forgetting of _____ material is much _____ than shown by his curve of forgetting.

28. Failure to encode _____ is a common cause of "forgetting."

29. Forgetting in sensory memory and STM probably reflects decay of memory _____ in the nervous system. Decay or _____ of memories may also account for some LTM loss, but most forgetting cannot be explained this way.

30. Often, forgetting is cue dependent. The power of cues to trigger memories is revealed by state-dependent _____ , in which bodily _____ at the time of learning and of retrieval affect memory.

31. Much _____ in both STM and LTM can be attributed to interference of memories with one another.

32. When recent learning _____ with retrieval of prior learning, retroactive interference has occurred. If old memories _____ with new memories, proactive interference has occurred.

- ## *How accurate are everyday memories?*

Recite and Review: Pages 267–269

33. Repression is the _____ of painful, embarrassing, or traumatic memories.

34. Repression is thought to be unconscious, in contrast to suppression, which is a _____ attempt to avoid thinking about something.

35. Experts are currently debating the validity of childhood memories of _____ that reappear after apparently being repressed for decades.

36. Canadian researchers have shown that preschoolers can be susceptible to _____ when the interviewer is _____ , when asked detailed questions, and when false events are suggested many times.

37. Independent evidence has verified that some recovered memories are _____ . However, others have been shown to be _____ .

38. In the absence of confirming or disconfirming _____ , there is currently no way to separate true memories from fantasies. Caution is advised for all concerned with attempts to retrieve supposedly hidden memories.

39. Flashbulb memories, which seem especially vivid, are created at emotionally significant times. While such memories may not be accurate, we tend to place great _____ in them.

- ### *What happens in the brain when memories are formed?*

Recite and Review: Pages 269—271

40. Retrograde _____ and the effects of electroconvulsive _____ (ECS) may be explained by the concept of consolidation.

41. Consolidation theory holds that engrams (permanent _____ _____) are formed during a critical period after learning. Until they are consolidated, long-term memories are easily destroyed.

42. The hippocampus is a _____ structure associated with the consolidation of memories.

43. The search within the brain for engrams has now settled on changes in individual _____ cells.

44. The best-documented changes are alterations in the amounts of transmitter _____ released by nerve cells.

- ### *How can memory be improved?*

Recite and Review: Pages 271—275 & Psychology in Action

45. Memory can be improved by using feedback, recitation, and rehearsal, by selecting and _____ information, and by using the progressive _____ method, spaced practice, overlearning, and active search strategies.

46. The effects of serial _____ , sleep, review, cues, and elaboration should also be kept in mind when studying or memorizing.

47. Mnemonic systems, such as the _____ method, use mental images and unusual associations to link new information with familiar memories already stored in _____ . Such strategies give information personal meaning and make it easier to recall.

Connections

1.	_____ echoes and icons	a.	STM
2.	_____ working memory	b.	constructive processing
3.	_____ 7 information bits	c.	network model
4.	_____ chunking	d.	sensory memory
5.	_____ revised memories	e.	false memories
6.	_____ memory structure	f.	recoding
7.	_____ pseudo-memories	g.	better recall
8.	_____ self-reference effect	h.	magic number

9. _____ selective attention
10. _____ long-term memory
11. _____ incoming information
12. _____ encoding for LTM
13. _____ sensory memory
14. _____ short-term memory
15. _____ rehearsal buffer

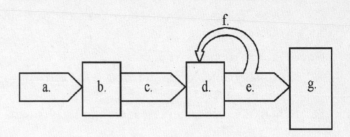

16. _____ semantic memory
17. _____ long-term memory
18. _____ procedural memory
19. _____ sensory memory
20. _____ episodic memory
21. _____ short-term memory
22. _____ declarative memory

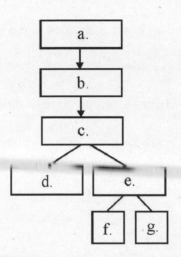

Check Your Memory

Check Your Memory: Pages 248–250

1. Incoming information must be encoded before it is stored in memory.
   True or False

2. Sensory memories last for a few minutes or less.
   True or False

3. A memory that cannot be retrieved has little value.
   True or False

4. Selective attention influences what information enters STM.
   True or False

5. Working memory is another name for sensory memory.
   True or False

6. Doing two things at the same time could interfere with STM.
   True or False

7. Errors in long-term memory tend to focus on the sounds of words.
   True or False

8. Generally, the more you know, the more new information you can store in long-term memory.
   True or False

Check Your Memory: Pages 251-254

9. For many kinds of information, STM can store an average of 5 bits of information.
   True or False

10. Chunking recodes information into smaller units that are easier to fit into STM.
    True or False

11. The more times a short-term memory is rehearsed, the better its chance of being stored in LTM.
    True or False

12. On average, short-term memories last only about 18 minutes, unless they are rehearsed.
    True or False

13. Maintenance rehearsal keeps memories active in sensory memory.
    True or False

14. The surface of the brain records the past like a movie, complete with sound track.
    True or False

15. It is easier to remember new information if the meaning is personally relevant.
    True or False

16. Being confident about a memory tells little about the true accuracy of the memory.
    True or False

17. Hypnosis increases false memories more than it does true ones.
    True or False

18. Long-term memories appear to be organized alphabetically for speedy access.
    True or False

Check Your Memory: Pages 254–256

19. Knowing how to swing a golf club is a type of declarative memory.
    True or False

20. A person lacking declarative memory might still remember how to solve a mechanical puzzle.
    True or False

21. Endel Tulving is an influential Canadian memory researcher.
    True or False

22. Semantic memories are almost immune to forgetting.
    True or False

23. Semantic memories are a type of declarative memory.
    True or False

24. Episodic memories have no connection to particular times and places.
    True or False

Check Your Memory: Pages 257–259

25. Remembering the first sound of a name you are trying to recall is an example
    of the tip-of-the-tongue state.
    True or False

26. Tests of recognition require verbatim memory.
    True or False

27. The serial position effect measures the strength of the feeling of knowing.
    True or False

28. Recognition tends to be a more sensitive test of memory than recall.
    True or False

29. False positives and distractors greatly affect the accuracy of relearning tests.
    True or False

30. Recall, recognition, and relearning are used to measure explicit memories.
    True or False

31. Priming is used to activate explicit (hidden) memories.
    True or False

Check Your Memory: Pages 259—262

32. Eidetic images last for 30 seconds or more.
    True or False

33. About 8 percent of all children have eidetic images.
    True or False

34. Eidetic imagery becomes rare by adulthood.
    True or False

35. Mr. S (the mnemonist) had virtually unlimited eidetic imagery.
    True or False

36. Practice in remembering one type of information increases the capacity of STM
    to store other types of information, too.
    True or False

37. All contestants in the World Memory Championship performed poorly on tasks
    that prevented the use of learned strategies.
    True or False

Check Your Memory: Pages 262—266

38. Ebbinghaus chose to learn nonsense syllables so that they would all be the same length.
    True or False

39. Ebbinghaus's curve of forgetting levels off after 2 days, showing little further memory loss after that.
    True or False

40. Encoding failure was shown when students were asked to draw a penny but not when
    asked to recall the layout of push-button telephones.
    True or False

41. Decay of memory traces clearly applies to information in STM.
    True or False

42. Disuse theories of forgetting answer the question: Have I been storing the information in the first place?
    True or False

43. The presence of memory cues almost always improves memory.
    True or False

44. Information learned under the influence of a drug may be best remembered when the drugged state occurs again.
    True or False

45. If you are in a bad mood, you are more likely to remember unpleasant events.
    True or False

46. Categorizing a person as a member of a group tends to limit the accuracy of memories about the person's appearance.
    True or False

47. Sleeping tends to interfere with retaining new memories.
    True or False

48. You learn information A and then information B. If your memory of B is lowered by having first learned A, you have experienced retroactive interference.
    True or False

Check Your Memory: Pages 267–269

49. Unconsciously forgetting painful memories is called negative transfer.
    True or False

50. A conscious attempt to put a memory out of mind is called repression.
    True or False

51. Suggestion and fantasy are elements of many techniques used in attempts to recover repressed memories.
    True or False

52. Unless a memory can be independently confirmed, there is no way to tell if it is real or not.
    True or False

53. Flashbulb memories tend to be formed when an event is surprising or emotional.
    True or False

54. The confidence we have in flashbulb memories is well placed—they are much more accurate than most other memories.
    True or False

Check Your Memory: Pages 269–271

55. Retrograde amnesia is a gap in memories of events preceding a head injury.
    True or False

56. Consolidation of new information will still happen even if an electroconvulsive shock is given after the new information.
    True or False

57. People with damage to the hippocampus typically cannot remember events that occurred before the damage.
    True or False

58. In the early 1920s, Karl Lashley found the location of engrams in the brain.
    True or False

59. Storing memories alters the activity, structure, and chemistry of the brain.
    True or False

Check Your Memory: Pages 271–275 & Psychology in Action

60. Recitation is a good way to generate feedback while studying.
    True or False

61. Elaborative rehearsal involving "why" questions improves memory.
    True or False

62. Overlearning is inefficient; you should stop studying at the point of initial mastery of new information.
    True or False

63. Massed practice is almost always superior to spaced practice.
    True or False

64. When learning, it helps to gradually extend how long you remember new information before reviewing it again.
    True or False

65. Recalling events from different viewpoints is part of doing a cognitive interview.
    True or False

66. *Roy G. Biv* is a mnemonic for the notes on a musical staff.
    True or False

67. Many mnemonics make use of mental images or pictures.
    True or False

68. Mnemonics often link new information to familiar memories.
    True or False

69. The keyword method is superior to rote learning for memorizing vocabulary words in another language.
    True or False

Final Survey and Review

• *Is there more than one type of memory?*

1. Memory is an active system. Information is first _____ (changed into the form in which it will be retained).

2. Next it is stored in memory. Later it must be _____ to be put to use.

3. Humans appear to have 3 interrelated memory systems. These are _____ memory, _____ memory (STM), and long-term memory (LTM).

4. Sensory memory holds an exact copy of what is seen or heard, in the form of an _____ (image) or _____ (sound sensation).

5. _____ memories tend to be stored as sounds. _____ memories are stored on the basis of meaning, or importance.

6. _____ acts as a temporary storehouse for small amounts of information. It provides a _____ memory where thinking, mental arithmetic, and the like take place. LTM acts as a permanent storehouse for _____ information.

7. _____ memory is exact, but very brief, lasting only a few seconds or less. Through _____ _____ , some information is transferred to STM.

• *What are the features of each type of memory?*

8. The _____ test reveals that STM has an average upper limit of about 7 bits of information. However, this can be extended by chunking, or _____ information into larger units or groups.

9. Short-term memories are brief and very sensitive to interruption , or _____ ; however, they can be prolonged by _____ rehearsal (silent repetition).

10. _____ rehearsal, which emphasizes meaning, helps transfer information from STM to LTM.

11. LTM seems to have an almost unlimited storage capacity. However, LTM is subject to _____ processing, or ongoing revision and updating. As a result, people often have _____ (false memories) that they believe are true.

12. LTM is highly organized to allow retrieval of needed information. The pattern, or structure, of memory _____ is the subject of current memory research. _____ models portray LTM as a system of linked ideas.

• *Is there more than one type of long-term memory?*

13. Within long-term memory, _____ memories for facts seem to differ from _____ memories for skills.

14. Declarative memories may be further categorized as _____ memories or _____ memories.

15. _____ memories consist of basic factual knowledge that is almost immune to forgetting.

16. _____ memories record personal experiences that are associated with specific times and places.

• *How is memory measured?*

17. The _____ -of-the- _____ state shows that memory is not an all-or-nothing event. Memories may be revealed by recall, _____ , or relearning.

18. In _____ , memory proceeds without specific cues, as in an essay exam. Remembering a list of information often reveals a _____ _____ effect (middle items on the list are most subject to errors).

19. A common test of recognition is the _____ -choice question. Recognition is very sensitive to the kinds of _____ (wrong choices) used.

20. In _____ , "forgotten" material is learned again, and memory is indicated by a savings score.

21. Recall, recognition, and relearning mainly measure _____ memories that we are aware of having. Other techniques, such as priming, are necessary to reveal _____ memories, which are unconscious.

• *What are "photographic" memories?*

22. _____ _____ (photographic memory) occurs when a person is able to project an image onto an external surface. Such images allow brief, nearly complete recall by some children.

23. _____ _____ is rarely found in adults. However, many adults have internal images, which can be very vivid and a basis for remembering.

24. _____ memory can be learned by finding ways to directly store information in LTM. Learning has no effect on the _____ of STM. Some people may have naturally superior memory abilities that exceed what can be achieved through learning.

• *What causes forgetting?*

25. Forgetting and memory were extensively studied by Herman _____ , whose curve of forgetting shows that forgetting is typically most rapid immediately after learning.

26. He used _____ syllables to study memory. The forgetting of meaningful material is much slower than shown by his curve of forgetting.

27. Failure to _____ information is a common cause of "forgetting."

28. Forgetting in _____ memory and _____ probably reflects decay of memory traces in the nervous system. Decay or disuse of memories may also account for some _____ loss, but most forgetting cannot be explained this way.

29. Often, forgetting is _____ dependent. The power of _____ to trigger memories is revealed by _____ learning, in which bodily states at the time of learning and of retrieval affect memory.

30. Much forgetting in both STM and LTM can be attributed to _____ of memories with one another.

31. When recent learning interferes with retrieval of prior learning, _____ interference has occurred. If old memories interfere with new memories, _____ interference has occurred.

• *How accurate are everyday memories?*

32. _____ is the motivated forgetting of painful, embarrassing, or traumatic memories.

33. _____ is thought to be unconscious, in contrast to _____ , which is a conscious attempt to avoid thinking about something.

34. Experts are currently debating the validity of childhood memories of abuse that reappear after apparently being _____ for decades.

35. Preschoolers can be influenced by suggestion if the interviewer is biased, if they are asked _____ questions, and if false events are suggested _____ .

36. Independent evidence has verified that some _____ memories are true. However, others have been shown to be false.

37. In the absence of confirming or disconfirming evidence, there is currently no way to separate true memories from _____ . Caution is advised for all concerned with attempts to retrieve supposedly hidden memories.

38. _____ memories, which seem especially vivid, are created at emotionally significant times. While such memories may not be _____ , we tend to place great confidence in them.

• *What happens in the brain when memories are formed?*

39. _____ amnesia and the effects of _____ shock (ECS) may be explained by the concept of consolidation.

40. Consolidation theory holds that _____ (permanent memory traces) are formed during a critical period after learning. Until they are _____ , long-term memories are easily destroyed.

41. The _____ is a brain structure associated with the consolidation of memories.

42. The search within the brain for engrams has now settled on changes in individual _____ _____ .

43. The best-documented changes are alterations in the amounts of _____ chemicals released by nerve cells.

• *How can memory be improved?*

44. Memory can be improved by using _____ (knowledge of results), recitation, and rehearsal, by _____ and organizing information, and by using the progressive part method, spaced practice, overlearning, and active _____ strategies.

45. The effects of _____ position, sleep, review, cues, and _____ (connecting new information to existing knowledge) should also be kept in mind when studying or memorizing.

46. _____ systems, such as the keyword method, use mental images and unusual associations to link new information with familiar memories already stored in LTM. Such strategies give information personal meaning and make it easier to recall.

Mastery Test

1. The meaning and importance of information has a strong impact on
   a. sensory memory
   b. eidetic memory
   c. long-term memory
   d. procedural memory

2. Pseudo-memories are closely related to the effects of
   a. repression
   b. suppression
   c. semantic forgetting
   d. constructive processing

3. The occurrence of _____ implies that consolidation has been prevented.
   a. retrograde amnesia
   b. hippocampal transfer
   c. suppression
   d. changes in the activities of individual nerve cells

4. Most of the techniques used to recover supposedly repressed memories involve
   a. redintegration and hypnosis
   b. suggestion and fantasy
   c. reconstruction and priming
   d. coercion and fabrication

5. Most daily memory chores are handled by
   a. sensory memory and LTM
   b. STM and working memory
   c. STM and LTM
   d. STM and declarative memory

6. Three key processes in memory systems are
   a. storage, organization, recovery
   b. encoding, attention, reprocessing
   c. storage, retrieval, encoding
   d. retrieval, reprocessing, reorganization

7. Procedural memories are to skills as _____ memories are to facts.
   a. declarative
   b. short-term
   c. redintegrative
   d. eidetic

8. An ability to answer questions about distances on a map you have seen only once implies that some memories are based on
   a. constructive processing
   b. redintegration
   c. internal images
   d. episodic processing

9. The first potential cause of forgetting that may occur is
   a. engram decay
   b. disuse
   c. cue-dependent forgetting
   d. encoding failure

10. The persistence of icons and echoes is the basis for
    a. sensory memory
    b. short-term memory
    c. long-term memory
    d. working memory

11. Priming is most often used to reveal
    a. semantic memories
    b. episodic memories
    c. implicit memories
    d. eidetic memories

12. "Projection" onto an external surface is most characteristic of
    a. sensory memories
    b. eidetic images
    c. flashbulb memories
    d. mnemonic images

13. Chunking helps especially to extend the capacity of
    a. sensory memory
    b. STM
    c. LTM
    d. declarative memory

14. There is presently no way to tell if a "recovered" memory is true or false unless independent _____ exists.
    a. evidence
    b. amnesia
    c. elaboration
    d. consolidation

15. Taking an essay test inevitably requires a person to use
    a. recall
    b. recognition
    c. relearning

    d.   priming

16. A savings score is used in what memory task?
    a. recall
    b. recognition
    c. relearning
    d. priming

17. _____ rehearsal helps link new information to existing memories by concentrating on meaning.
    a. Redintegrative
    b. Constructive
    c. Maintenance
    d. Elaborative

18. Middle items are neither held in STM nor moved to LTM. This statement explains the
    a. feeling of knowing
    b. serial position effect
    c. tip-of-the-tongue state
    d. semantic forgetting curve

19. According to the curve of forgetting, the greatest decline in the amount recalled occurs during the _____ after learning.
    a. first hour
    b. second day
    c. third to sixth days
    d. retroactive period

20. Work with brain stimulation, truth serums, and hypnosis suggests that long-term memories are
    a. stored in the hippocampus
    b. relatively permanent
    c. unaffected by later input
    d. permanent only for facts

21. Which of the following is most likely to improve the accuracy of memory?
    a. hypnosis
    b. constructive processing
    c. the serial position effect
    d. memory cues

22. To qualify as repression, forgetting must be
    a. retroactive
    b. proactive
    c. unconscious
    d. explicit

23. Which of the following typically is NOT a good way to improve memory?
    a. massed practice
    b. overlearning

    c.   rehearsal

    d.   recall strategies

24. A witness to a crime is questioned in ways that re-create the context of the crime and that provide many memory cues. It appears that she is undergoing

    a.   retroactive priming

    b.   the progressive part method

    c.   retroactive consolidation

    d.   a cognitive interview

25. One thing that is clearly true about flashbulb memories is that

    a.   they are unusually accurate

    b.   we place great confidence in them

    c.   they apply primarily to public tragedies

    d.   they are recovered by using visualization and hypnosis

26. One common mnemonic strategy is the

    a.   serial position technique

    b.   feeling of knowing tactic

    c.   network procedure

    d.   keyword method

27. An adult hockey fanatic in your family knows all the names of hockey players and their sweater numbers since the beginning of the NHL. This individual's capacity shows

    a.   that memory skills can be learned

    b.   what one can do with eidetic memory

    c.   that such feats can only be accomplished with procedural knowledge (memory)

    d.   the importance of sensory memory in memorizing information

28. Which of the following is NOT considered a part of long-term memory?

    a.   echoic memory

    b.   semantic memory

    c.   episodic memory

    d.   declarative memory

29. You are very thirsty. Suddenly you remember a time years ago when you became very thirsty while hiking. This suggests that your memory is

    a.   proactive

    b.   state dependent

    c.   still not consolidated

    d.   eidetic

30. After memorizing 5 lists of words you recall less of the last list than a person who only memorized list number five. This observation is explained by

    a.   reactive processing

    b.   reconstructive processing

    c.   proactive interference

    d.   retroactive interference

Memory

31. Which group of people would be least affected by suggestion according to Canadian researchers?
    a.   the elderly
    b.   children
    c.   alcoholics
    d.   young adults

Solutions

Recite and Review

1. system, Information
2. stored
3. 3, short-term, long-term
4. exact, image
5. sounds, meaning
6. temporary, permanent
7. seconds, STM
8. bits, larger
9. interruption, repetition
10. STM, memories
11. updating, false
12. organized, models
13. facts, skills
14. Declarative
15. forgetting
16. personal
17. state, recall
18. essay, middle
19. recognition, Recognition
20. savings
21. memories, memories
22. Priming, cues
23. image
24. adults
25. LTM, STM
26. curve, after
27. meaningful, slower
28. information
29. traces, disuse
30. learning, states
31. forgetting
32. interferes, interfere
33. forgetting
34. conscious
35. abuse
36. suggestion, biased
37. true, false
38. evidence
39. confidence
40. amnesia, shock
41. memory, traces
42. brain
43. nerve
44. chemicals
45. organizing, part
46. position
47. keyword, LTM

Connections

1. D
2. A
3. H
4. F
5. B
6. C
7. E
8. G
9. C
10. G
11. A
12. E
13. B
14. D
15. F
16. F or G
17. C
18. D
19. A
20. F or G
21. B
22. E

Check Your Memory

1. T
2. F
3. T
4. T
5. F
6. T
7. F
8. T
9. T
10. F
11. T
12. F
13. F
14. F
15. T
16. T
17. T
18. F
19. F
20. T
21. T
22. T
23. T
24. F
25. T
26. F
27. F
28. T
29. F

30. T	**66.** F	**30.** interference
31. F	**67.** T	**31.** retroactive, proactive
32. T	**68.** T	**32.** Repression
33. T	**69.** T	**33.** Repression, suppression
34. T		**34.** repressed
35. F		**35.** specific, repeatedly
36. F	**Final Survey and Review**	**36.** recovered
37. F		**37.** fantasies
38. F	**1.** encoded	**38.** Flashbulb, accurate
39. T	**2.** retrieved	**39.** Retrograde, electroconvulsive
40. F	**3.** sensory, short-term	**40.** engrams, consolidated
41. T	**4.** icon, echo	**41.** hippocampus
42. F	**5.** Short-term, Long-term	**42.** nerve, cells
43. T	**6.** STM, working, meaningful	**43.** transmitter
44. T	**7.** Sensory, selective, attention	**44.** feedback, selecting, search
45. T	**8.** digit-span, recoding	**45.** serial, elaboration
46. T	**9.** interference, maintenance	**46.** Mneumonic
47. F	**10.** Elaborative	
48. F	**11.** constructive, pseudo-memories	
49. F	**12.** networks, Network	**Mastery Test**
50. F	**13.** declarative, procedural	
51. T	**14.** semantic, episodic	**1.** C (p. 250)
52. T	**15.** Semantic	**2.** D (p. 253)
53. T	**16.** Episodic	**3.** A (p. 269)
54. F	**17.** tip, tongue, recognition	**4.** B (p. 267)
55. T	**18.** recall, serial, position	**5.** C (p. 250)
56. F	**19.** multiple, distractors	**6.** C (p. 249)
57. F	**20.** relearning	**7.** A (p. 255)
58. F	**21.** explicit, implicit	**8.** C (p. 259)
59. T	**22.** Eidetic, imagery	**9.** D (p. 263)
60. T	**23.** Eidetic, imagery	**10.** A (p. 248)
61. T	**24.** Exceptional, limits	**11.** C (p. 259)
62. F	**25.** Ebbinghaus	**12.** B (p. 259)
63. F	**26.** nonsense	**13.** B (p. 251)
64. T	**27.** encode	**14.** A (p. 268)
65. T	**28.** sensory, STM, LTM	**15.** A (p. 257)
	29. cue, cues, state-dependent	**16.** C (p. 258)

17. D (p. 252)
18. B (p. 272)
19. A (p. 262)
20. B (p. 252)
21. D (p. 273)
22. C (p. 267)
23. A (p. 273)
24. D (p. 274)
25. B (p. 268)
26. D (p. 277)
27. A (p. 261)
28. A (p. 255)
29. B (p. 265)
30. C (p. 266)
31. B (p. 268)

Chapter 8

Cognition, Intelligence, and Creativity

Chapter Overview

Thinking is the mental manipulation of images, concepts, and language (or symbols). Most people use internal images (including kinesthetic images) for thinking. A concept is a generalized idea of a class of objects or events. We learn concepts from positive and negative instances and from rules. Different types of concepts are used. Prototypes are often used to identify concepts. Language translates events into symbols, which are combined using the rules of grammar and syntax. True languages are productive. Studies suggest that, with training, primates are capable of some language use.

The solution to a problem may be arrived at mechanically (by trial and error or by rote). Solutions by understanding usually begin with discovering the general properties of an answer. Problem solving is frequently aided by analogies and heuristics, which can guide and narrow the search for solutions. When understanding leads to a rapid solution, insight has occurred. Insight can be blocked by fixations. Work on artificial intelligence has focused on computer simulations and expert systems. Human expertise is based on organized knowledge and acquired strategies.

Intelligence refers to a general capacity to act purposefully, think rationally, and deal effectively with the environment. In practice, intelligence is operationally defined by creating tests. The first practical individual intelligence test was assembled by Alfred Binet. A modern version is the Stanford-Binet Intelligence Scale. A second major intelligence test is the Wechsler Adult Intelligence Scale. Culture-fair and group intelligence tests are also available. Intelligence is expressed as an intelligence quotient (IQ) or as a deviation IQ. The distribution of IQ scores approximates a normal curve. Intelligence reflects the combined effects of heredity and environment.

People with IQs in the gifted or "genius" range tend to be superior in many respects. In addition, many children are gifted or talented in other ways. The terms mentally retarded and developmentally disabled apply to persons who have an IQ below 70 or who lack various adaptive behaviours. About 50 percent of the cases of mental retardation are organic; the remaining cases are of undetermined cause (many are thought to be familial).

Creative solutions are practical, sensible, and original. Creative thinking requires divergent thought, characterized by fluency, flexibility, and originality. Tests of creativity measure these qualities. Five stages often seen in creative problem solving are orientation, preparation, incubation, illumination, and verification. There is only a small positive correlation between IQ and creativity.

Intuitive thinking often leads to errors. Wrong conclusions may be drawn when an answer seems highly representative of what we already believe is true. A second problem is ignoring the base rate of an event. Clear thinking is usually aided by stating or framing a problem in broad terms. Major sources of thinking errors include rigid mental sets, faulty logic, and over-simplifications. Various strategies, including brainstorming, tend to enhance creative problem solving.

Learning Objectives

1. Define the terms *cognition* and *cognitive psychology*.

2. List three basic units of thought.

3. Describe mental imagery (including the concepts of mental rotation and reverse vision). Explain how both stored and created images may be used to solve problems.

4. Explain how the size of a mental image is important.

5. Explain how kinesthetic imagery aids thinking.

6. Define the terms *concept* and *concept formation*, explain how concepts aid thinking, and describe how they are learned. Define the term *conceptual rule*.

7. Define the terms *conjunctive concept*, *relational concept*, *disjunctive concept*, and *exemplars*.

8. Explain the importance of prototypes.

9. Explain the difference between the denotative and the connotative meaning of a word or concept, and describe how the connotative meaning of a word is measured.

10. Define *semantics* and explain how semantic problems may arise.

11. Briefly describe the following three requirements of a language and their related concepts:
    a. symbols
       i) phonemes
       ii) morphemes
    b. grammar
       i) syntax
       ii) transformation rules
    c. productivity

12. Describe the research involving attempts to teach primates to use language. Describe the criticisms and practical value of such attempts.

13. Compare and contrast mechanical problem solving with problem solving through understanding. Describe the role of analogies in problem solving.

14. Define the term *heuristic* and contrast it with random search strategies.

15. Describe how insight may be used as a problem-solving technique.

16. List and describe the three abilities involved in insight.

17. Explain how fixation and functional fixedness block problem solving, and give an example of each.

18. List and explain four common barriers to creative thinking.

19. Define the term *artificial intelligence* and state the principle that makes it possible.

20. Explain how computer simulations and expert systems are used.

21. Explain the differences between experts and novices.

22. Describe Binet's role in intelligence testing.

23. State Wechsler's description of intelligence.

24. Explain what an operational definition of intelligence is.

25. Generally describe the construction of the Stanford-Binet Intelligence Scale.

26. Define *intelligence quotient*, and use an example to show how it was computed. Explain the purpose of deviation IQ scores.

27. Distinguish the Wechsler tests from the Stanford-Binet tests, and distinguish between group and individual intelligence tests.

28. Define the term *culture-fair test*, and explain how IQ tests may be unfair to certain groups.

29. Describe the pattern of distribution of IQ scores observed in the general population.

30. Discuss the relationship between IQ and achievement.

31. Briefly describe Terman's study of gifted children. State how successful subjects differed from the less successful ones.

32. List seven early signs of giftedness.

33. Describe Howard Gardner's broader view of intelligence and list the eight different kinds of intelligence he discusses.

34. State the dividing line between normal intelligence and retardation (or developmental disability), list the degrees of retardation, and describe the similarities between people of normal intelligence and those regarded as retarded.

35. Differentiate between organic and familial retardation.

36. Explain how twin (identical and fraternal) studies can be used to support either side of the heredity/environment controversy.

37. Describe some evidence that strongly supports the environmental view of intelligence.

38. Describe some studies that indicate how much environmental influences can alter intelligence.

39. Discuss how the heredity/environment debate is currently viewed.

40. Describe the following four kinds of thought:
    a. inductive
    b. deductive
    c. logical
    d. illogical

41. Describe the following characteristics of creative thinking:
    a. fluency
    b. flexibility
    c. originality

42. Explain how creativity is related to divergent and convergent thinking. Describe how the ability to think divergently can be measured.

43. List and describe five stages of creative thinking and relate them to a problem that you have solved.

44. List five conclusions about creative people.

45. Define *intuition*.

46. Explain the following errors made when using intuition:
    a. representativeness
    b. base rate (underlying odds)
    c. framing

47. Describe eight practical steps for encouraging creativity.

48. Describe the process of brainstorming and explain how it can be used to solve problems.

Practice Quizzes

Recite and Review

• *What is the nature of thought?*

Recite and Review: Page 284

1. Cognitive psychology is the study of human _____ processing (thinking, language, and problem solving).

2. Thinking is the manipulation of _____ representations of external problems or situations.

3. Three basic units of thought are images, concepts, and _____ or symbols.

• *In what ways are images related to thinking?*

Recite and Review: Pages 284–286

4. Most people have internal images of one kind or another. Images may be based on information stored in memory or they may be _____ .

5. The size of images used in problem solving may _____ . Images may be three-dimensional and they may be rotated in _____ to answer questions.

6. Many of the systems in the brain that are involved in processing _____ images work in reverse to create mental images.

7. Kinesthetic images are created from produced, remembered, or imagined _____ sensations. _____ sensations and micromovements seem to help structure thinking for many people.

• *How are concepts learned?*

Recite and Review: Pages 286–289

8. A concept is a generalized idea of a _____ of objects or events.

9. Forming concepts may be based on experiences with _____ and negative instances.

10. Concepts may also be acquired by learning rules that define the _____ .

11. In practice, we frequently use prototypes (general _____ of the concept class) to identify concepts.

12. Concepts may be classified as conjunctive ("_____" concepts), disjunctive ("_____" concepts), relational concepts, or exemplars (past _____).

13. The denotative meaning of a word or concept is its exact _____ . Connotative meaning is _____ or emotional.

14. Connotative meaning can be measured with the semantic differential. Most connotative meaning involves the dimensions _____ , strong-weak, and active-passive.

● *What is the role of language in thinking?*

Recite and Review: Pages 289–290

15. Language allows events to be encoded into _____ for easy mental manipulation.

16. Language is built out of phonemes (basic speech _____) and morphemes (speech sounds collected into _____ units).

17. Thinking in language is influenced by meaning. The study of _____ is called semantics.

18. Language carries meaning by combining a set of symbols or signs according to a set of _____ (grammar), which includes rules about word _____ (syntax).

19. Various sentences are created by applying transformation _____ to simple statements.

20. A true language is productive, and can be used to generate new ideas or possibilities. American Sign Language (ASL) and other _____ languages used by the deaf are true languages.

● *Can animals be taught to learn language?*

Recite and Review: Pages 290–292

21. Animal communication is relatively limited because it lacks symbols that can be rearranged easily. As a result, it does not have the productive quality of _____ language.

22. Attempts to teach chimpanzees ASL and other non-verbal systems suggest to some that primates are capable of language use. However, others believe that the chimps are merely using _____ responses to get food and other reinforcers.

23. Studies that make use of lexigrams (_____ word-symbols) provide the best evidence yet of animal language use.

● *What do we know about problem solving?*

Recite and Review: Pages 292–297

24. The solution to a problem may be found mechanically (by trial and error or by _____ application of rules). However, mechanical solutions are frequently inefficient or ineffective, except where aided by _____ .

25. Solutions by understanding usually involves a _____ comprehension of the problem. Using _____ has been shown to help find solutions.

26. Problem solving is frequently aided by heuristics. These are strategies that typically _____ the search for solutions.

27. When understanding leads to a rapid _____ , insight has occurred. Three elements of insight are _____ encoding, selective combination, and selective comparison.

28. Insights and other problem solving attempts can be blocked by fixation (a tendency to repeat _____ solutions).

29. Functional fixedness is a common _____ , but emotional blocks, cultural values, learned conventions, and perceptual _____ are also problems.

- ### *What is artificial intelligence?*

Recite and Review: Pages 297—298

30. Artificial intelligence refers to computer _____ that can perform tasks that require _____ when done by people.

31. Two principal areas of artificial intelligence research are _____ simulations and expert systems.

32. Expert human problem solving is based on organized _____ and acquired strategies, rather than some general improvement in thinking ability.

- ### *How is human intelligence defined and measured?*

Recite and Review: Pages 298—303

33. Intelligence refers to one's general capacity to act purposefully, think _____ , and deal effectively with the _____ .

34. In practice, writing an intelligence test provides an operational _____ of intelligence.

35. The first practical _____ _____ was assembled in 1904, in Paris, by Alfred Binet.

36. A modern version of Binet's test is the *Stanford-Binet* _____ _____ , Fourth Edition.

37. The Stanford-Binet measures _____ reasoning, quantitative reasoning, abstract/visual reasoning, and short-term _____ .

38. Intelligence is expressed in terms of an intelligence _____ (IQ). IQ is defined as mental age (MA) divided by chronological age (CA) and then multiplied by _____ .

39. An "average" IQ of _____ occurs when mental age _____ chronological age.

40. Modern IQ tests no longer calculate _____ directly. Instead, the final score reported by the test is a deviation IQ, which gives a person's _____ intellectual standing in his or her age group.

41. A second major intelligence test is the *Wechsler* _____ *Intelligence Scale*, Third Edition (WAIS-III). The WAIS-III measures both verbal and performance (_____) intelligence.

42. Intelligence tests have also been produced for use with _____ of people. The Scholastic Assessment Test (SAT), measures a variety of _____ aptitudes and it can be used to estimate intelligence.

- ### *How do IQ scores relate to achievement and thinking ability?*

Recite and Review: Pages 303—308

43. When graphed, the distribution (percentage of people receiving each score) of IQ scores approximates a normal (_____ -shaped) _____ .

44. While researchers agree that men and women do not differ in _____ intelligence, a debate still exists as to whether specific differences are due to _____ or due to biological influences in men and women.

45. People with IQs above 140 are considered to be in the _____ or "genius" range.

46. Studies done by Lewis Terman showed that the gifted tend to have a higher _____ between IQ score and real-world success.

47. By criteria other than _____ , a large proportion of children might be considered gifted or talented in one way or another.

48. Howard Gardner believes that _____ IQ tests define intelligence too narrowly. According to Gardner, intelligence consists of abilities in language, logic and _____ , _____ and spatial thinking, music, kinesthetic skills, intrapersonal skills, interpersonal skills, and naturalist skills.

49. The terms mentally _____ and developmentally disabled are applied to those whose IQ falls below _____ or who lack various adaptive behaviours.

50. Further classifications of retardation are: _____ (50-55 to 70), moderate (35-40 to 50-55), _____ (20-25 to 35-40), and profound (below 20-25).

51. About _____ percent of the cases of mental retardation are organic, being caused by _____ injuries, fetal damage, metabolic disorders, or genetic abnormalities. The remaining cases are of undetermined cause.

52. Many cases of subnormal intelligence are thought to be the result of familial retardation (a low level of _____ stimulation in the home, poverty, and poor nutrition).

53. Studies of family relationships in humans, especially comparisons between fraternal twins and identical twins (who have identical _____), also suggest that intelligence is partly _____ .

54. However, environment is also important, as revealed by changes in tested intelligence induced by _____ environments and improved education.

55. _____ therefore reflects the combined effects of heredity and environment.

56. Differences in the average IQ scores for various racial groups are based on environmental differences, not _____ .

• *What is the nature of creative thinking?*

Recite and Review: Pages 309–313

57. To be creative, a solution must be _____ and sensible as well as original.

58. _____ may be deductive or inductive, logical or illogical.

59. Creative thinking requires divergent thought, characterized by fluency, flexibility, and _____ .

60. Tests of _____ , such as the Unusual Uses Test, the Consequences Test, and the Anagrams Test, measure the capacity for divergent thinking.

61. Five stages often seen in creative problem solving are orientation, _____ , incubation, illumination, and verification.

62. Studies suggest that creative persons share a number of identifiable general traits, _____ abilities, thinking _____ , and personality characteristics. There is only a small correlation between IQ and creativity.

• *How accurate is intuition?*

Recite and Review: Pages 313–315

63. Intuitive thinking often leads to _____ . Wrong conclusions may be drawn when an answer seems highly representative of what we already believe is _____ . (That is, when people apply the representativeness heuristic.)

64. A second problem is ignoring the base rate (or underlying _____) of an event.

65. Clear thinking is usually aided by stating or framing a problem in _____ terms.

• *What can be done to improve thinking and to promote creativity?*

Recite and Review: Psychology in Action

66. _____ sets can act as major barriers to creative _____ .

67. Creativity can be enhanced by defining problems _____ , by establishing a creative atmosphere, restating a problem in _____ ways, by allowing _____ for incubation, by seeking _____ input, by taking sensible risks, and by looking for analogies.

68. Brainstorming, in which the production and criticism of ideas is kept _____ , also tends to enhance creative problem solving.

Connections

1. _____ cognition
2. _____ language
3. _____ examplar
4. _____ mental rotation
5. _____ reverse vision
6. _____ stored images
7. _____ kinesthetic imagery
8. _____ concept
9. _____ prototype
10. _____ connotative meaning

a. 3-D images
b. remembered perceptions
c. images created by brain
d. mental class
e. implicit actions
f. thinking
g. ideal or model
h. emotional meaning
i. representation of past experiences
j. symbols and rules

11. _____ word meanings
12. _____ morpheme
13. _____ phoneme
14. _____ "hidden" grammar rules
15. _____ Washoe
16. _____ insight
17. _____ Kanzi
18. _____ trial-and-error
19. _____ heuristic
20. _____ fixation

a. meaningful unit
b. ASL
c. semantics
d. lexigrams
e. language sound
f. mechanical solution
g. thinking strategy
h. blind to alternatives
i. sudden solution
j. transformation rules

21. _____ Binet
22. _____ identical twins
23. _____ IQ
24. _____ deviation IQ
25. _____ verbal reasoning
26. _____ memory test
27. _____ WAIS
28. _____ culture-fair test
29. _____ group test
30. _____ normal curve

a. same genes
b. relative standing
c. Wechsler test
d. first intelligence test
e. ethnic minority
f. Scholastic Assessment Test (SAT)
g. bell shape
h. digit span
i. MA/CA x 100
j. comprehension

171

31.	_____ fixation	a.	knowledge plus rules
32.	_____ expert system	b.	many types of solutions
33.	_____ fluency	c.	one correct answer
34.	_____ flexibility	d.	moment of insight
35.	_____ originality	e.	underlying odds
36.	_____ convergent thinking	f.	affects decisions
37.	_____ Anagrams Test	g.	many solutions
38.	_____ illumination	h.	blind to alternatives
39.	_____ base rate	i.	measures divergent thinking
40.	_____ framing	j.	novelty of solutions

Check your memory

Check Your Memory: Page 284

1. Cognitive psychology is the study of sensation memory, and learning.
   True or False

2. Images, concepts, and language may be used to mentally represent problems.
   True or False

3. Images are generalized ideas of a class of related objects or events.
   True or False

4. Blindfolded chess players mainly use concepts to represent chess problems and solutions.
   True or False

Check Your Memory: Pages 284–286

5. Images are used to make decisions, change feelings, and to improve memory.
   True or False

6. Mental images may be used to improve memory and skilled actions.
   True or False

7. The visual cortex is activated when a person has a mental image.
   True or False

8. The more the image of a shape has to be rotated in space, the longer it takes to tell if it matches another view of the same shape.
   True or False

9. Women perform better than men on mental rotation tasks.
   True or False

10. The smaller a mental image is, the harder it is to identify its details.
    True or False

11. People with good kinesthetic imagery tend to learn sports skills faster than average.
    True or False

Check Your Memory: Pages 286–289

12. Concept formation is typically based on examples and rules.
    True or False

13. Prototypes are very strong negative instances of a concept.
    True or False
14. "Greater than" and "lopsided" are relational concepts.
    True or False
15. The semantic differential is used to rate the objective meanings of words and concepts.
    True or False

Check Your Memory: Pages 289—290

16. Encoding is the study of the meanings of language.
    True or False
17. The study of meaning in language is called semantics.
    True or False
18. Morphemes are the basic speech sounds of a language.
    True or False
19. Syntax is a part of grammar.
    True or False
20. Noam Chomsky believes that a child who says, "I drinked my juice," has applied the semantic differential to a simple, core sentence.
    True or False
21. ASL has 600,000 root signs.
    True or False
22. True languages are productive, thus ASL is not a true language.
    True or False

Check Your Memory: Pages 290—292

23. Animal communication can be described as productive.
    True or False
24. Chimpanzees have never learned to speak even a single word.
    True or False
25. One of Sarah chimpanzee's outstanding achievements was mastery of sentences involving transformational rules.
    True or False
26. Some "language" use by chimpanzees appears to be no more than simple operant responses.
    True or False
27. Only a minority of the things that language-trained chimps "say" have anything to do with food.
    True or False
28. Language-trained chimps have been known to hold conversations when no humans were present.
    True or False
29. Kanzi's use of grammar is on a par with that of a 2-year-old child.
    True or False

Check Your Memory: Pages 292—297

30. Except for the simplest problems, mechanical solutions are typically best left to computers.
    True or False
31. Karl Dunker's famous tumour problem could only be solved by trial-and-error.
    True or False

32. Research has shown that politicians and journalists rarely use analogies spontaneously when looking for the solution to a problem.
True or False

33. Working backward from the desired goal to the starting point can be a useful heuristic.
True or False

34. In problem solving, rapid insights are more likely to be correct than those that develop slowly.
True or False

35. Selective encoding refers to bringing together seemingly unrelated bits of useful information.
True or False

36. Functional fixedness is an inability to see new uses for familiar objects.
True or False

Check Your Memory: Pages 297—298

37. AI is frequently based on a set of rules applied to a body of information.
True or False

38. Computer simulation programs can be used to create a model of the organization and processes involved in a business such as a magazine publishing company.
True or False

39. Much human expertise is based on acquired strategies for solving problems.
True or False

40. Chess experts have an exceptional ability to remember the positions of chess pieces placed at random on a chessboard.
True or False

Check Your Memory: Pages 298—303

41. Alfred Binet's first test was designed to measure mechanical aptitude.
True or False

42. When asked to give examples of intelligent people, students nominated people that were similar to their parents in attitudes and occupations.
True or False

43. Lewis Terman helped write the Stanford-Binet intelligence test.
True or False

44. Mental age refers to average mental ability for a person of a given age.
True or False

45. Mental age can't be higher than chronological age.
True or False

46. An IQ will be greater than 100 when CA is larger than MA.
True or False

47. Average intelligence is defined as an IQ from 90 to 109.
True or False

48. Modern IQ tests give scores as deviation IQs.
True or False

49. The WISC is designed to test adult performance intelligence.
True or False

50. The digit symbol task is considered a performance subtest of the WAIS.
    True or False

51. The Stanford-Binet, Wechsler's, and the SAT are all group intelligence tests.
    True or False

Check Your Memory: Pages 303—308

52. In a normal curve, a majority of scores are found near the average.
    True or False

53. An IQ above 130 is described as "bright normal."
    True or False

54. The correlation between IQ scores and school grades is .5.
    True or False

55. Only 12 people out of 100 score above 130 on IQ tests.
    True or False

56. Some of the gender differences on spatial test performance is due to the role of biology rather than learning.
    True or False

57. Gifted children tend to get average IQ scores by the time they reach adulthood.
    True or False

58. Gifted persons are more susceptible to mental illness.
    True or False

59. Talking in complete sentences at age 2 is regarded as a sign of giftedness.
    True or False

60. The moderately retarded can usually learn routine self-help skills.
    True or False

61. The IQs of identical twins are more alike than those of fraternal twins.
    True or False

62. Adult intelligence is approximately 50 percent hereditary.
    True or False

Check Your Memory: Pages 309—313

63. In inductive thinking, a general rule is inferred from specific examples.
    True or False

64. Fluency and flexibility are measures of convergent thinking.
    True or False

65. Creative thinkers typically apply reasoning and critical thinking to novel ideas after they produce them.
    True or False

66. Creative ideas combine originality with feasibility.
    True or False

67. Creative problem solving temporarily stops during the incubation period.
    True or False

68. Creative people have an openness to experience and they have a wide range of knowledge and interests.
    True or False

Check Your Memory: Pages 313—315

69. Intuition is a quick, impulsive insight into the true nature of a problem and its solution.
    True or False

70. The probability of two events occurring together is lower than the probability
    of either one occurring alone.
    True or False

71. The representativeness heuristic is the strategy of stating problems in broad terms.
    True or False

72. Framing refers to the way in which a problem is stated or structured.
    True or False

Check Your Memory: Psychology in Action

73. Creative problem solving involves defining problems as narrowly as possible.
    True or False

74. It is wise to allow time for incubation if you are seeking a creative solution to a problem.
    True or False

75. Edward de Bono suggests that digging deeper with logic is a good way to increase your creativity.
    True or False

76. People seeking creative solutions should avoid taking risks; doing so just leads to dead-ends.
    True or False

77. Delaying evaluation during the early stages of creative problem solving tends to lead to poor thinking.
    True or False

78. The cross-stimulation effect is an important part of brainstorming in groups.
    True or False

Final Survey and Review

• *What is the nature of thought?*

1. _____ psychology is the study of human information processing (thinking,
   _____ , and problem solving).

2. Thinking is the manipulation of internal _____ of external problems or situations.

3. Three basic units of thought are _____ , _____ , and language or _____ .

• *In what ways are images related to thinking?*

4. Most people have internal images of one kind or another. Images may be based on
   _____ _____ in memory or they may be created.

5. The _____ of images used in problem solving may change. Images may be three-dimensional
   and they may be _____ in space to answer questions.

6. Many of the systems in the _____ that are involved in processing _____
   images work in reverse to create _____ images.

7. Kinesthetic _____ are created from produced, remembered, or imagined muscular sensations.
   Kinesthetic sensations and _____ seem to help structure thinking for many people.

• *How are concepts learned?*

8. A concept is a _____ idea of a class of objects or events.

9. Forming concepts may be based on experiences with positive and _____ _____ .

10. Concepts may also be acquired by learning _____ that define the concept.

11. In practice, we frequently use _____ (general models of the concept class) to identify concepts.

12. Concepts may be classified as _____ ("and" concepts), _____ ("either-or" concepts), relational concepts, or _____ (past experiences).

13. The _____ meaning of a word or concept is its exact definition. _____ meaning is personal or emotional.

14. Connotative meaning can be measured with the _____ differential. Most connotative meaning involves the dimensions good-bad, _____ , and _____ .

• *What is the role of language in thinking?*

15. Language allows events to be _____ into symbols for easy mental manipulation.

16. Language is built out of _____ (basic speech sounds) and _____ (speech sounds collected into meaningful units).

17. Thinking in language is influenced by meaning. The study of meaning is called _____ .

18. Language carries meaning by combining a set of symbols or signs according to a set of rules (_____), which includes rules about word order (_____).

19. Various sentences are created by applying _____ rules to simple statements.

20. A true language is _____ , and can be used to generate new ideas or possibilities. _____ _____ Language (ASL) and other gestural languages used by the deaf are true languages.

• *Can animals be taught to use language?*

21. _____ communication is relatively limited because it lacks symbols that can be rearranged easily. As a result, it does not have the _____ quality of human language.

22. Attempts to teach chimpanzees ASL and other non-verbal systems suggest to some that _____ are capable of language use. However, others believe that the chimps are merely using operant responses to get food and other _____ .

23. Studies that make use of _____ (geometric word-symbols) provide the best evidence yet of animal language use.

• *What do we know about problem solving?*

24. The solution to a problem may be found _____ (by trial and error or by rote application of rules). However, _____ solutions are frequently inefficient or ineffective, except where aided by computer.

25. Solutions by _____ usually involves a deeper comprehension of the problem. Using _____ can help find solutions.

26. Problem solving is frequently aided by _____ . These are strategies that typically narrow the search for solutions.

27. When understanding leads to a rapid solution, _____ has occurred. Three elements of _____ are selective _____ , selective combination and selective comparison.

28. Insights and other problem solving attempts can be blocked by _____ (a tendency to repeat wrong solutions).

29. _____ fixedness is a common fixation, but emotional _____ , cultural _____ , learned conventions, and perceptual habits are also problems.

• *What is artificial intelligence?*

30. Artificial intelligence refers to _____ _____ that can perform tasks that require intelligence when done by _____ .

31. Two principal areas of artificial intelligence research are computer simulations and _____ _____ .

32. Expert human problem solving is based on _____ knowledge and acquired _____ , rather than some general improvement in thinking ability.

• *How is human intelligence defined and measured?*

33. Intelligence refers to one's general capacity to act _____ , _____ rationally, and deal effectively with the environment.

34. In practice, writing an intelligence test provides an _____ definition of intelligence.

35. The first practical intelligence test was assembled in 1904, in Paris, by _____ _____ .

36. A modern version of that test is the _____ Intelligence Scale, Fourth Edition.

37. The Stanford-Binet measures verbal reasoning, _____ reasoning, _____ /visual reasoning, and short-term memory.

38. Intelligence is expressed in terms of an intelligence quotient (IQ). IQ is defined as _____ _____ (MA) divided by _____ _____ (CA) and then multiplied by 100.

39. An "average" IQ of 100 occurs when _____ age equals _____ age.

40. Modern IQ tests no longer calculate IQ directly. Instead, the final score reported by the test is a _____ _____ , which gives a person's relative intellectual standing in his or her age group.

41. A second major intelligence test is the _____ *Adult Intelligence Scale-III* (WAIS-III). The WAIS-III measures both _____ and _____ (non-verbal) intelligence.

42. Intelligence tests have also been produced for use with groups of people. The _____ _____ Test (SAT), measures a variety of mental _____ and it can be used to estimate intelligence.

• *How do IQ scores relate to achievement and thinking ability?*

43. When graphed, the _____ (percentage of people receiving each score) of IQ scores approximates a _____ (bell-shaped) curve.

44. While researchers _____ that men and women do not differ in overall intelligence, a debate still exists as to whether _____ differences are due to learning or biological influences.

45. People with IQs above _____ are considered to be in the gifted or "genius" range.

46. Studies done by Lewis _____ showed that the _____ tend to have a higher correlation between IQ score and real world _____ .

47. By criteria other than IQ, a large proportion of children might be considered _____ or _____ in one way or another.

48. Howard _____ believes that traditional IQ tests define intelligence too narrowly. According to Gardner, intelligence consists of abilities in _____ , logic and math, visual and spatial thinking, _____ , kinesthetic skills, intrapersonal skills, interpersonal skills, and _____ skills.

49. The terms mentally retarded and _____ disabled are applied to those whose IQ falls below 70 or who lack various _____ behaviours.

50. Further classifications of retardation are: mild (50-55 to 70), _____ (35-40 to 50-55), severe (20-25 to 35-40), and _____ (below 20-25).

51. About 50 percent of the cases of mental retardation are _____ , being caused by birth injuries, fetal damage, metabolic disorders, or _____ abnormalities. The remaining cases are of undetermined cause.

52. Many cases of subnormal intelligence are thought to be the result of _____ retardation (a low level of intellectual stimulation in the home, poverty, and poor nutrition).

53. Studies of family relationships in humans, especially comparisons between _____ twins and _____ twins, suggest that intelligence is partly hereditary.

54. However, _____ is also important, as revealed by changes in tested intelligence induced by stimulating _____ and improved education.

55. Intelligence therefore reflects the combined effects of _____ and _____ .

56. Differences in the average IQ scores for various racial groups are based on _____ differences, not heredity.

• *What is the nature of creative thinking?*

57. To be creative, a solution must be practical and sensible as well as _____ .

58. Thinking may be deductive or _____ , _____ or illogical.

59. Creative thinking requires _____ thought, characterized by _____ , flexibility, and originality.

60. Tests of creativity, such as the *Unusual* _____ *Test*, the *Consequences Test*, and the *Anagrams Test*, measure the capacity for _____ thinking.

61. Five stages often seen in creative problem solving are orientation, preparation, _____ , _____ , and verification.

62. Studies suggest that creative persons share a number of identifiable general traits, thinking abilities, thinking styles, and _____ characteristics. There is only a small _____ between IQ and creativity.

• *How accurate is intuition?*

63. Intuitive thinking often leads to errors. Wrong conclusions may be drawn when an answer seems highly _____ of what we already believe is true. (That is, when people apply the representativeness _____ .)

64. A second problem is ignoring the _____ _____ (or underlying probability) of an event.

65. Clear thinking is usually aided by stating or _____ a problem in broad terms.

• *What can be done to improve thinking and to promote creativity?*

66. Mental _____ can act as major barriers to _____ thinking.

67. Creativity can be enhanced by defining problems broadly, by establishing a creative atmosphere, by allowing time for _____ , by restating a problem in different ways, by seeking varied _____ , by taking sensible _____ , and by looking for analogies.

68. _____ , in which the production and criticism of ideas is kept separate, also tends to enhance creative problem solving.

Mastery Test

1. The mark of a true language is that it must be
   a. spoken
   b. productive
   c. based on spatial grammar and syntax
   d. capable of encoding conditional relationships

2. Computer simulations and expert systems are two major applications of
   a. AI
   b. ASL
   c. brainstorming
   d. problem framing

3. Failure to wear automobile seat belts is an example of which intuitive thinking error?
   a. allowing too much time for incubation
   b. framing a problem broadly
   c. ignoring base rates
   d. recognition that two events occurring together are more likely than either one alone

4. One thing that images, concepts, and symbols all have in common is that they are
   a. morphemes
   b. internal representations
   c. based on reverse vision
   d. translated into micromovements

5. To decide if a container is a cup, bowl, or vase, most people compare it to
   a. a prototype
   b. its connotative meaning
   c. a series of negative instances
   d. a series of relevant phonemes

6. During problem solving, being "cold," "warm," or "very warm" is closely associated with
   a. insight
   b. fixation
   c. automatic processing
   d. rote problem solving

7. The *Anagrams Test* measures
   a. mental sets
   b. inductive thinking
   c. logical reasoning
   d. divergent thinking

8. "Either-or" concepts are
   a. conjunctive
   b. disjunctive
   c. relational

d.   prototypical

9.   Which term does not belong with the others?

    a.   selective comparison

    b.   functional fixedness

    c.   learned conventions

    d.   emotional blocks

10.   Separate collections of verbal and performance subtests are a feature of the

    a.   WAIS

    b.   Gardner-8

    c.   CQT

    d.   Stanford-Binet

11.   Mental retardation is formally defined by deficiencies in

    a.   aptitudes and self-help skills

    b.   intelligence and scholastic aptitudes

    c.   language and spatial thinking

    d.   IQ and adaptive behaviours

12.   A 12-year-old child, with an IQ of 100, must have an MA of

    a.   100

    b.   12

    c.   10

    d.   15

13.   The difference between prime beef and dead cow is primarily a matter of

    a.   syntax

    b.   conjunctive meaning

    c.   semantics

    d.   the productive nature of language

14.   Culture-fair tests attempt to measure intelligence without being affected by a person's

    a.   verbal skills

    b.   cultural background

    c.   educational level

    d.   all of the preceding

15.   Which of the listed terms does NOT correctly complete this sentence: Insight involves selective_____.

    a.   encoding

    b.   combination

    c.   comparison

    d.   fixation

16.   Which of the following is LEAST likely to predict that a person is creative?

    a.   high IQ

    b.   a preference for complexity

   c.   fluency in combining ideas

   d.   use of mental images

17.   "Try working backward from the desired goal to the starting point or current state." This advice describes a

   a.   syllogism

   b.   heuristic

   c.   prototype

   d.   dimension of the semantic differential

18.   Language allows events to be _____ into _____.

   a.   translated, concepts

   b.   fixated, codes

   c.   rearranged, lexigrams

   d.   encoded, symbols

19.   "A triangle must be a closed shape with three sides made of straight lines." This statement is an example of a

   a.   prototype

   b.   positive instance

   c.   conceptual rule

   d.   disjunctive concept

20.   Fluency, flexibility, and originality are all measures of

   a.   inductive thinking

   b.   selective comparison

   c.   intuitive framing

   d.   divergent thinking

21.   The form of imagery that is especially important in music, sports, dance, and martial arts is

   a.   kinesthetic imagery

   b.   semantic imagery

   c.   prototypical imagery

   d.   conjunctive imagery

22.   Among animals trained to use language, Kanzi has been unusually accurate at

   a.   using proper syntax

   b.   substituting gestures for lexigrams

   c.   expressing conditional relationships

   d.   forming chains of operant responses

23.   The largest number of people are found in which IQ range?

   a.   80-89

   b.   90-109

   c.   110-119

   d.   below 70

24. Looking for analogies and delaying evaluation are helpful strategies for increasing
    a. divergent thinking
    b. convergent thinking
    c. functional fixedness
    d. concept formation

25. Comparing 2 three-dimensional shapes to see if they match is easiest if only a small amount of _____ is required.
    a. conceptual recoding
    b. mental rotation
    c. concept formation
    d. kinesthetic transformation

26. The good-bad dimension on the semantic differential is closely related to a concept's
    a. disjunctive meaning
    b. conjunctive meaning
    c. connotative meaning
    d. denotative meaning

27. Questions about vocabulary, comprehension, and absurdities would be found in which ability area of the Stanford-Binet?
    a. verbal reasoning
    b. quantitative reasoning
    c. abstract/visual reasoning
    d. short-term memory

28. The directions "modify, magnify, rearrange, and suspend judgment" could be expected to aid a group engaged in
    a. a means-ends analysis
    b. base rate framing
    c. brainstorming
    d. solving delayed response problems

29. According to Noam Chomsky, surface sentences are created by applying _____ to simple sentences.
    a. encoding grammars
    b. transformation rules
    c. conditional prototypes
    d. selective conjunctions

30. The occurrence of an insight corresponds to which stage of creative thinking?
    a. verification
    b. incubation
    c. illumination
    d. fixation

31. Which of the following animals (this category includes humans) has mental images and is capable of rotating them?

    a. bees

    b. pigeons

    c. humans

    d. all of the above

32. A recent Canadian study found that success among artists was related to

    a. a life completely focused on one's art

    b. a high score on neurotic traits

    c. narcissistic tendencies and isolation

    d. a strong ability for fantasy thinking.

Solutions

Recite and Review

1. information
2. internal
3. language
4. created
5. change, space
6. visual
7. muscular, Kinesthetic
8. class
9. positive
10. concept
11. models
12. and, either-or, experiences
13. definition, personal
14. good-bad
15. symbols
16. sounds, meaningful
17. meaning
18. order, rules
19. rules
20. gestural
21. human
22. operant
23. geometric
24. rote, computer
25. deeper, analogies
26. narrow
27. solution, selective
28. wrong
29. fixation, habits
30. programs, intelligence
31. computer

32. knowledge
33. rationally, environment
34. definition
35. intelligence, test
36. Intelligence, Scale
37. verbal, memory
38. quotient, 100
39. 100, equals
40. IQs, relative
41. Adult, non-verbal
42. groups, mental
43. bell, curve
44. overall, learning
45. gifted
46. correlation
47. IQ
48. traditional, math, visual
49. retarded, 70
50. mild, severe
51. 50, birth
52. intellectual
53. genes, heredity
54. stimulating
55. Intelligence
56. genetics (or heredity)
57. practical
58. Thinking
59. originality
60. creativity
61. preparation
62. thinking, styles
63. errors, true
64. probability
65. broad
66. Mental, thinking

67. broadly, different, time, varied
68. separate

Connections

1. F
2. J
3. I
4. A
5. C
6. B
7. E
8. D
9. G
10. H
11. C
12. A
13. E
14. J
15. B
16. I
17. D
18. F
19. G
20. H
21. D
22. A
23. I
24. B
25. J
26. H
27. C
28. E
29. F
30. G

31. H	**23.** F	**58.** F
32. A	**24.** F	**59.** T
33. G	**25.** F	**60.** F
34. B	**26.** T	**61.** T
35. J	**27.** T	**62.** T
36. C	**28.** T	**63.** T
37. I	**29.** T	**64.** F
38. D	**30.** T	**65.** T
39. E	**31.** F	**66.** T
40. F	**32.** F	**67.** F
	33. T	**68.** T

Check your memory

	34. T	**69.** F
	35. F	**70.** T
1. F	**36.** T	**71.** F
2. T	**37.** T	**72.** T
3. F	**38.** T	**73.** F
4. F	**39.** T	**74.** T
5. T	**40.** F	**75.** F
6. T	**41.** F	**76.** F
7. T	**42.** F	**77.** F
8. T	**43.** T	**78.** T
9. F	**44.** T	
10. T	**45.** F	
11. T	**46.** F	
12. T	**47.** T	## Final Survey and Review
13. F	**48.** T	
14. T	**49.** F	**1.** Cognitive, language
15. F	**50.** T	**2.** representations
16. F	**51.** F	**3.** images, concepts, symbols
17. T	**52.** T	**4.** information, stored
18. F	**53.** F	**5.** size, rotated
19. T	**54.** T	**6.** brain, visual, mental
20. F	**55.** F	**7.** images, micromovements
21. F	**56.** T	**8.** generalized
22. F	**57.** F	**9.** negative, instances
		10. rules
		11. prototypes

12. conjunctive, disjunctive, exemplars

13. denotive, Connotative

14. semantic, strong-weak, active-passive

15. encoded

16. phonemes, morphemes

17. sematics

18. grammar, syntax

19. transformation

20. productive, American, Sign

21. Animal, productive

22. primates, reinforcers

23. lexigrams

24. mechanically, mechanical

25. understanding, analogies

26. heuristics

27. insight, insight, encoding

28. fixation

29. Functional, blocks, values

30. computer, programs, people

31. expert, systems

32. organized, strategies

33. purposefully, think

34. operational

35. Alfred, Binet

36. Stanford-Binet

37. quantitative, abstract

38. mental, age, chronological, age

39. mental, chronological

40. Deviation , IQ

41. Wechsler, verbal, performance

42. Scholastic, Assessment, aptitudes

43. distribution, normal

44. agree, specific

45. 140

46. Terman, gifted, success

47. gifted, talented

48. Gardner, language, music, naturalist

49. developmentally, adaptive

50. moderate, profound

51. organic, genetic

52. familial

53. fraternal, identical

54. environment, environments

55. heredity, environment

56. environmental

57. original

58. inductive, logical

59. divergent, fluency

60. Uses, divergent

61. incubation, illumination

62. personality, correlation

63. representative, heuristic

64. base, rate

65. framing

66. sets, creative

67. incubation, input, risks

68. Brainstorming

Mastery Test

1. B (p. 290)

2. A (p. 297)

3. C (p. 314)

4. B (p. 284)

5. A (p. 288)

6. A (p. 295)

7. D (p. 310)

8. B (p. 387)

9. A (p. 295)

10. A (p. 302)

11. D (p. 305)

12. B (p. 300)

13. C (p. 289)

14. D (p. 302)

15. D (p. 295)

16. A (p. 312)

17. B (p. 295)

18. D (p. 289)

19. C (p. 287)

20. D (p. 309)

21. A (p. 286)

22. A (p. 292)

23. B (p. 303)

24. A (p. 309)

25. B (p. 285)

26. C (p. 288)

27. A (p. 300)

28. C (p. 318)

29. B (p. 290)

30. C (p. 311)

31. D (p. 280)

32. C (p. 312)

Chapter 9

Motivation and Emotion

Chapter Overview

Motivation typically involves needs, drives, goals, and goal attainment. Three types of motives are primary motives, stimulus motives, and secondary motives. Most primary motives maintain homeostasis.

Hunger is influenced by the stomach, blood sugar levels, metabolism in the liver, fat stores in the body, activity in the hypothalamus, diet, and other factors. Eating disorders are serious and sometimes fatal problems. Behavioural dieting uses self-control techniques to change basic eating patterns and habits.

Thirst and other basic motives are affected by many factors, but they are primarily controlled by the hypothalamus. Pain avoidance is episodic and partially learned. The sex drive is non-homeostatic.

Sexual arousal is related to stimulation of the body's erogenous zones, but arousal is strongly influenced by mental factors. There is little difference in male and female sexual responsiveness. Sexual orientation refers to whether a person is heterosexual, homosexual, or bisexual. A combination of hereditary, biological, social, and psychological influences combine to produce one's sexual orientation. Human sexual response can be divided into four phases: (1) excitement; (2) plateau; (3) orgasm; and (4) resolution, which apply to both males and females and to people of all sexual orientations.

The stimulus motives include drives for information, exploration, manipulation, and sensory input. Drives for stimulation are partially explained by arousal theory. Optimal performance on a task usually occurs at moderate levels of arousal. Circadian rhythms are closely tied to sleep, activity, and energy cycles.

Social motives, which are learned, account for much of the diversity of human motivation. The need for achievement is a social motive correlated with success in many situations.

Maslow's hierarchy of motives categorizes needs as basic or growth oriented. Self-actualization, the highest and most fragile need, is reflected in meta-needs. In many situations, extrinsic motivation can lower intrinsic motivation, enjoyment, and creativity.

Emotions are linked to basic adaptive behaviours. Other major elements of emotion are bodily changes, emotional expressions, and emotional feelings. Physiological changes during emotion are caused by adrenaline and the autonomic nervous system (ANS). The sympathetic branch of the ANS arouses the body and the parasympathetic branch quiets it. Basic emotional expressions are unlearned. Facial expressions are central to emotion. Body gestures and movements (body language) also express feelings. A variety of theories have been proposed to explain emotion.

Subjective well-being (happiness) is a combination of general life satisfaction and positive emotions. Making progress toward your goals is associated with happiness, especially if the goals express your personal interests and values.

Learning Objectives

1. Define *motivation*.
2. Describe or analyze a motivational sequence using the need-reduction model.

3. Explain how the incentive value of a goal can affect motivation and describe how incentive value is related to internal need.

4. List and describe the three major types of motives and give an example of each.

5. Define *homeostasis*.

6. Discuss why hunger cannot be fully explained by the contractions of an empty stomach.

7. Describe the relationship of each of the following to hunger:
   a. blood sugar
   b. liver
   c. hypothalamus
      i) feeding system (lateral hypothalamus)
      ii) satiety system (ventromedial hypothalamus)
      iii) blood sugar regulator (paraventricular nucleus)
   d. NPY, GLP-1, and leptin

8. Explain how a person's set point is related to obesity.

9. Describe the impact of external eating cues and dietary content on obesity.

10. Explain the paradox of yo-yo dieting.

11. Define *overweight* and *obesity*.

12. Explain what is meant by behavioural dieting, and describe the techniques which can enable you to control your weight.

13. Describe how cultural factors, taste, and taste aversions relate to hunger.

14. Describe the essential features of the eating disorders anorexia nervosa and bulimia nervosa. Explain what causes them and what treatment is available for them. Define reverse anorexia.

15. Name the brain structure that appears to control thirst (as well as hunger). Differentiate extracellular and intracellular thirst.

16. Explain how the drive to avoid pain and the sex drive differ from other primary drives. Include a brief explanation of the non-homeostatic nature of the sex drive.

17. Define *erogenous zone*, and explain how it relates to sexual behaviour.

18. Define the term *sexual orientation* and discuss the various types of sexual orientation. Discuss the combination of influences that produces homosexuality.

19. List in order and briefly describe the four phases of sexual response in men and women.

20. Describe the basic female and male sexual responses, and state the basic differences in sexual response styles of men and women.

21. Describe the evidence for the existence of stimulus drives.

22. Explain the arousal theory of motivation and the characteristics of sensation-seekers. Describe the inverted U function. Relate arousal to the Yerkes-Dodson law and give an example of it.

23. Describe the two major components of test anxiety and describe four ways to reduce it.

24. Explain how circadian rhythms affect energy levels, motivation, and performance. Include an explanation of how and why shift work and jet lag may adversely affect a person and how to minimize the effects of shifting one's rhythms.

25. Define *need for achievement* (nAch) and differentiate it from the need for power.

26. Describe people who are achievers, and relate nAch to risk-taking.

27. Briefly describe the results of the subliminal tape experiment.

28. Explain the influences of drive and determination in the development of success for high achievers.

29. List seven steps to enhancing self-confidence.

30. List (in order) the needs found in Maslow's hierarchy of motives, and distinguish between basic needs and growth needs.

31. Explain why the lower (physiological) needs in Maslow's hierarchy are considered prepotent.

32. Define *meta-need* and give an example of one.

33. Distinguish between intrinsic and extrinsic motivation, and explain how each type of motivation may affect the person's interest in work, leisure activities, and creativity.

34. Explain why emotions aid survival.

35. List and describe the three major elements of emotions.

36. List the eight primary emotions proposed by Plutchik and explain his concept of mixing them.

37. State which side of the brain processes positive versus negative emotion.

38. Describe the effects of the sympathetic and parasympathetic branches of the ANS during and after emotion.

39. Define *parasympathetic rebound* and discuss its possible involvement in cases of sudden death.

40. Explain how the polygraph is supposed to detect lies.

41. Discuss the limitations and/or accuracy of lie detector devices.

42. Understand that emotional expressions have evolved to aid our survival. Describe the evidence that supports the conclusion that most emotional expressions are universal. Include a brief description of cultural and gender differences in emotion.

43. Define *kinesics*. List and describe the emotional messages conveyed by facial expressions (include the three basic dimensions) and body language. Explain how overall posture can indicate one's emotional state.

44. Briefly describe the James-Lange theory of emotion.

45. Briefly describe the Cannon-Bard theory of emotion.

46. Briefly describe Schachter's cognitive theory of emotion and give experimental evidence to support his theory.

47. Describe and give an example of how attribution affects emotion.

48. Briefly describe the facial feedback hypothesis.

49. Discuss the role of appraisal in contemporary models of emotion.

50. Describe the concept of emotional intelligence and how it may enhance one's life.

51. Briefly discuss the concept of subjective well-being.

52. Discuss the relationship of personal factors (such as wealth and personality) to happiness.

53. Briefly discuss McGregor and Little's findings regarding integrity, goals, and happiness.

Practice Quizzes

Recite and Review

- ### *What is motivation? Are there different types of motives?*

Recite and Review: Pages 325–328

1. Motives _____ (begin), sustain (perpetuate), and direct _____ .

2. Motivation typically involves the sequence _____ , drive, _____ , and goal attainment (need reduction).

3. Behaviour can be activated either by needs (_____) or by goals (_____).

4. The attractiveness of a _____ and its ability to initiate action are related to its incentive value (its value above and beyond its capacity to fill a _____).

5. Three principal types of motives are primary motives, stimulus motives, and _____ motives.

6. Most _____ motives operate to maintain a _____ state of bodily equilibrium called homeostasis.

- ### *What causes hunger? Overeating? Eating disorders?*

Recite and Review: Pages 328–334

7. Hunger is influenced by a complex interplay between distention (fullness) of the _____ , hypoglycemia (low _____ sugar), metabolism in the _____ , and fat stores in the body.

8. The most direct control of eating is exerted by the hypothalamus, which has areas that act like feeding (_____) and satiety (_____) systems for hunger and eating.

9. The lateral hypothalamus acts as a _____ system; the ventromedial hypothalamus is part of a _____ system; the paraventricular nucleus influences both hunger and satiety.

10. Other factors influencing hunger are the set point for the proportion of _____ in the body, external eating cues, the attractiveness and variety of _____ .

11. Hunger is also influenced by emotions, learned _____ preferences and _____ aversions, and cultural values.

12. A person is considered overweight if 25% or more of their body weight is made up of _____ and is considered obese if this proportion is more than _____ percent.

13. Anorexia nervosa (self-inflicted _____) and bulimia nervosa (_____ and purging) are two prominent eating disorders.

14. Reverse anorexia is seen in some well-muscled _____ who, unlike anorexics, have the unreal perception that their body is too _____ .

15. These eating disorders tend to involve conflicts about self-image, self-control, and _____ .

• *Is there more than one type of thirst? In what ways are pain avoidance and the sex drive unusual?*

Recite and Review: Pages 334—336

16. Like hunger, thirst and other basic motives are affected by a number of _____ factors, but are primarily under the central control of the hypothalamus in the _____ .

17. Thirst may be either intracellular (when _____ is lost from inside _____) or extracellular (when _____ is lost from the spaces between _____).

18. Pain avoidance is unusual because it is episodic (associated with particular conditions) as opposed to cyclic (occurring in regular _____).

19. Pain is best described as a _____ (neuromatrix) that responds to both pain intensity and the _____ components (i.e. memory, what the wound looks like, etc.) that surround the event.

20. Pain avoidance and pain tolerance are partially _____ (influenced by training).

21. The sex drive in many lower animals is related to estrus (or "heat") in _____ . The sex drive is unusual in that it is non-homeostatic (relatively _____ of needs in the body).

22. Sex _____ in both males and females may be related to bodily levels of androgens.

• *What are typical patterns of human sexual response?*

Recite and Review: Pages 336—339

23. Sexual arousal is related to stimulation of the body's erogenous zones (areas that produce erotic _____), but cognitive elements such as _____ and images are equally important.

24. There is little difference in sexual _____ between males and females.

25. Evidence suggests that the sex drive peaks at a _____ age for females than it does for males, although this difference is diminishing.

26. Sexual orientation refers to one's degree of emotional and erotic attraction to members of the same _____ , opposite _____ , or both _____ .

27. A person may be heterosexual, _____ , or bisexual.

28. A combination of hereditary, biological, social, and psychological influences combine to produce one's _____ _____ .

29. As a group, homosexual men and women do not differ psychologically from _____ .

30. In a series of landmark studies, William _____ and Virginia Johnson directly observed sexual response in a large number of adults.

31. Human sexual response can be divided into four phases: (1) _____ ; (2) plateau; (3) _____ ; and (4) resolution.

32. Both males and females may go through all four stages in _____ minutes. But during lovemaking, most females typically take longer than this.

33. Males experience a refractory period after _____ and ejaculation. Only 5 percent of men are _____ -orgasmic.

• *How does arousal relate to motivation?*

Recite and Review: Pages 340—343

34. The stimulus drives reflect needs for information, exploration, manipulation, and _____ input.

35. Drives for stimulation are partially explained by arousal theory, which states that an ideal level of _____ _____ will be maintained if possible.

36. The desired level of _____ or stimulation varies from person to person, as measured by the Sensation-Seeking Scale.

37. Optimal performance on a task usually occurs at _____ levels of arousal. This relationship is described by an inverted U function.

38. The Yerkes-Dodson law further states that for _____ tasks the ideal arousal level is higher, and for _____ tasks it is lower.

39. Circadian _____ within the body are closely tied to sleep, activity levels, and energy cycles. Time zone travel and shift work can seriously disrupt _____ and bodily rhythms.

40. If you anticipate a _____ in body rhythms, you can gradually preadapt to your new _____ over a period of days.

• *What are social motives? Why are they important?*

Recite and Review: Pages 343—345

41. _____ motives are learned through socialization and cultural conditioning.

42. One of the most prominent social motives is the _____ for achievement (nAch).

43. High nAch is correlated with _____ in many situations, with occupational choice, and with moderate _____ taking.

44. Self-confidence affects _____ because it influences the challenges you will undertake, the _____ you will make, and how long you will _____ when things don't go well.

• *Are some motives more basic than others?*

Recite and Review: Pages 345—348

45. Maslow's hierarchy (rank ordering) of motives categorizes needs as _____ and growth oriented.

46. _____ needs in the hierarchy are assumed to be prepotent (dominant) over _____ needs.

47. _____ -actualization, the highest and most fragile need, is reflected in meta- _____ .

48. In many situations, extrinsic motivation (that which is induced by obvious _____ rewards) can reduce intrinsic motivation, enjoyment, and creativity.

• *What happens during emotion? Can "lie detectors" really detect lies?*

Recite and Review: Pages 348—352

49. Emotions are linked to many basic adaptive _____ , such as attacking, retreating, feeding, and reproducing.

50. Other major elements of emotion are physiological changes in the body, emotional expressions, and emotional _____ .

51. The following are considered to be primary emotions: fear, surprise, _____ , disgust, _____ , anticipation, joy, and acceptance. Other emotions seem to represent mixtures of the primaries.

52. Physical changes associated with emotion are caused by the action of adrenaline, a _____ released into the bloodstream, and by activity in the autonomic _____ _____ (ANS).

53. The sympathetic _____ of the ANS is primarily responsible for arousing the body, the parasympathetic _____ for quieting it.

54. Sudden death due to prolonged and intense emotion is probably related to parasympathetic _____ (excess activity). Heart attacks caused by sudden intense emotion are more likely due to sympathetic _____ .

55. The polygraph, or "lie detector," measures _____ _____ by monitoring heart rate, blood pressure, breathing rate, and the galvanic skin response (GSR).

56. Asking a series of _____ and irrelevant questions may allow the detection of _____ , but overall, the accuracy of the lie detector has been challenged by many researchers.

- ### *How accurately are emotions expressed by "body language" and the face?*

Recite and Review: Pages 352—355

57. Basic emotional expressions, such as smiling or baring one's teeth when angry, appear to be _____ .

58. Facial expressions of _____ , anger, disgust, _____ , and happiness are recognized by people of all cultures.

59. Body gestures and movements (body language) also express _____ , mainly by communicating emotional _____ .

60. Three dimensions of _____ expressions are pleasantness-unpleasantness, attention-rejection, and activation.

61. The study of _____ _____ is known as kinesics.

- ### *How do psychologists explain emotions?*

Recite and Review: Pages 355—360

62. The James-Lange theory of emotion says that emotional experience _____ an awareness of the bodily reactions of emotion.

63. In contrast, the Cannon-Bard theory says that bodily reactions and emotional experience occur _____ _____ _____ _____ and that emotions are organized in the brain.

64. Schachter's cognitive theory of emotion emphasizes the importance of _____ , or interpretations, applied to feelings of bodily arousal.

65. Also important is the process of attribution, in which bodily _____ is attributed to a particular person, object, or situation.

66. The facial feedback hypothesis holds that sensations and information from emotional _____ help define what emotion a person is feeling.

67. Contemporary views of emotion place greater emphasis on how _____ are appraised. Also, all of the elements of emotion are seen as interrelated and interacting.

68. Emotional intelligence can be seen as the equivalent of Howard Gardner's intelligence. This _____ intelligence refers to skills such as empathy, self-control, _____ , sensitivity to the feelings of others, _____ , and self-motivation.

- ### *What factors contribute most to a happy and fulfilling life?*

Recite and Review: Psychology in Action

69. Subjective well being (_____) occurs when _____ emotions outnumber _____ emotions and a person is satisfied with his or her life.

70. Happiness is only mildly related to _____ , education, marriage, religion, age, sex, and work. However, people who have an extraverted, optimistic _____ do tend to be happier.

71. People who are making progress toward their long-term _____ tend to be happier. This is especially true if the _____ have integrity and personal meaning.

Connections

1. _____ physiological needs
2. _____ safety and security
3. _____ self-actualization
4. _____ lateral hypothalamus
5. _____ basic needs
6. _____ esteem and self-esteem
7. _____ paraventricular nucleus
8. _____ growth needs
9. _____ love and belonging
10. _____ ventromedial hypothalamus

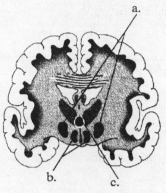

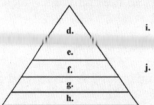

11. _____ need	a.	steady state
12. _____ incentive value	b.	lateral hypothalamus
13. _____ secondary motives	c.	internal deficiency
14. _____ homeostasis	d.	learned goals
15. _____ satiety system	e.	estrogen levels
16. _____ feeding system	f.	yo-yo dieting
17. _____ hunger and satiety	g.	about a day
18. _____ weight cycling	h.	paraventricular nucleus
19. _____ estrus	i.	ventromedial hypothalamus
20. _____ circadian	j.	goal desirability

21.	_____ changes eating habits	a.	standards of excellence
22.	_____ need for achievement	b.	prolonged mild emotion
23.	_____ facial expressions	c.	assigning causes to events
24.	_____ mood	d.	behavioural dieting
25.	_____ sympathetic branch	e.	emotional competence
26.	_____ attribution	f.	emotion
27.	_____ body language	g.	appraisal of threat
28.	_____ sadness	h.	facial feedback hypothesis
29.	_____ anxiety	i.	kinesics
30.	_____ emotional intelligence	j.	fight or flight

Check Your Memory

Check Your Memory: Pages 325—328

1. The terms need and drive are used interchangeably to describe motivation.
   True or False

2. Overeating is an adaptive response that evolved to compensate for the times when food is scarce.
   True or False

3. Incentive value refers to the "pull" of valued goals.
   True or False

4. Primary motives are based on needs that must be met for survival.
   True or False

5. Much of the time, homeostasis is maintained by automatic reactions within the body.
   True or False

Check Your Memory: Pages 328—334

6. Cutting the sensory nerves from the stomach abolishes hunger
   True or False

7. Lowered levels of glucose in the blood can cause hunger.
   True or False

8. The body's hunger centre is found in the thalamus.
   True or False

9. The paraventricular nucleus is sensitive to neuropeptide Y.
   True or False

10. Both glucagon-like peptide 1 (GLP-1) and leptin act as stop signals that inhibit eating.
    True or False

11. Dieting speeds up the body's metabolic rate.
    True or False

12. Overweight means that at least 30% of one's weight is made up of fat.
    True or False

13. Obesity is increasing in North America.
    True or False

14. People who diet intensely every other day lose as much weight as those who diet moderately every day.
    True or False

15. Exercise makes people hungry and tends to disrupt dieting and weight loss.
    True or False

16. Behavioural dieting changes habits without reducing the number of calories consumed.
    True or False

17. Charting daily progress is a basic behavioural dieting technique.
    True or False

18. Taste aversions may be learned after longer time delays than in other forms of classical conditioning.
    True or False

19. Many victims of anorexia nervosa overestimate their body size.
    True or False

Check Your Memory: Pages 334—336

20. Bleeding, vomiting, or sweating can cause extracellular thirst.
    True or False

21. Intracellular thirst is best satisfied by a slightly salty liquid.
    Truc or False

22. Tolerance for pain is largely unaffected by learning.
    True or False

23. Castration of a male animal typically abolishes the sex drive.
    True or False

24. Getting drunk *decreases* sexual desire, arousal, pleasure, and performance.
    True or False

Check Your Memory: Pages 336—339

25. Male and female patterns of sexual behaviour have continued to become less alike in recent years.
    True or Falsc

26. Your sexual orientation is revealed, in part, by who you have erotic fantasies about.
    True or False

27. Gay males are converted to homosexuality during adolescence by other homosexuals.
    True or False

28. Sexual orientation is a very stable personal characteristic.
    True or False

29. Sexual orientation is influenced by heredity.
    True or False

30. Masters and Johnson's data on human sexuality was restricted to questionnaires and interviews.
    True or False

31. During the excitement phase of sexual response, the nipples become erect in both males and females.
    True or False

32. In males, orgasm is always accompanied by ejaculation.
    True or False

33. Almost all women experience a short refractory period after ejaculation.
    True or False

197

34. Both orgasm and resolution tend to last longer in females than they do in males.
    True or False

35. Women tend to go through the phases of sexual response more slowly than men do.
    True or False

36. Sexual scripts determine when, where, and with whom we are likely to express sexual feelings.
    True or False

Check Your Memory: Pages 340–343

37. It is uncomfortable to experience both very high and very low levels of arousal.
    True or False

38. Disinhibition and boredom susceptibility are characteristics of sensation-seeking persons.
    True or False

39. For nearly all activities, the best performance occurs at high levels of arousal.
    True or False

40. Test anxiety is a combination of arousal and excessive worry.
    True or False

41. Being overprepared is a common cause of test anxiety.
    True or False

42. Changes in body temperature are closely related to circadian rhythms.
    True or False

43. Subjective mood appears to follow the highs and lows of body temperature.
    True or False

44. Adapting to rapid time zone changes is easiest when a person travels east, rather than west.
    True or False

Check Your Memory: Pages 343–345

45. The need for achievement refers to a desire to have impact on other people.
    True or False

46. People high in nAch generally prefer "long shots" or "sure things."
    True or False

47. Subliminal motivational tapes are no more effective than placebo tapes that lack any "hidden messages."
    True or False

48. Benjamin Bloom found that high achievement is based as much on hard work as it is on talent.
    True or False

49. For many activities, self-confidence is one of the most important sources of motivation.
    True or False

Check Your Memory: Pages 345–348

50. Maslow's hierarchy of needs places self-esteem at the top of the pyramid.
    True or False

51. Maslow believed that needs for safety and security are more potent than needs for love and belonging.
    True or False

52. Meta-needs are the most basic needs in Maslow's hierarchy.
    True or False

53. Intrinsic motivation occurs when obvious external rewards are provided for engaging in an activity.
    True or False

54. People are more likely to be creative when they are intrinsically motivated.
    True or False

Check Your Memory: Pages 348—352

55. Most physiological changes during emotion are related to the release of adrenaline into the brain.
    True or False

56. Robert Plutchik's theory lists contempt as a primary emotion.
    True or False

57. For most students, elevated moods tend to occur on Saturdays and Tuesdays.
    True or False

58. Positive emotions are processed mainly in the left hemisphere of the brain.
    True or False

59. The sympathetic branch of the ANS is under voluntary control and the parasympathetic branch is involuntary.
    True or False

60. The parasympathetic branch of the ANS slows the heart and lowers blood pressure.
    True or False

61. A parasympathetic rebound could cause death if very severe.
    True or False

62. The polygraph measures the body's unique physical responses to lying.
    True or False

63. Only a guilty person should react emotionally to irrelevant questions.
    True or False

64. Control questions used in polygraph exams are designed to make almost everyone anxious.
    True or False

65. The lie detector's most common error is to label innocent persons guilty.
    True or False

Check Your Memory: Pages 352—355

66. Children born deaf and blind express emotions with their faces in about the same way as other people do.
    True or False

67. The "A-okay" hand gesture means "everything is fine" around the world.
    True or False

68. Facial blends mix two or more basic expressions.
    True or False

69. Humans have evolved to identify a smiling face (non-threatening) more quickly than an angry face (threatening).
    True or False

70. Gestures such as rubbing hands, twisting hair, and biting lips are consistently related to lying.
    True or False

71. People from Asian cultures are more likely to express anger in public than people from Western cultures.
    True or False

72. In Western cultures, men tend to be more emotionally expressive than women.
    True or False

Check Your Memory: Pages 355—360

73. The James-Lange theory of emotion says that we see a bear, feel fear, are aroused, and then run.
    True or False

74. According to Schachter's cognitive theory, arousal must be labeled in order to become an emotion.
    True or False

75. Making facial expressions can actually cause emotions to occur and alter physiological activities in the body.
    True or False

76. Emotional appraisal refers to deciding if your own facial expressions are appropriate for the situation you are in.
    True or False

77. Emotional intelligence refers to the ability to use primarily the right cerebral hemisphere to process emotional events.
    True or False

Check Your Memory: Psychology in Action

78. Subjective well being is primarily a matter of having relatively few negative emotions.
    True or False

79. A person who agrees that "The conditions of my life are excellent," would probably score high in life satisfaction.
    True or False

80. Wealthier people are generally happier people.
    True or False

81. You are likely to be happy if you are making progress on smaller goals that relate to long-term, life goals.
    True or False

82. Usually, a good life is one that is happy and meaningful.
    True or False

Final Survey and Review

- *What is motivation? Are there different types of motives?*

1. Motives initiate (begin), _____ (perpetuate), and _____ activities.
2. Motivation typically involves the sequence need, _____ , response, and goal _____ (need reduction).
3. Behaviour can be activated either by _____ (push) or by _____ (pull).
4. The attractiveness of a goal and its ability to initiate action are related to its _____ .
5. Three principal types of motives are _____ motives, _____ motives, and _____ motives.
6. Most primary motives operate to maintain a steady state of bodily equilibrium called _____ .

- *What causes hunger? Overeating? Eating disorders?*

7. Hunger is influenced by a complex interplay between _____ (fullness) of the stomach, _____ (low blood sugar), metabolism in the liver, and fat stores in the body.

8. The most direct control of eating is exerted by the _____ , which has areas that act like feeding (start) and _____ (stop) systems for hunger and eating.

9. The _____ hypothalamus acts as a feeding system; the _____ hypothalamus is part of a satiety system; the paraventricular _____ influences both hunger and satiety.

10. Other factors influencing hunger are the _____ _____ for the proportion of fat in the body, external eating _____ , the attractiveness and variety of diet.

11. Hunger is also influenced by emotions, learned taste preferences, taste _____ and _____ values.

12. A person is considered _____ if 25% or more of their body weight is made up of fat and _____ if this proportion is at least 30%.

13. _____ nervosa (self-inflicted starvation) and _____ nervosa (gorging and purging) are two prominent eating disorders.

14. _____ anorexia is seen in some well-muscled bodybuilders who have the belief that their bodies are too small.

15. These eating disorders tend to involve conflicts about _____ , self-control, and anxiety.

• *Is there more than one type of thirst? In what ways are pain avoidance and the sex drive unusual?*

16. Like hunger, thirst and other basic motives are affected by a number of bodily factors, but are primarily under the central control of the _____ in the brain.

17. Thirst may be either _____ (when fluid is lost from inside cells) or _____ (when fluid is lost from the spaces between cells).

18. Pain avoidance is unusual because it is _____ (associated with particular conditions) as opposed to _____ (occurring in regular cycles).

19. Pain is best described as a system (_____) that responds to both pain _____ and psychological components (i.e. _____ , what wound looks like, etc.).

20. Pain _____ and pain _____ are partially learned.

21. The sex drive in many lower animals is related to _____ (or "heat") in females. The sex drive is unusual in that it is non- _____ (relatively independent of body needs).

22. Sex drive in both males and females may be related to bodily levels of _____ .

• *What are the typical patterns of human sexual response?*

23. Sexual arousal is related to stimulation of the body's _____ zones (areas that produce erotic pleasure), but _____ elements such as thoughts and images are equally important.

24. There is little _____ in sexual behaviour between males and females.

25. Evidence suggests that the sex drive peaks at a later age for _____ than it does for _____ , although this difference is diminishing.

26. Sexual _____ refers to one's degree of emotional and erotic attraction to members of the same sex, opposite sex, or both sexes.

27. A person may be _____ , homosexual, or _____ .

28. A combination of _____ , biological, _____ , and psychological influences combine to produce one's sexual orientation.

29. As a group, _____ men and women do not differ psychologically from _____ .

201

30. In a series of landmark studies, William Masters and Virginia _____ directly observed sexual response in a large number of adults.

31. Human sexual response can be divided into four phases: (1) excitement; (2) _____ ; (3) orgasm; and (4) _____ .

32. Both males and females may go through all four stages in 4 minutes. But during lovemaking, most _____ typically take longer than this.

33. Males experience a _____ period after orgasm and ejaculation. Only 5 percent of men are multi- _____ .

• *How does arousal relate to motivation?*

34. The _____ drives reflect needs for information, _____ , manipulation, and sensory input.

35. Drives for stimulation are partially explained by _____ _____ , which states that an ideal level of bodily arousal will be maintained if possible.

36. The desired level of arousal or stimulation varies from person to person, as measured by the _____ Scale.

37. Optimal performance on a task usually occurs at moderate levels of arousal. This relationship is described by an _____ _____ function.

38. The _____ law further states that for simple tasks the ideal arousal level is higher, and for complex tasks it is lower.

39. _____ rhythms within the body are closely tied to sleep, activity levels, and energy cycles. Travel across _____ _____ and shift work can seriously disrupt sleep and bodily rhythms.

40. If you anticipate a change in body rhythms, you can gradually _____ to your new schedule over a period of days.

• *What are social motives? Why are they important?*

41. Social motives are learned through _____ and cultural conditioning.

42. One of the most prominent social motives is the need for _____ (nAch).

43. _____ nAch is correlated with success in many situations, with occupational choice, and with _____ risk taking.

44. _____ affects motivation because it influences the challenges you will undertake, the effort you will make, and how long you will persist when things don't go well.

• *Are some motives more basic than others?*

45. Maslow's _____ (rank ordering) of motives categorizes needs as basic and _____ oriented.

46. Lower needs in the hierarchy are assumed to be _____ (dominant) over higher needs.

47. Self- _____ , the highest and most fragile need, is reflected in _____ -needs.

48. In many situations, _____ motivation (that which is induced by obvious external rewards) can reduce _____ motivation, enjoyment, and creativity.

• *What happens during emotion? Can "lie detectors" really detect lies?*

49. Emotions are linked to many basic _____ behaviours, such a attacking, retreating, feeding, and reproducing.

50. Other major elements of emotion are physiological changes in the body, emotional _____ , and emotional feelings.

51. The following are considered to be _____ emotions: fear, surprise, sadness, disgust, anger, anticipation, joy, and acceptance.

52. Physical changes associated with emotion are caused by the action of _____ , a hormone released into the bloodstream, and by activity in the _____ nervous system (ANS).

53. The _____ branch of the ANS is primarily responsible for arousing the body, the _____ branch for quieting it.

54. Sudden death due to prolonged and intense emotion is probably related to _____ rebound (excess activity). Heart attacks caused by sudden intense emotion are more likely due to _____ arousal.

55. The _____ , or "lie detector," measures emotional arousal by monitoring heart rate, blood pressure, breathing rate, and the _____ skin response (GSR).

56. Asking a series of _____ and _____ questions may allow the detection of lies, but overall, the accuracy of the lie detector has been challenged by many researchers.

• *How accurately are emotions expressed by "body language" and the face?*

57. Basic emotional _____ , such as smiling or baring one's teeth when angry, appear to be unlearned.

58. _____ expressions of fear, anger, disgust, sadness, and happiness are recognized by people of all cultures.

59. Body _____ and movements (body language) also express feelings, mainly by communicating emotional tone.

60. Three dimensions of facial expressions are pleasantness-unpleasantness, attention-rejection, and _____ .

61. The study of body language is known as _____ .

• *How do psychologists explain emotions?*

62. The _____ -Lange theory of emotion says that emotional experience follows an awareness of the bodily reactions of emotion.

63. In contrast, the _____ -Bard theory says that bodily reactions and emotional experience occur at the same time and that emotions are organized in the brain.

64. Schachter's _____ theory of emotion emphasizes the importance of labels, or interpretations, applied to feelings of bodily _____ .

65. Also important is the process of _____ , in which bodily arousal is attributed to a particular person, object, or situation.

66. The _____ _____ hypothesis holds that sensations and information from emotional expressions help define what emotion a person is feeling.

67. Contemporary views of emotion place greater emphasis on how situations are _____ (evaluated). Also, all of the elements of emotion are seen as interrelated and interacting.

68. _____ intelligence can be seen as the equivalent of Howard Gardner's personal intelligence. It involves skills such as _____ , self-control, self-awareness, sensitivity to the feelings of others, persistence and _____ .

- ## *What factors contribute most to a happy and fulfilling life?*

69. _____ _____ _____ (happiness) occurs when positive emotions outnumber negative emotions and a person is satisfied with his or her life.

70. Happiness is only mildly related to wealth, education, marriage, religion, age, sex, and work. However, people with _____ , optimistic personalities do tend to be happier.

71. People who are making progress toward their long-term goals tend to be happier. This is especially true if the goals have _____ and personal _____ .

Mastery Test

1. Which of the following is NOT one of the signs of emotional arousal recorded by a polygraph?
    a. heart rate
    b. blood pressure
    c. pupil dilation
    d. breathing rate

2. Plain water is most satisfying when a person has _____ thirst.
    a. intracellular
    b. hypothalamic
    c. extracellular
    d. homeostatic

3. When expectations of a friendly first date clash with an attempted seduction the problem can be attributed to differences in
    a. gender roles
    b. erogenous confrontation
    c. gender myths
    d. sexual scripts

4. Strong external rewards tend to undermine
    a. extrinsic motivation
    b. intrinsic motivation
    c. prepotent motivation
    d. stimulus motivation

5. Activity in the ANS is directly responsible for which element of emotion?
    a. emotional feelings
    b. emotional expressions
    c. physiological changes
    d. misattributions

6. The first two phases of the sexual response cycle are
    a. excitement, arousal
    b. arousal, orgasm
    c. excitement, plateau
    d. stimulation, arousal

7. Motivation refers to the ways in which activities are initiated, sustained, and
   a. acquired
   b. valued
   c. directed
   d. aroused

8. The psychological state or feeling we call thirst corresponds to which element of motivation?
   a. need
   b. drive
   c. deprivation
   d. incentive value

9. People who score high on the SSS generally prefer
   a. low levels of arousal
   b. moderate levels of arousal
   c. high levels of arousal
   d. the middle of the V function

10. Which facial expression is NOT recognized by people of all cultures?
    a. anger
    b. disgust
    c. optimism
    d. fear

11. Learning to weaken eating cues is useful in
    a. self-selection feeding
    b. yo-yo dieting
    c. rapid weight cycling
    d. behavioural dieting

12. Jet lag occurs when a traveler's _____ are out of synchrony with local time.
    a. biorhythms
    b. circadian rhythms
    c. sensation-seeking patterns
    d. opponent processes

13. Which theory holds that emotional feelings, arousal, and behaviour are generated simultaneously in the brain?
    a. James-Lange
    b. Cannon-Bard
    c. cognitive
    d. attribution

14. Compared with people in North America, people in Asian cultures are less likely to express which emotion?
    a. anger
    b. jealousy
    c. curiosity

    d.   fear

15. Binge eating is most associated with

    a.   bulimia nervosa

    b.   bait shyness

    c.   low levels of NPY

    d.   anorexia nervosa

16. Goals that are desirable are high in

    a.   need reduction

    b.   incentive value

    c.   homeostatic valence

    d.   motivational "push"

17. _____ is to pain avoidance as _____ is to the sex drive.

    a.   Non-homeostatic, episodic

    b.   Episodic, non-homeostatic

    c.   Non-homeostatic, cyclic

    d.   Cyclic, non-homeostatic

18. A specialist in kinesics could be expected to be most interested in

    a.   facial blends

    b.   circadian rhythms

    c.   sensation seeking

    d.   primary motives

19. Coping statements are a way to directly correct which part of test anxiety?

    a.   overpreparation

    b.   under-arousal

    c.   excessive worry

    d.   compulsive rehearsal

20. Drives for exploration and activity are categorized as

    a.   primary motives

    b.   secondary motives

    c.   stimulus motives

    d.   extrinsic motives

21. Sudden death following a period of intense fear may occur when _____ slows the heart to a stop.

    a.   a sympathetic overload

    b.   adrenaline poisoning

    c.   opponent-process feedback

    d.   a parasympathetic rebound

22. Research on well being suggests that a good life is one that combines happiness and

    a.   financial success

    b.   educational achievement

    c.   an introverted personality

    d.   achieving meaningful goals

23.   You could induce eating in a laboratory rat by activating the

    a.   lateral hypothalamus

    b.   corpus callosum

    c.   rat's set point

    d.   ventromedial hypothalamus

24.   People think cartoons are funnier if they see them while holding a pen crosswise in their teeth. This observation supports

    a.   the James-Lange theory

    b.   the Cannon-Bard theory

    c.   Schachter's cognitive theory

    d.   the facial feedback hypothesis

25.   Basic biological motives are closely related to

    a.   nAch

    b.   homeostasis

    c.   activity in the thalamus

    d.   levels of melatonin in the body

26.   Self-actualization is to _____ needs as safety and security are to _____ needs.

    a.   growth, basic

    b.   basic, meta-

    c.   prepotent, basic

    d.   meta-, extrinsic

27.   Which of the following is NOT a core element of emotion?

    a.   physiological changes

    b.   emotional expressions

    c.   emotional feelings

    d.   misattributions

28.   The effects of a "supermarket diet" on eating are related to the effects of _____ on eating.

    a.   anxiety

    b.   incentive value

    c.   metabolic rates

    d.   stomach distention

29.   According to the Yerkes-Dodson law, optimum performance occurs at _____ levels of arousal for simple tasks and _____ levels of arousal for complex tasks.

    a.   higher, lower

    b.   lower, higher

    c.   minimum, high

    d.   average, high

30. Contemporary models of emotion place greater emphasis on _____, or the way situations are evaluated.

    a.   appraisal

    b.   attribution

    c.   feedback

    d.   emotional tone

31. Which Canadian ethnic group is more at risk of developing type 2 diabetes due to obesity?

    a.   Italian

    b.   French

    c.   Jewish

    d.   Native

32. According to the Canadian researcher, Ronald Melzack, our pain system is best described as a combination of

    a.   only pain avoidance

    b.   both pain level and psychological components

    c.   psychological components and perception of experience

    d.   pain tolerance and pain avoidance

33. Emotional intelligence can be seen as the equivalent of which of Howard Gardner's types of intelligence?

    a.   Bodily-kinesthetic skills

    b.   Naturalist skills

    c.   Intrapersonal and interpersonal skills

    d.   Self-awareness skills

Solutions

Recite and Review

1. initiate, activities
2. need, goal
3. push, pull
4. goal, need
5. secondary
6. primary, steady
7. stomach, blood, liver
8. start, stop
9. feeding, satiety
10. fat, diet
11. taste, taste
12. fat, 30
13. starvation, gorging
14. bodybuilders, small
15. anxiety
16. bodily, brain
17. fluid, cells, fluid, cells
18. cycles
19. system, psychological
20. learned
21. females, independent
22. drive
23. pleasure, thoughts
24. responsiveness
25. later
26. sex, sex, sexes
27. homosexual
28. sexual, orientation
29. heterosexuals
30. Masters
31. excitement, orgasm
32. 4
33. orgasm, multi
34. sensory
35. physical, arousal
36. arousal
37. moderate
38. simple, complex
39. rhythms, sleep
40. change, schedule
41. Social
42. need
43. success, risk
44. motivation, effort, persist
45. basic
46. Lower, higher
47. Self, needs
48. external
49. behaviours
50. feelings
51. sadness, anger
52. hormone, nervous, system
53. branch, branch
54. rebound, arousal
55. emotional, arousal
56. relevant, lying
57. unlearned
58. fear, sadness
59. feelings, tone
60. facial
61. body, language
62. follows
63. at, the, same, time
64. labels
65. arousal
66. expressions
67. situations
68. personal, self-awareness, persistence
69. happiness, positive, negative
70. wealth, personality
71. goals, goals

Connections

1. H
2. G
3. D
4. A
5. J
6. E
7. C
8. I
9. F
10. B
11. C
12. J
13. D
14. A
15. I
16. B
17. H
18. F
19. E
20. G
21. D
22. A
23. H
24. B
25. J
26. C

27. I

28. F

29. G

30. E

Check Your Memory

1. F

2. T

3. T

4. T

5. T

6. F

7. T

8. F

9. T

10. T

11. F

12. F

13. T

14. T

15. F

16. F

17. T

18. T

19. T

20. T

21. F

22. F

23. T

24. T

25. F

26. T

27. F

28. T

29. T

30. F

31. T

32. F

33. F

34. T

35. T

36. T

37. T

38. T

39. F

40. T

41. F

42. T

43. T

44. F

45. F

46. F

47. T

48. T

49. T

50. F

51. T

52. F

53. F

54. T

55. F

56. F

57. F

58. T

59. F

60. T

61. T

62. F

63. F

64. T

65. T

66. T

67. F

68. T

69. F

70. F

71. F

72. F

73. F

74. T

75. T

76. F

77. F

78. F

79. T

80. F

81. T

82. T

Final Survey and Review

1. sustain, direct

2. drive, attainment

3. needs, goals

4. incentive

5. primary, stimulus, secondary

6. homeostasis

7. distention, hypoglycemia

8. hypothalamus, satiety

9. lateral, ventromedial, nucleus

10. set, point, cues

11. aversions, cultural

12. overweight, obese

13. Anorexia, bulimia

14. Reverse

15. self-image

16. hypothalamus

17. intracellular, extracellular
18. episodic, cyclic
19. neuromatrix, intensity, memory
20. avoidance, tolerance
21. estrus, homeostatic
22. androgens
23. erogenous, cognitive
24. difference
25. females, males
26. orientation
27. heterosexual, bisexual
28. heredity, social
29. homosexual, heterosexuals
30. Johnson
31. plateau, resolution
32. females
33. refractory, orgasmic
34. stimulus, exploration
35. arousal, theory
36. Sensation-seeking
37. inverted, U
38. Yerkes-Dodson
39. Circadian, time, zones
40. preadapt
41. socialization
42. achievement
43. High, moderate
44. Self-confidence
45. hierarchy, growth
46. prepotent
47. actualization, meta
48. extrinsic, intrinsic
49. adaptive

50. expressions
51. primary
52. adrenaline, autonomic
53. sympathetic, parasympathetic
54. parasympathetic, sympathetic
55. polygraph, galvanic
56. relevant, irrelevant
57. expressions
58. Facial
59. gestures
60. activation
61. kinesics
62. James
63. Cannon
64. cognitive, arousal
65. attribution
66. facial, feedback
67. appraised
68. Emotional, empathy, self-motivation
69. Subjective, well, being
70. extraverted
71. integrity, meaning

Mastery Test

1. C (p. 351)
2. A (p. 334)
3. D (p. 339)
4. B (p. 341)
5. C (p. 350)
6. C (p. 337)
7. C (p. 325)
8. B (p. 325)
9. C (p. 340)
10. C (p. 353)
11. D (p. 332)
12. B (p. 343)
13. B (p. 355)
14. A (p. 354)
15. A (p. 333)
16. B (p. 326)
17. B (p. 335)
18. A (p. 354)
19. C (p. 342)
20. C (p. 340)
21. D (p. 350)
22. D (p. 362)
23. A (p. 329)
24. D (p. 357)
25. B (p. 357)
26. A (p. 346)
27. D (p. 348)
28. B (p. 326)
29. A (p. 341)
30. A (p. 358)
31. D (p. 330)
32. B (p. 335)
33. C (p. 359)

Chapter 10

Personality

Chapter Overview

Personality refers to unique and enduring behaviour patterns. Character is personality evaluated. Temperament refers to the hereditary and physiological aspects of one's emotional nature. Personality traits are lasting personal qualities. Personality types are categories defined by groups of shared traits. Behaviour is also influenced by self-concept. Personality theories combine various ideas and principles to explain personality.

Allport's trait theory classifies traits as common, individual, cardinal, central, or secondary. Cattell's trait theory attributes visible surface traits to the existence of 16 underlying source traits. The five-factor model reduces traits to 5 dimensions. Traits appear to interact with situations to determine behaviour. Behavioural genetics suggests that heredity influences personality traits.

Like other psychodynamic approaches, Sigmund Freud's psychoanalytic theory emphasizes unconscious forces and conflicts within the personality. Behavioural theories of personality emphasize learning, conditioning, and the immediate effects of the environment. Social learning theory adds cognitive elements, such as perception, thinking, and understanding to the behavioural view. Many differences between males and females are based on social learning. Psychological androgyny is related to greater behavioural adaptability and flexibility. Humanistic theory emphasizes subjective experiences and needs for self-actualization.

Techniques typically used for personality assessment are interviews, direct observation, questionnaires, and projective tests.

Shyness is a mixture of social inhibition and social anxiety. It is marked by heightened public self-consciousness and a tendency to regard one's shyness as a lasting trait. Shyness can be lessened by changing self-defeating beliefs and by improving social skills.

Learning Objectives

1. Define the term *personality* and explain how personality differs from character and temperament. Discuss the stability of personality.

2. Define the term *trait*. Describe the trait approach and the type approach to personality. Explain the main shortcoming of the type approach.

3. Explain the concepts *self-concept* and *self-esteem* and how they affect behaviour and personal adjustment.

4. Briefly discuss differences in the basis of self-esteem in Eastern and Western cultures.

5. Define the term *personality theory*. List and describe the four broad perspectives of personality included in this chapter.

6. Characterize the general approach to the study of personality taken by trait theorists.

7. Distinguish common traits from individual traits.

8. Define and give examples of Allport's cardinal traits, central traits, and secondary traits.

9. Distinguish between surface traits and source traits, and state how Cattell measured source traits.

10. Explain how Cattell's approach to personality traits differed from Allport's approach.

11. Discuss the five-factor model of personality.

12. Explain what a trait-situation interaction is.

13. Explain how twin studies are used to assess the relative contributions of heredity and environment to personality. Discuss how the similarities in the personalities of twins can be explained.

14. Assess the relative contributions of heredity and environment to the makeup of personality.

15. List and describe the three parts of the personality according to Freud.

16. Describe the dynamic conflict between the three parts of personality, and relate neurotic and moral anxiety to the conflict.

17. Describe the relationships among the three parts of personality and the three levels of awareness.

18. List and describe Freud's four psychosexual stages. In your answer include an explanation of fixation and the age range for each stage.

19. Discuss the positive and the negative aspects of Freud's developmental theory.

20. Explain how behaviourists view personality and traits. Include a definition of the term *situational determinants*.

21. Explain how learning theorists view the structure of personality. Include in your discussion the terms *habit, drive, cue, response,* and *reward.*

22. Explain how learning theory and social learning theory differ. Include in your discussion a description of the terms *psychological situation, expectancy, reinforcement value,* and *self-reinforcement.* Explain how self-reinforcement is related to self-esteem and depression.

23. Using the behaviouristic view of development, explain why feeding, toilet training, sex training, and learning to express anger or aggression may be particularly important to personality formation.

24. Describe the role of social reinforcement, imitation, and identification in personality development.

25. Discuss the concept of androgyny and its relationship to masculinity, femininity, and adaptability.

26. Briefly explain how the humanists set themselves apart from the Freudian and behaviourist views of personality.

27. Describe the development of Maslow's interest in self-actualization.

28. Use at least five of the characteristics of self-actualizers listed in your text to describe a self-actualizing person. Use the complete list to evaluate yourself and explain what may be helping or hindering your self-actualization.

29. List and briefly explain or describe (where applicable) eight steps to promote self-actualization.

30. Differentiate Freud's and Rogers's views of the normal or fully functioning individual.

31. Describe Rogers's view of an incongruent person.

32. Explain how "possible selves" help translate our hopes, dreams, and fears and ultimately direct our future behaviour.

33. Explain how "conditions of worth," "positive self-regard," and "organismic valuing" may affect personality formation.

34. Discuss the following assessment techniques in terms of purpose, method, advantages, and limitations:
    a. unstructured and structured interviews
    b. direct observation (Include rating scales, behavioural assessment, and situational testing.)
    c. personality questionnaires (Include validity, reliability, and a description of the MMPI-2.)
    d. honesty tests
    e. projective tests (Include descriptions of the Rorschach and TAT.)

35. Describe the personality characteristics of sudden murderers, and explain how their characteristics are related to the nature of their homicidal actions.

36. List and describe the three elements of shyness. State what usually causes shyness.

37. Compare the personality characteristics of the shy and the non-shy. Include the concepts "labelling" and "self-esteem".

38. List and discuss the three major areas that can help reduce shyness.

Practice Quizzes

Recite and Review

• *How do psychologists use the term personality? What core concepts make up the psychology of personality?*

Recite and Review: Pages 369–372

1. Personality is made up of one's unique and relatively stable _____ patterns.

2. Character is personality that has been judged or _____ . That is, it is the possession of desirable qualities.

3. Temperament refers to the _____ and physiological aspects of one's emotional nature.

4. Personality traits are lasting personal qualities that are inferred from _____ .

5. A personality type is a style of personality defined by having a group of related _____ or similar characteristics.

6. Two widely recognized personality _____ are an introvert (shy, self-centred person) and an extrovert (bold, outgoing person).

7. Behaviour is influenced by self-concept, which is a person's perception of his or her own _____ traits.

8. _____ theories combine interrelated assumptions, ideas, and principles to explain personality.

9. Four major types of personality theories are: _____ , psychodynamic, behaviouristic, and humanistic.

- ## *Are some personality traits more basic or important than others?*

Recite and Review: Pages 372—378

10. Trait _____ attempt to specify qualities of personality that are most lasting or characteristic of a person.

11. Gordon Allport made useful distinctions between common traits (which are shared by most members of a culture) and _____ traits (characteristics of a single person).

12. Allport also identified cardinal traits (a trait that influences nearly all of a person's activities), central traits (core traits of personality), and _____ traits (superficial traits).

13. The theory of Raymond Cattell attributes visible _____ traits to the existence of 16 underlying source traits (which he identified using factor _____).

14. Source traits are measured by the Sixteen _____ _____ Questionnaire (16 PF).

15. The outcome of the 16 PF and other personality tests may be graphically presented as a _____ profile.

16. The five-factor model of personality reduces traits to 5 _____ dimensions of personality.

17. The five factors are: extroversion, _____ , conscientiousness, neuroticism, and openness to _____ .

18. _____ interact with situations to determine behaviour.

19. Heredity is responsible for 25 to 50 percent of the variation in personality _____ .

20. Studies of separated _____ twins suggest that heredity contributes significantly to adult personality traits. Overall, however, personality is shaped as much, or more by differences in environment.

- ## *How do psychodynamic theories explain personality?*

Recite and Review: Pages 378—382

21. Psychodynamic theories focus on the inner workings of personality, especially hidden or _____ forces and internal conflicts.

22. According to Sigmund Freud's psychoanalytic theory, personality is made up of the id, _____ , and superego.

23. The id operates on the pleasure _____ . The ego is guided by the reality _____ .

24. The _____ is made up of the conscience and the ego ideal.

25. Libido, derived from the _____ instincts, is the primary _____ running the personality.

26. Conflicts within the personality may cause neurotic _____ or moral _____ and motivate use of ego-defense mechanisms.

27. The personality operates on three levels, the _____ , preconscious, and unconscious.

28. The id is completely _____ ; the ego and superego can operate at all three levels of awareness.

29. The Freudian view of personality development is based on a series of psychosexual _____ : the _____ , anal, phallic, and genital.

30. Fixations (unresolved emotional conflicts) at any stage can leave a lasting imprint on _____ .

31. Freud's theory pioneered the idea that feeding, toilet training, and early sexual experiences leave an imprint on _____ .

215

Personality

- ## *What do behaviourists emphasize in their approach to personality?*

Recite and Review: Pages 382—388

32. Behavioural theories of personality emphasize _____ , conditioning, and immediate effects of the environment.

33. Learning theorists generally stress the effects of prior learning and _____ determinants of behaviour.

34. Learning theorists John Dollard and Neal Miller consider _____ the basic core of personality. _____ express the combined effects of drive, cue, response, and _____ .

35. _____ learning theory adds cognitive elements, such as perception, thinking, and understanding to the behavioural view of personality.

36. Examples of social learning concepts are the _____ situation (the situation as it is perceived), expectancies (expectations about what effects a response will have), and reinforcement _____ (the subjective value of a reinforcer or activity).

37. Some social learning theorists treat "conscience" as a case of _____ -reinforcement.

38. The behaviouristic view of personality development holds that social reinforcement in four situations is critical. The critical situations are _____ , toilet or cleanliness training, sex training, and _____ or aggression training.

39. Identification (feeling emotionally connected to a person) and _____ (mimicking another person's behaviour) are of particular importance in sex (or gender) training.

40. Research conducted by Sandra Bem indicates that roughly one third of all persons are androgynous (they possess both _____ and _____ traits).

41. Androgyny is measured with the Bem _____ _____ Inventory (BSRI).

42. Being _____ means that a person is independent and assertive.

43. Being _____ means that a person is nurturant and interpersonally oriented.

44. Psychological _____ appears related to greater adaptability or flexibility in behaviour.

- ## *How do humanistic theories differ from other perspectives?*

Recite and Review: Pages 389—392

45. Humanistic theory views human nature as _____ , and emphasizes subjective experience, _____ choice, and needs for self-actualization.

46. Abraham Maslow's study of self-actualizers identified characteristics they share, ranging from efficient perceptions of reality to frequent _____ _____ (temporary moments of self-actualization).

47. Carl Rogers's theory views the _____ as an entity that emerges when experiences that match the self- _____ are symbolized (admitted to consciousness), while those that are incongruent are excluded.

48. The incongruent person has a highly unrealistic _____ and/or a mismatch between the _____ and the ideal self.

49. The congruent or _____ functioning person is flexible and open to experiences and feelings.

50. In the development of personality, humanists are primarily interested in the emergence of a _____ and in self-evaluations.

51. As parents apply conditions of _____ (standards used to judge thoughts, feelings, and actions) to a child, the child begins to do the same.

52. Internalized conditions of worth contribute to incongruence, they damage _____ self-regard, and they disrupt the organismic _____ process.

• *How do psychologists measure personality?*

Recite and Review: Pages 393—401

53. Techniques typically used for personality assessment are _____ , observation, questionnaires, and projective _____ .

54. Structured and unstructured _____ provide much information, but they are subject to _____ bias and misperceptions. The halo effect may also _____ accuracy.

55. Direct observation, sometimes involving situational tests, behavioural assessment, or the use of _____ scales, allows evaluation of a person's actual _____ .

56. Personality questionnaires, such as the _____ _____ Personality Inventory-2 (MMPI-2), are objective and _____ , but their validity is open to question.

57. Honesty tests, which are essentially personality _____ , are widely used by businesses to make hiring decisions. Their validity is hotly debated.

58. Projective tests ask a subject to project thoughts or feelings onto an ambiguous _____ or unstructured situation.

59. The *Rorschach*, or _____ test, is a well-known projective technique. A second is the _____ Apperception Test (TAT).

60. The validity and objectivity of projective tests are quite _____ . Nevertheless, projective techniques are considered useful by many clinicians, particularly as part of a _____ battery.

• *What causes shyness? What can be done about It?*

Recite and Review: Psychology in Action

61. Shyness is a mixture of _____ inhibition and _____ anxiety.

62. Shy persons tend to lack social skills and they feel social anxiety (because they believe they are being _____ by others).

63. Shy persons also have a self-defeating bias in their _____ (they tend to blame _____ for social failures).

64. Shyness is marked by heightened _____ self-consciousness (awareness of oneself as a _____ object) and a tendency to regard shyness as a lasting trait.

65. Shyness can be lessened by changing self-defeating _____ and by improving _____ skills.

Connections

1.	_____ character	a.	heart-attack risk
2.	_____ trait	b.	system of concepts
3.	_____ Type A	c.	personality judged
4.	_____ cardinal trait	d.	traits of Big Five
5.	_____ choleric	e.	source traits
6.	_____ phlegmatic	f.	culturally typical
7.	_____ facet traits	g.	sluggish
8.	_____ 16 PF	h.	universal dimensions
9.	_____ common traits	i.	relates to all of a person's activities
10.	_____ Big Five	j.	lasting personal quality

11.	_____ trait-situation	a.	mouth
12.	_____ Thanatos	b.	pride
13.	_____ Eros	c.	genitals
14.	_____ conscience	d.	female confilict
15.	_____ ego ideal	e.	interaction
16.	_____ oral stage	f.	male conflict
17.	_____ anal stage	g.	death instinct
18.	_____ phallic stage	h.	elimination
19.	_____ Oedipus	i.	life instinct
20.	_____ Electra	j.	guilt

21.	_____ habits	a.	interview problem
22.	_____ androgyny	b.	evaluation fears
23.	_____ Maslow	c.	shoot-don't-shoot
24.	_____ Rogers	d.	personality questionnaire
25.	_____ social learning	e.	same score each time
26.	_____ halo effect	f.	fully functioning person
27.	_____ MMPI	g.	self-actualization
28.	_____ reliability	h.	BSRI
29.	_____ social anxiety	i.	cognitive behaviourism
30.	_____ situational test	j.	learned behaviour patterns

Check Your Memory

Check Your Memory: Pages 369—372

1. The term *personality* refers to charisma or personal style.
   True or False

2. Personality is a person's relatively stable pattern of attitudes.
   True or False

3. Character refers to the inherited "raw material" from which personality is formed.
   True or False

4. In Asian cultures, self-esteem is strongly tied to personal achievement, rather than group success.
   True or False

5. Traits are stable or lasting qualities of personality, displayed in most situations.
   True or False

6. Personality traits typically become quite stable by age 30.
   True or False

7. Paranoid, dependent, and antisocial personalities are regarded as personality types.
   True or False

8. Two major dimensions of Eysenck's personality theory are stable-unstable and calm-moody.
   True or False

9. Japanese people living in Canada have a lower self-esteem than those living in Japan.
   True or False

10. Trait theories of personality stress subjective experience and personal growth.
    True or False

Check Your Memory: Pages 372—378

11. Extroverted students tend to study in noisy areas of the library.
    True or False

12. Nearly all of a person's activities can be traced to one or two common traits.
    True or False

13. Roughly 7 central traits are needed, on the average, to describe an individual's personality.
    True or False

14. Allport used factor analysis to identify central traits.
    True or False

15. The 16 PF is designed to measure surface traits.
    True or False

16. Judging from scores on the 16 PF, airline pilots have traits that are similar to creative artists.
    True or False

17. As one of the Big Five factors, neuroticism refers to having negative, upsetting emotions.
    True or False

18. To predict someone's behaviour it would be better to look at a person's facet traits
    than where they rate on a Big Five dimension.
    True or False

19. The expression of personality traits tends to be influenced by external situations.
    True or False

20. Similarities between reunited identical twins show that personality is mostly shaped by genetics.
    True or False

21. Studies of identical twins show that personality traits are approximately 70 percent hereditary.
    True or False

22. Some of the coincidences shared by identical twins appear to be based on the fallacy of positive instances.
    True or False

Check Your Memory: Pages 378—382

23. The id is totally unconscious.
    True or False

24. The ego is guided by the pleasure principle.
    True or False

25. The superego is the source of feelings of guilt and pride.
    True or False

26. Threats of punishment from the Thanatos cause moral anxiety.
    True or False

27. Oral-dependent persons are gullible.
    True or False

28. Vanity and narcissism are traits of the anal-retentive personality.
    True or False

29. The genital stage occurs between the ages of 3 and 6, just before latency.
    True or False

30. Boys are more likely to develop a strong conscience if their fathers are affectionate and accepting.
    True or False

31. Freud regarded latency as the most important stage of psychosexual development.
    True or False

32. Erik Erikson's psychosocial stages were derived, in part, from Freud's psychosexual stages.
    True or False

Check Your Memory: Pages 382—388

33. Behaviourists view personality as a collection of learned behaviour patterns.
    True or False

34. Behaviourists attribute our actions to prior learning and specific situations.
    True or False

35. According to Dollard and Miller, habits are acquired through observational learning.
    True or False

36. Cues are signals from the environment that guide responses.
    True or False

37. An expectancy refers to the anticipation that making a response will lead to reinforcement.
    True or False

38. People who are depressed tend to engage in a high rate of self-reinforcement
    to make themselves feel better.
    True or False

39. Social reinforcement is based on attention and approval from others.
    True or False

40. In elementary school, misbehaving boys typically get more attention from teachers than girls do.
    True or False

41. The BSRI consists of 20 masculine traits and 20 feminine traits.
    True or False

42. About 50 percent of all people who take the BSRI are scored as androgynous.
    True or False

43. Masculine men and feminine women consistently choose to engage in sex-appropriate activities.
    True or False

44. Masculine men and women are not so good at understanding their feelings but are quite good at understanding the feelings of others.
    True or False

45. Androgynous persons tend to be more satisfied with their lives than non-androgynous persons are.
    True or False

Check Your Memory: Pages 389—392

46. Humanists believe that humans are capable of free choice.
    True or False

47. To investigate self-actualization, Maslow studied eminent men and women exclusively.
    True or False

48. Self-actualizers usually try to avoid task centering.
    True or False

49. Personal autonomy is a characteristic of the self-actualizing person.
    True or False

50. Information inconsistent with one's self-image is described as incongruent.
    True or False

51. Poor self-knowledge is associated with high self-esteem because people do not have to think about their own faults.
    True or False

52. Congruence represents a close correspondence between self-image, the ideal self, and the true self.
    True or False

53. Images of possible selves typically cause feelings of incongruence.
    True or False

54. Rogers believed that organismic valuing is healthier than trying to meet someone else's conditions of worth.
    True or False

Check Your Memory: Pages 393—401

55. Planned questions are used in a structured interview.
    True or False

56. The halo effect may involve either a positive or a negative impression.
    True or False

57. Personality questionnaires are used to do behavioural assessments.
    True or False

58. Judgmental firearms training is a type of honesty test.
    True or False

59. Items on the MMPI-2 were selected for their ability to identify persons with psychiatric problems.
    True or False

60. The validity scale of the MMPI-2 is used to rate Type A behaviour.
    True or False

61. The psychasthenia scale of the MMPI-2 detects the presence of phobias and compulsive actions.
    True or False

62. It is very easy to fake responses to a projective test.
    True or False

63. The TAT is a situational test.
    True or False

64. Habitually violent prison inmates are aggressive and overcontrolled.
    True or False

Check Your Memory: Psychology in Action

65. Shyness is closely related to private self-consciousness.
    True or False

66. Non-shy persons believe that external situations cause their occasional feelings of shyness.
    True or False

67. The odds of meeting someone interested in socializing are about the same wherever you are.
    True or False

68. Open-ended questions help keep conversations going.
    True or False

Final Survey and Review

• *How do psychologists use the term personality? What core concepts make up the psychology of personality?*

1. _____ is made up of one's unique and relatively stable behaviour _____ .

2. _____ is personality that has been judged or evaluated. That is, it is the possession of desirable qualities.

3. _____ refers to the hereditary and physiological aspects of one's emotional nature.

4. Personality _____ are lasting personal qualities that are inferred from behaviour.

5. A personality _____ is a style of personality defined by having a group of related traits or similar characteristics.

6. Two widely recognized personality types are an _____ (shy, self-centred person) and an _____ (bold, outgoing person).

7. Behaviour is influenced by _____ , which is a person's perception of his or her own personality traits.

8. Personality _____ combine interrelated assumptions, ideas, and principles to explain personality.

9. Four major types of personality theories are: trait, _____ , behaviouristic, and _____ .

• *Are some personality traits more basic or important than others?*

10. _____ theories attempt to specify qualities of personality that are most lasting or characteristic of a person.

11. Gordon _____ made useful distinctions between _____ traits (which are shared by most members of a culture) and individual traits (characteristics of a single person).

12. He also identified _____ traits (a trait that influences nearly all of a person's activities), _____ traits (core traits of personality), and secondary traits (superficial traits).

13. The theory of Raymond _____ attributes visible surface traits to the existence of 16 underlying _____ traits (which he identified using _____ analysis).

14. _____ _____ are measured by the Sixteen Personality Factor Questionnaire (16 PF).

15. The outcome of the 16 PF and other personality tests may be graphically presented as a trait _____ .

16. The _____ model of personality reduces traits to 5 universal dimensions of personality.

17. They are: _____ , agreeableness, conscientiousness, _____ , and openness to experience.

18. Traits _____ with _____ to determine behaviour.

19. Heredity is responsible for _____ to _____ percent of the variation in personality traits.

20. Studies of separated identical twins suggest that _____ contributes significantly to adult personality traits. Overall, however, personality is shaped as much, or more by differences in _____ .

• *How do psychodynamic theories explain personality?*

21. Psychodynamic theories focus on the inner workings of _____ , especially hidden or unconscious forces and internal _____ .

22. According to Sigmund Freud's _____ theory, personality is made up of the _____ , ego, and _____ .

23. The id operates on the _____ principle. The ego is guided by the _____ principle.

24. The superego is made up of the _____ and the _____ ideal.

25. _____ , derived from the life _____ , is the primary energy running the personality.

26. Conflicts within the personality may cause _____ anxiety or _____ anxiety and motivate use of ego-defense mechanisms.

27. The personality operates on three levels, the conscious, _____ , and _____ .

28. The _____ is completely unconscious; the _____ and _____ can operate at all three levels of awareness.

29. The Freudian view of personality development is based on a series of _____ stages: the oral, anal, _____ , and genital.

30. _____ (unresolved emotional conflicts) at any stage can leave a lasting imprint on personality.

31. Freud's theory pioneered the idea that _____ , _____ training, and early sexual experiences leave an imprint on personality.

• *What do behaviourists emphasize in their approach to personality?*

32. _____ theories of personality emphasize learning, conditioning, and immediate effects of the environment.

33. Learning theorists generally stress the effects of prior learning and situational _____ of behaviour.

34. Learning theorists John Dollard and Neal Miller consider habits the basic core of personality. Habits express the combined effects of _____ , _____ , response, and reward.

35. Social learning theory adds _____ elements, such as perception, thinking, and understanding to the behavioural view of personality.

36. Examples of social learning concepts are the psychological situation (the situation as it is perceived), _____ (expectations about what effects a response will have), and _____ value (the subjective value of a reinforcer or activity).

37. Some social learning theorists treat "conscience" as a case of self- _____ .

38. The behaviouristic view of personality development holds that social reinforcement in four situations is critical. The critical situations are feeding, _____ _____ , sex training, and anger or _____ training.

39. _____ (feeling emotionally connected to a person) and imitation (mimicking another person's behaviour) are of particular importance in sex (or gender) training.

40. Research conducted by Sandra Bem indicates that roughly one _____ of all persons are _____ (they possess both masculine and feminine traits).

41. Androgyny is measured with the _____ Sex Role _____ (BSRI).

42. Being masculine means that a person is _____ and assertive.

43. Being feminine means that a person is _____ (helpful and comforting) and interpersonally oriented.

44. Psychological androgyny appears related to greater _____ or flexibility in behaviour.

• *How do humanistic theories differ from other perspectives?*

45. Humanistic theory views human nature as good, and emphasizes _____ experience, free choice, and needs for self- _____ .

46. Abraham _____ study of _____ identified characteristics they share, ranging from efficient perceptions of reality to frequent peak experiences.

47. Carl Rogers's theory views the self as an entity that emerges when experiences that match the self-image are _____ (admitted to consciousness), while those that are _____ are excluded.

48. The _____ person has a highly unrealistic self-image and/or a mismatch between the self-image and the _____ self.

49. The _____ or fully functioning person is flexible and open to experiences and feelings.

50. In the development of personality, humanists are primarily interested in the emergence of a self-image and in _____ .

51. As parents apply _____ of worth (standards used to judge thoughts, feelings, and actions) to a child, the child begins to do the same.

52. Internalized _____ _____ _____ contribute to incongruence, they damage positive self-regard, and they disrupt the _____ valuing process.

• *How do psychologists measure personality?*

53. Techniques typically used for personality assessment are interviews, direct _____ , questionnaires, and _____ tests.

54. Structured and _____ interviews provide much information, but they are subject to interviewer _____ and misperceptions. The halo effect may also lower the accuracy of an interview.

55. Direct observation, sometimes involving _____ tests, _____ assessment, or the use of rating scales, allows evaluation of a person's actual behaviour.

56. Personality questionnaires, such as the *Minnesota Multiphasic _____ _____ -2* (MMPI-2), are objective and reliable, but their _____ is open to question.

57. _____ tests, which are essentially personality questionnaires, are widely used by businesses to measure integrity and make hiring decisions.

58. _____ tests ask subjects to react to an ambiguous stimulus or unstructured situation.

59. The _____ , or inkblot test, is a well-known projective technique. A second is the Thematic _____ Test (TAT).

60. The _____ and objectivity of projective tests are quite low. Nevertheless, projective techniques are considered useful by many clinicians, particularly as part of a test _____ .

• *What causes shyness? What can be done about it?*

61. Shyness is a mixture of social _____ and social anxiety.

62. Shy persons tend to lack social _____ and they feel social anxiety (because they believe they are being evaluated by others).

63. Shy persons also have a _____ bias in their thinking (they tend to blame themselves for social failures).

64. Shyness is marked by heightened public self-_____ (awareness of oneself as a _____ object) and a tendency to regard shyness as a lasting _____ .

65. Shyness can be lessened by changing _____ beliefs and by improving social _____ .

Mastery Test

1. The hereditary aspects of a person's emotional nature define his or her
   a. character
   b. personality
   c. cardinal traits
   d. temperament

2. Two parts of the psyche that operate on all three levels of awareness are the
   a. id and ego
   b. ego and superego
   c. id and superego
   d. id and ego ideal

3. The four critical situations Miller and Dollard consider important in the development of personality are feeding, toilet training,
   a. sex, and aggression
   b. cleanliness, and language
   c. attachment, and imitation
   d. social learning

4. Scales that rate a person's tendencies for depression, hysteria, paranoia, and mania are found on the
   a. MMPI-2
   b. Rorschach
   c. TAT
   d. 16 PF

5. In the five-factor model, people who score high on openness to experience are
   a. intelligent
   b. extroverted
   c. choleric
   d. a personality type

6. Maslow used the term _____ to describe the tendency to make full use of personal potentials.
   a. full functionality
   b. self-potentiation
   c. ego-idealization
   d. self-actualization

7. Studies of reunited identical twins support the idea that
   a. personality traits are 70 percent hereditary
   b. fixations influence the expression of personality traits
   c. personality traits are altered by selective mating and placement in families of comparable status
   d. personality is shaped as much or more by environment as by heredity

8. A person's perception of his or her own personality is the core of
   a. temperament
   b. source traits
   c. self-concept
   d. trait-situation interactions

9. Which of the following concepts is NOT part of Dollard and Miller's behavioural model of personality?
   a. drive
   b. expectancy
   c. cue
   d. reward

10. The terms *structured* and *unstructured* apply most to
    a. the halo effect
    b. interviews
    c. questionnaires
    d. honesty tests

11. Behavioural theorists account for the existence of a conscience with the concept of
    a. traits of honesty and integrity
    b. the superego
    c. self-reinforcement
    d. conditions of worth

12. Feelings of pride come from the _____, a part of the _____.
    a. libido, conscience
    b. ego ideal, superego
    c. reality principle, superego

d.   superego, ego

13.   Four types of temperament recognized by the early Greeks are: melancholic, choleric, phlegmatic and
   a.   sanguine
   b.   sardonic
   c.   sagittarian
   d.   sagacious

14.   Freud believed that boys identify with their fathers in order to resolve the _____ conflict.
   a.   Animus
   b.   Electra
   c.   Oedipus
   d.   Persona

15.   Maslow regarded peak experiences as temporary moments of
   a.   task-centering
   b.   congruent selfhood
   c.   self-actualization
   d.   organismic valuing

16.   Ambiguous stimuli are used primarily in the
   a.   MMPI-2
   b.   Shoot-Don't-Shoot Test
   c.   Rorschach
   d.   16 PF

17.   A person who is generally extroverted is more outgoing in some situations than in others. This observation supports the concept of
   a.   trait-situation interactions
   b.   behavioural genetic determinants
   c.   situational fixations
   d.   possible selves

18.   Allport's concept of central traits is most closely related to Cattell's
   a.   surface traits
   b.   source traits
   c.   secondary traits
   d.   cardinal traits

19.   According to Freud, tendencies to be orderly, obstinate, and stingy are formed during the _____ stage.
   a.   genital
   b.   anal
   c.   oral
   d.   phallic

20.   Which of the following is NOT part of Carl Rogers's view of personality?
   a.   possible selves
   b.   organismic valuing

    c.   conditions of worth

    d.   congruence

21.   Rating scales are primarily used in which approach to personality assessment?

    a.   projective testing

    b.   direct observation

    c.   questionnaires

    d.   the TAT technique

22.   Which theory of personality places the greatest emphasis on the effects of the environment?

    a.   trait

    b.   psychodynamic

    c.   behaviouristic

    d.   humanistic

23.   Freudian psychosexual stages occur in the order:

    a.   oral, anal, genital, phallic

    b.   oral, phallic, anal, genital

    c.   genital, oral, anal, phallic

    d.   oral, anal, phallic, genital

24.   Rogers described mismatches between one's self-image and reality as a state of

    a.   moral anxiety

    b.   incongruence

    c.   basic anxiety

    d.   negative symbolization

25.   All but one of the following are major elements of shyness; which does not apply?

    a.   private self-consciousness

    b.   social anxiety

    c.   self-defeating thoughts

    d.   belief that shyness is a lasting trait

26.   People who all grew up in the same culture would be most likely to have the same _____ traits.

    a.   cardinal

    b.   common

    c.   secondary

    d.   source

27.   A trait profile is used to report the results of

    a.   the 16 PF

    b.   situational tests

    c.   the TAT

    d.   the inkblot test

28. An emphasis on the situational determinants of actions is a key feature of _____ theories of personality.
    a. psychodynamic
    b. projective
    c. behaviourist
    d. humanist

29. Expectancies and the psychological situation are concepts important to
    a. the five-factor model
    b. development of the superego
    c. social learning theory
    d. Maslow

30. A policeman who accepts emotional support from others, especially from women, would most likely be scored as _____ on the BSRI.
    a. masculine
    b. feminine
    c. androgynous
    d. expressive-nurturant

31. The subcategories of the Big Five dimensions are called
    a. common traits
    b. secondary traits
    c. sublevel traits
    d. facet traits

Solutions

Recite and Review

1. behaviour
2. evaluated
3. hereditary
4. behaviour
5. traits
6. types
7. personality
8. Personality
9. trait
10. theories
11. individual
12. secondary
13. surface, analysis
14. Personality, Factor
15. trait
16. universal
17. agreeableness, experience
18. Traits
19. traits
20. identical
21. unconscious
22. ego
23. principle, principle
24. superego
25. life, energy
26. anxiety, anxiety
27. conscious
28. unconscious
29. stages, oral
30. personality
31. personality

32. learning
33. situational
34. habits, Habits, reward
35. Social
36. psychological, value
37. self
38. feeding, anger
39. imitation
40. masculine, feminine
41. Sex, Role
42. masculine
43. feminine
44. androgyny
45. good, free
46. peak , experiences
47. self, image
48. self-image, self-image
49. fully
50. self-image
51. worth
52. positive, valuing
53. interviews, tests
54. interviews, interviewer, lower
55. rating, behaviour
56. Minnesota, Multiphasic, reliable
57. questionnaires
58. stimulus
59. inkblot, Thematic
60. low, test
61. social, social
62. evaluated
63. thinking, themselves
64. public, social
65. beliefs, social

Connections

1. C
2. J
3. A
4. I
5. B
6. G
7. D
8. E
9. F
10. H
11. E
12. G
13. I
14. J
15. B
16. A
17. H
18. C
19. F
20. D
21. J
22. H
23. G
24. F
25. I
26. A
27. D
28. E
29. B
30. C

Check Your Memory

1. F

2. F	38. F	3. Temperament
3. F	39. T	4. traits
4. F	40. T	5. type
5. T	41. F	6. introvert, extrovert
6. T	42. F	7. Self-concept
7. T	43. T	8. theories
8. F	44. F	9. psychodynamic, humanistic
9. F	45. T	10. Trait
10. F	46. T	11. Allport, common
11. T	47. F	12. cardinal, central
12. F	48. F	13. Cattell, source, factor
13. T	49. T	14. Source, traits
14. F	50. T	15. profile
15. F	51. F	16. Five-factor
16. F	52. T	17. extroversion, neuroticism
17. T	53. F	18. interact, situations
18. T	54. T	19. 25, 30
19. T	55. T	20. heredity, environment
20. F	56. T	21. personality, conflicts
21. F	57. F	22. psychoanalytical, id, superego
22. T	58. F	23. pleasure, reality
23. T	59. T	24. conscience, ego
24. F	60. F	25. Libido, instincts
25. T	61. T	26. neurotic, moral
26. F	62. F	27. preconscious, unconscious
27. T	63. F	28. id, ego, superego
28. F	64. F	29. psyhosexual, phallic
29. F	65. F	30. Fixations
30. T	66. T	31. feeding, toilet
31. F	67. F	32. Behavioural
32. T	68. T	33. determinants
33. T		34. drive, cue
34. T		35. cognitive
35. F	**Final Survey and Review**	36. expectancies, reinforcement
36. T		37. reinforcement
37. T	1. Personality, patterns	38. toilet, training, aggression
	2. Character	

231

39. Identification

40. third, androgynous

41. Bem, Inventory

42. independent

43. nurturant

44. adaptability

45. subjectivity, actualization

46. Maslow's, self-actualizers

47. symbolized, incongruent

48. incongruent, ideal

49. congruent

50. Self-evaluations

51. conditions

52. conditions, of, worth, organismic

53. observation, projective

54. unstructured, bias

55. situational, behavioural

56. Personality, Inventory, validity

57. Honesty

58. Projective

59. Rorschach, Apperception

60. validity, battery

61. inhibition

62. skills

63. self-defeating

64. consciousness, social, trait

65. self-defeating, skills

5. A (p. 375)

6. D (p. 389)

7. D (p. 377)

8. C (p. 370)

9. B (p. 384)

10. B (p. 394)

11. C (p. 385)

12. B (p. 379)

13. A (p. 372)

14. C (p. 381)

15. C (p. 390)

16. C (p. 398)

17. A (p. 376)

18. B (p. 373)

19. B (p. 381)

20. A (p. 391)

21. B (p. 394)

22. C (p. 383)

23. D (p. 381)

24. B (p. 390)

25. A (p. 402)

26. B (p. 373)

27. A (p. 374)

28. C (p. 383)

29. C (p. 384)

30. C (p. 386)

31. D (p. 375)

Mastery Test

1. D (p. 369)

2. B (p. 378)

3. A (p. 385)

4. A (p. 397)

Chapter 11

Health, Stress, and Coping

Chapter Overview

Health psychologists study behavioural risk factors and health-promoting behaviours. Various "lifestyle" diseases are directly related to unhealthy personal habits. Sexually transmitted diseases are a good example of how behavioural risk factors contribute to health risks. Stress is also a major risk factor. At work, prolonged stress can lead to burnout. Emotional appraisals greatly affect our stress reactions and coping attempts.

Frustration and conflict are common sources of stress. Major behavioural reactions to frustration include persistence, more vigorous responding, circumvention, direct aggression, displaced aggression and escape or withdrawal. Five major types of conflict are approach-approach, avoidance-avoidance, approach-avoidance, double approach-avoidance, and multiple approach-avoidance.

Anxiety, threat, or feelings of inadequacy frequently lead to the use of defense mechanisms. Common defense mechanisms include compensation, denial, fantasy, intellectualization, isolation, projection, rationalization, reaction formation, regression, repression, and sublimation. Learned helplessness explains some depression and some failures to cope with threat. Mastery training acts as an antidote to helplessness.

A large number of life changes can increase susceptibility to illness. However, immediate health is more closely related to the severity of daily hassles or microstressors. Intense or prolonged stress may cause psychosomatic problems. Biofeedback may be used to combat stress and psychosomatic illnesses. People with Type A personalities run a heightened risk of suffering a heart attack. People with hardy personality traits are resistant to stress. The body reacts to stress in a pattern called the general adaptation syndrome (G.A.S.). In addition, stress may lower the body's immunity to disease.

A number of coping skills can be applied to manage stress. Most focus on bodily effects, ineffective behaviours, and upsetting thoughts.

Learning Objectives

1. Define the terms *health psychology* and *behavioural medicine*.

2. List twelve behavioural risk factors that can adversely affect one's health.

3. Describe the disease-prone personality.

4. Briefly describe health-promoting behaviours that increase life expectancy.

5. Explain how health psychologists work to lessen behavioural risks to health. Describe the impact of refusal-skills training and community health programs on illness prevention.

6. Explain the cause, methods of transmission, and ways of preventing STDs.

7. Define the term *wellness* by listing five characteristics of wellness.

8. Explain the similarity between your body's stress reaction and emotion.

9. List five aspects of stress that make it more intense and damaging.

233

10. Describe burnout. List and describe the three aspects of the problem. Describe three things that can be done to help reduce it.

11. Give an example of how primary and secondary appraisal are used in coping with a threatening situation.

12. Explain how the perception of control of a stressor influences the amount of threat felt.

13. Differentiate problem-focused coping from emotion-focused coping and explain how they may help or hinder each other.

14. List and describe the two different kinds of frustration.

15. List four factors that increase frustration.

16. List and describe five common reactions to frustration.

17. Explain how scapegoating is a special form of displaced aggression.

18. Describe and give an example of each of the following four types of conflict:
    a. approach-approach
    b. avoidance-avoidance
    c. approach-avoidance (include the terms *ambivalence* and *partial approach*)
    d. double approach-avoidance (include the term *vacillation*)

19. Define the term *defense mechanism* and discuss the positive and negative aspects of using them.

20. Describe the following defense mechanisms and give an example of each:
    a. denial
    b. repression
    c. reaction formation
    d. regression
    e. projection
    f. rationalization
    g. compensation
    h. sublimation

21. Describe the development of learned helplessness and relate this concept to attribution and depression. Explain how helplessness may be "unlearned."

22. Describe the problems that typically contribute to depression among college students.

23. List the five conditions of depression and describe how it can be combatted.

24. Discuss the relationship between life changes and long-term health. Describe the Social Readjustment Rating Scale (SRRS).

25. Explain how hassles are related to immediate health.

26. Distinguish between psychosomatic disorders and hypochondria.

27. List the causes of psychosomatic disorders and name several of the most common types of psychosomatic problems.

28. Discuss biofeedback in terms of the process involved, its possible applications, and the contradictory evidence as to its value in aiding relaxation.

29. Differentiate between Type A and Type B personalities. Be aware of the twelve strategies for reducing hostility and be able to apply them.

30. Describe what a hardy personality is and list the three ways such people view the world.

31. Explain the concept of the general adaptation syndrome. List and describe its three stages.

32. Explain how stress affects the immune system and list some ways to boost the immune system.

33. List the three types of responses that are triggered by stress.

34. Discuss the stress management techniques that can be used to diminish or break the cycle of stress responses. Include a discussion of the effective ways to avoid frustration.

35. Define *stereotyped response* and explain how it differs from persistence.

36. Discuss three effective ways to avoid frustration and four strategies for coping with conflict.

Practice Quizzes

Recite and Review

- ### *What is health psychology? How does behaviour affect health?*

Recite and Review: Pages 410–416

1. Health psychologists are interested in _____ that helps maintain and promote health. The related field of behavioural medicine applies psychology to _____ treatment and problems.

2. Most people today die from lifestyle diseases caused by unhealthy personal _____ .

3. Studies have identified a number of behavioural risk factors, which increase the chances of _____ or injury.

4. A general disease-prone personality pattern also raises the risk of _____ .

5. Health-promoting _____ tend to maintain good health. They include practices such as getting regular exercise, controlling _____ and alcohol use, maintaining a balanced _____ , getting good medical care, avoiding _____ deprivation, and managing stress.

6. During the last 20 years there has been a steady increase in the incidence of sexually transmitted _____ (STDs).

7. Part of this increase is due to the emergence of _____ _____ deficiency syndrome (AIDS) caused by the human immunodeficiency _____ (HIV).

8. STDs have had a sizable impact on patterns of sexual behaviour, including increased awareness of high- _____ behaviours and some curtailment of _____ taking.

9. Health psychologists attempt to promote wellness (a positive state of _____) through community health _____ that educate people about risk factors and healthful behaviours.

- ### *What is stress? What factors determine its severity?*

Recite and Review: Pages 417–420

10. Stress occurs when we are forced to _____ or adapt to external demands.

11. Stress is more damaging in situations involving pressure (responding at full capacity for long periods), a lack of _____ , unpredictability of the stressor, and _____ or repeated emotional shocks.

12. _____ is intensified when a situation is perceived as a threat and when a person does not feel competent to cope with it.

13. In _____ settings, prolonged stress can lead to burnout, marked by emotional _____ , depersonalization (detachment from others), and reduced personal accomplishment.

14. The _____ (initial) appraisal of a situation greatly affects our emotional response to it. Stress reactions, in particular, are related to an appraisal of _____ .

15. During a _____ appraisal some means of coping with a situation is selected. Coping may be either problem-focused (managing the situation) or emotion-focused (managing one's emotional reactions) or both.

• *What causes frustration and what are typical reactions to it?*

Recite and Review: Pages 420–422

16. Frustration is the negative emotional state that occurs when progress toward a _____ is _____ . Sources of frustration may be external or personal.

17. External frustrations are based on delay, failure, rejection, loss, and other direct blocking of motives. Personal frustration is related to _____ characteristics over which one has little control.

18. Frustrations of all types become more _____ as the strength, urgency, or importance of the blocked motive increases.

19. Major behavioural reactions to frustration include persistence, more _____ responding, and circumvention of barriers.

20. Other reactions to frustration are _____ aggression, displaced aggression (including scapegoating), and escape, or _____ .

• *Are there different types of conflict? How do people react to conflict?*

Recite and Review: Pages 422–424

21. _____ occurs when we must choose between contradictory alternatives.

22. Three basic types of conflict are approach-approach (choice between two _____ alternatives), avoidance-avoidance (both alternatives are _____), and approach-avoidance (a goal or activity has both positive and negative aspects).

23. More complex conflicts are: double approach-avoidance (both alternatives have _____ and _____ qualities) and multiple approach-avoidance (several alternatives each have good and bad qualities).

24. Approach-approach conflicts are usually the _____ to resolve.

25. Avoidance conflicts are _____ to resolve and are characterized by inaction, indecision, freezing, and a desire to escape (called _____ the field).

26. People usually remain in approach-avoidance conflicts, but fail to fully resolve them. Approach-avoidance conflicts are associated with ambivalence (_____ feelings) and _____ approach.

27. Vacillation (wavering between choices) is the most common reaction to double _____ conflicts.

- ## *What are defense mechanisms?*

Recite and Review: Pages 424–427

28. Anxiety, threat, or feelings of _____ frequently lead to the use of psychological defense mechanisms. These are habitual strategies used to avoid or reduce anxiety.

29. A number of defense mechanisms have been identified, including denial, fantasy, intellectualization, isolation, projection, rationalization, _____ formation, regression, and _____ (motivated forgetting).

30. Two defense mechanisms that have some _____ qualities are compensation and sublimation.

- ## *What do we know about coping with feelings of helplessness and depression?*

Recite and Review: Pages 427–430

31. Learned helplessness is a learned inability to overcome obstacles or to _____ punishment.

32. Learned helplessness explains the failure to cope with some threatening situations. The symptoms of learned helplessness and depression are nearly _____ .

33. Mastery _____ and hope act as antidotes to helplessness.

34. Depression (a state of deep sadness or despondency) is a serious emotional problem. Actions and thoughts that counter feelings of helplessness tend to _____ depression.

- ## *How is stress related to health and disease?*

Recite and Review: Pages 430–437

35. Work with the *Social Readjustment Rating Scale* (SRRS) indicates that a large number of life _____ units (LCUs) can increase susceptibility to _____ or illness.

36. Immediate health is more closely related to the intensity and severity of daily annoyances, known as _____ or microstressors.

37. Intense or prolonged stress may damage the body in the form of psychosomatic disorders (illnesses in which _____ factors play a part).

38. Psychosomatic (mind-body) disorders have no connection to hypochondria, the tendency to imagine that one has a _____ .

39. During biofeedback training, bodily processes are _____ and converted to a signal that indicates what the body is doing.

40. Biofeedback allows alteration of many bodily activities. It shows promise for promoting _____ , self-regulation, and for treating some psychosomatic illnesses.

41. People with Type A (_____ attack prone) personalities are competitive, striving, and frequently angry or hostile, and they have a chronic sense of _____ urgency.

42. _____ and hostility are especially likely to increase the chances of heart attack.

43. People who have traits of the hardy personality seem to be resistant to _____ , even if they also have Type A traits.

44. The body reacts to stress in a series of stages called the _____ adaptation syndrome (G.A.S.).

45. The stages of the G.A.S. are alarm, resistance, and exhaustion. The G.A.S. contributes to the development of _____ disorders.

46. Stress weakens the immune system and lowers the body's resistance to _____ .

- ### *What are the best strategies for managing stress?*

Recite and Review: Psychology in Action

47. Most stress management skills focus on one of three areas: bodily effects, ineffective _____ , and upsetting _____ .

48. Bodily effects can be managed with exercise, meditation, progressive _____ , and guided _____ .

49. The impact of ineffective behaviour can be remedied by slowing down, getting organized, striking a balance between "good stress" and _____ , accepting your limits, and seeking social support.

50. A good way to control upsetting thoughts is to replace negative self-statements with _____ coping statements.

Connections

1.	_____ risk factors	a.	a leading cause of death
2.	_____ tobacco	b.	ANS arousal
3.	_____ refusal skills	c.	blocked motive
4.	_____ stress reaction	d.	health-damaging habits
5.	_____ burnout	e.	psychological escape
6.	_____ primary appraisal	f.	scapegoat
7.	_____ frustration	g.	approach-avoidance
8.	_____ displaced aggression	h.	"Am I in trouble?"
9.	_____ apathy	i.	job stress
10.	_____ ambivalence	j.	smoking prevention

11. _____ compensation
12. _____ denial
13. _____ fantasy
14. _____ intellectualization
15. _____ isolation
16. _____ projection
17. _____ rationalization
18. _____ reaction formation
19. _____ regression
20. _____ repression
21. _____ sublimation

a. Fulfilling unmet desires in imagined activities.
b. Separating contradictory thoughts into "logic-tight" mental compartments.
c. Preventing actions by exaggerating opposite behaviour.
d. Justifying your behaviour by giving reasonable but false reasons for it.
e. Unconsciously preventing painful thoughts from entering awareness.
f. Counteracting a real or imagined weakness by seeking to excel.
g. Retreating to an earlier level of development.
h. Attributing one's own shortcomings or unacceptable impulses to others.
i. Protecting oneself from an unpleasant reality by refusing to perceive it.
j. Working off unacceptable impulses in constructive activities.
k. Thinking about threatening situations in impersonal terms.

22. _____ learned helplessness
23. _____ mastery training
24. _____ Social Readjustment Rating Scale
25. _____ hassle
26. _____ STD
27. _____ psychosomatic
28. _____ biofeedback
29. _____ Type A
30. _____ general adaptation syndrome

a. life change units
b. risky sexual behaviour
c. mind-body
d. self-regulation
e. cardiac personality
f. alarm reaction
g. microstressor
h. hope
i. shuttle box

Check Your Memory

Check Your Memory: Pages 410–416

1. Heart disease, lung cancer, and stroke are typical lifestyle diseases.
   True or False

2. Young Canadian adults aged 20 to 24 display less risky behaviours than those aged 15 to 19.
   True or False

3. People with disease-prone personalities are depressed, anxious, and hostile.
   True or False

4. Unhealthy lifestyles typically involve multiple risks.
   True or False

5. The first symptoms of AIDS may not appear for up to 7 years.
   True or False

6. HIV infections are spread by direct contact with body fluids.
   True or False

7. It is unwise to count on a partner for protection from HIV infection.
   True or False

8. Many people suffering from STDs are asymptomatic.
   True or False

9. Community health campaigns provide refusal skills training to large numbers of people.
   True or False

10. Wellness can be described as an absence of disease.
    True or False

Check Your Memory: Pages 417—420

11. Unpleasant activities produce stress, whereas, pleasant activities do not.
    True or False

12. Initial reactions to stressors are similar to those that occur during strong emotion.
    True or False

13. Short-term stresses rarely do any damage to the body.
    True or False

14. Unpredictable demands increase stress.
    True or False

15. Pressure occurs when we are faced with a stressor we can control.
    True or False

16. Burnout is especially a problem in helping professions.
    True or False

17. Stress is often related to the meaning a person places on events.
    True or False

18. The same situation can be a challenge or a threat, depending on how it is appraised.
    True or False

19. In a secondary appraisal, we decide if a situation is relevant or irrelevant, positive or threatening.
    True or False

20. When confronted by a stressor, it is best to choose one type of coping—problem focused or emotion focused.
    True or False

21. Emotion-focused coping is best suited to managing stressors you cannot control.
    True or False

Check Your Memory: Pages 420—422

22. Delays, rejections, and losses are good examples of personal frustrations.
    True or False

23. Varied responses and circumvention attempt to directly destroy or remove barriers that cause frustration.
    True or False

24. Scapegoating is a good example of escape or withdrawal.
    True or False

25. Abuse of drugs can be a way of psychologically escaping frustration.
    True or False

Check Your Memory: Pages 422—424

26. Approach-approach conflicts are fairly easy to resolve.
    True or False

27. Indecision, inaction, and freezing are typical reactions to approach-approach conflicts.
    True or False

28. People find it difficult to escape approach-avoidance conflicts.
    True or False

29. Wanting to eat, but not wanting to be overweight, creates an approach-approach conflict.
    True or False

30. People are very likely to vacillate when faced with a double approach-avoidance conflict.
    True or False

31. When deciding to be sexually active many young people are faced with an approach-avoidance conflict.
    True or False

Check Your Memory: Pages 424—427

32. Defense mechanisms are used to avoid or distort sources of threat or anxiety.
    True or False

33. Denial is a common reaction to bad news, such as learning that a friend has died.
    True or False

34. In reaction formation, a person fulfills unmet desires in imagined achievements.
    True or False

35. A child who becomes homesick while visiting relatives may be experiencing a mild regression.
    True or False

36. Denial and repression are the two most positive of the defense mechanisms.
    True or False

Check Your Memory: Pages 427—430

37. The deep depression experienced by prisoners of war appears to be related to learned helplessness.
    True or False

38. Learned helplessness occurs when events appear to be uncontrollable.
    True or False

39. Attributing failure to lasting, general factors, such as personal characteristics, tends to create the most damaging feelings of helplessness.
    True or False

40. Mastery training restores feelings of control over the environment.
    True or False

41. During the school year, Canadian students show no more distress than the general population.
    True or False

42. Depression is more likely when students find it difficult to live up to idealized images of themselves.
    True or False

241

43. Writing rational answers to self-critical thoughts can help counteract feelings of depression.
    True or False

Check Your Memory: Pages 430—437

44. Scores on the SRRS are expressed as life control units.
    True or False

45. A score of 300 LCUs on the SRRS is categorized as a major life crisis.
    True or False

46. According to the SRRS, being fired at work involves more LCUs than divorce does.
    True or False

47. Microstressors tend to predict changes in health 1 to 2 years after the stressful events took place.
    True or False

48. Psychosomatic disorders involve actual damage to the body or damaging changes in bodily functioning.
    True or False

49. A person undergoing biofeedback can sleep if he or she desires—the machine does all the work.
    True or False

50. Type B personalities are more than twice as likely to suffer heart attacks as Type A personalities.
    True or False

51. People with the hardy personality type tend to see life as a series of challenges.
    True or False

52. In the stage of resistance of the G.A.S., people have symptoms of headache, fever, fatigue, upset stomach, and the like.
    True or False

53. Serious health problems tend to occur when a person reaches the stage of exhaustion in the G.A.S.
    True or False

54. Stress management training can actually boost immune system functioning.
    True or False

Check Your Memory: Psychology in Action

55. Concern about being pregnant is the most stressful item listed on the *College Life Stress Inventory*.
    True or False

56. Exercising for stress management is most effective when it is done daily.
    True or False

57. Guided imagery is used to reduce anxiety and promote relaxation.
    True or False

58. Merely writing down thoughts and feelings about daily events can provide some of the benefits of social support.
    True or False

59. To get the maximum benefits, coping statements should be practised in actual stressful situations.
    True or False

60. Persistence must be flexible before it is likely to aid a person trying to cope with frustration.
    True or False

Final Survey and Review

- ## *What is health psychology? Hoes does behaviour affect health?*

1. Health psychologists are interested in behaviour that helps maintain and promote health. The related field of _____ _____ applies psychology to medical treatment and problems.

2. Most people today die from _____ diseases caused by unhealthy personal habits.

3. Studies have identified a number of behavioural _____ _____ , which increase the chances of disease or injury.

4. A general _____ personality pattern also raises the risk of illness.

5. Health- _____ behaviours tend to maintain good health. They include practices such as getting regular exercise, controlling smoking and alcohol use, maintaining a balanced diet, getting good medical care, avoiding sleep _____ , and managing _____ .

6. During the last 20 years there has been a steady increase in the incidence of _____ _____ diseases (STDs).

7. Part of this increase is due to the emergence of acquired immune _____ syndrome (AIDS) caused by the human _____ virus (HIV).

8. _____ have had a sizable impact on patterns of sexual behaviour, including increased awareness of high-risk behaviours and some curtailment of risk taking.

9. Health psychologists attempt to promote _____ (a positive state of health) through _____ _____ campaigns that educate people about risk factors and healthful behaviours.

- ## *What is stress? What factors determine its severity?*

10. Stress occurs when we are forced to adjust or _____ to external _____ .

11. Stress is more damaging in situations involving _____ (responding at full capacity for long periods), a lack of control, unpredictability of the _____ , and intense or repeated emotional shocks.

12. Stress is intensified when a situation is perccived as a _____ and when a person does not feel _____ to cope with it.

13. In work settings, prolonged stress can lead to _____ , marked by emotional exhaustion, _____ (detachment from others), and reduced personal accomplishment.

14. The primary _____ of a situation greatly affects our emotional response to it. Stress reactions, in particular, are related to an _____ of threat.

15. During a secondary appraisal some means of coping with a situation is selected. Coping may be either _____ -focused (managing the situation) or _____ -focused (managing one's emotional reactions) or both.

- ## *What causes frustration and what are typical reactions to it?*

16. _____ is the negative emotional state that occurs when progress toward a goal is blocked. Sources of frustration may be external or _____ .

17. _____ frustrations are based on delay, failure, rejection, loss, and other direct blocking of motives. _____ frustration is related to personal characteristics over which one has little control.

18. Frustrations of all types become more intense as the strength, urgency, or importance of the _____ _____ increases.

19. Major behavioural reactions to frustration include _____ , more vigorous responding, and _____ of barriers.

20. Other reactions to frustration are direct aggression, _____ aggression (including _____), and escape, or withdrawal.

• *Are there different types of conflict? How do people react to conflict?*

21. Conflict occurs when we must choose between _____ alternatives.

22. Three basic types of conflict are _____ (choice between two positive alternatives), _____ (both alternatives are negative), and approach-avoidance (a goal or activity has both positive and negative aspects).

23. More complex conflicts are: _____ approach-avoidance (both alternatives have positive and negative qualities) and _____ approach-avoidance (several alternatives each have good and bad qualities).

24. _____ conflicts are usually the easiest to resolve.

25. _____ conflicts are difficult to resolve and are characterized by inaction, indecision, freezing, and a desire to escape (called leaving the field).

26. People usually remain in approach-avoidance conflicts, but fail to fully resolve them. Approach-avoidance conflicts are associated with _____ (mixed feelings) and partial approach.

27. _____ (wavering between choices) is the most common reaction to double approach-avoidance conflicts.

• *What are defense mechanisms?*

28. Anxiety, threat, or feelings of inadequacy frequently lead to the use of psychological _____ _____ . These are habitual strategies used to avoid or reduce _____ .

29. A number of defense mechanisms have been identified, including _____ (refusing to perceive an unpleasant reality), fantasy, intellectualization, isolation, projection, _____ (justifying one's behaviour), reaction formation, regression, and repression.

30. Two defense mechanisms that have some positive qualities are _____ and _____ .

• *What do we know about coping with feelings of helplessness and depression?*

31. Learned _____ is a learned inability to overcome obstacles or to avoid _____ .

32. The symptoms of learned helplessness and _____ are nearly identical.

33. _____ training and hope act as antidotes to helplessness.

34. _____ (a state of deep sadness or despondency) is a serious emotional problem. Actions and thoughts that counter feelings of _____ tend to reduce depression.

• *How is stress related to health and disease?*

35. Work with the _____ _____ _____ Scale (SRRS) indicates that a large number of life change units (LCUs) can increase susceptibility to accident or illness.

36. Immediate health is more closely related to the intensity and severity of daily annoyances, known as hassles or _____ .

37. Intense or prolonged stress may damage the body in the form of _____ disorders (illnesses in which psychological factors play a part).

38. _____ (mind-body) disorders have no connection to _____ , the tendency to imagine that one has a disease.

39. During _____ training, bodily processes are monitored and converted to a _____ that indicates what the body is doing.

40. Biofeedback allows alteration of many bodily activities. It shows promise for promoting relaxation, self- _____ , and for treating some psychosomatic illnesses.

41. People with _____ _____ (heart attack prone) personalities are competitive, striving, and frequently _____ or hostile, and they have a chronic sense of time urgency.

42. Anger and hostility are especially likely to increase the chances of _____ _____ .

43. People who have traits of the _____ personality seem to be resistant to stress, even if they also have Type A traits.

44. The body reacts to stress in a series of stages called the general _____ _____ (G.A.S.).

45. The stages of the G.A.S. are _____ , resistance, and _____ . The G.A.S. contributes to the development of psychosomatic disorders.

46. Stress weakens the _____ system and lowers the body's resistance to illness.

• *What are the best strategies for managing stress?*

47. Most stress management skills focus on one of three areas: bodily effects, _____ behaviour, and _____ thoughts.

48. Bodily effects can be managed with exercise, meditation, _____ relaxation, and _____ imagery.

49. The impact of ineffective behaviour can be remedied by slowing down, getting organized, striking a balance between "good stress" and relaxation, accepting your _____ , and seeking _____ support.

50. A good way to control upsetting thoughts is to replace _____ self-statements with positive _____ statements.

Mastery Test

1. When stressful events appear to be uncontrollable, two common reactions are
   a. apathy and double-approach conflict
   b. helplessness and depression
   c. assimilation and marginalization
   d. psychosomatic disorders and hypochondria

2. The *College Life Stress Inventory* is most closely related to the
   a. SRRS
   b. G.A.S.
   c. K.I.S.
   d. *Disease-Prone Personality Scale*

3. We answer the question "Am I okay or in trouble?" when making
   a. negative self-statements
   b. coping statements
   c. a primary appraisal
   d. a secondary appraisal

245

4.   Which of the following is NOT a major symptom of burnout?
     a.   emotional exhaustion
     b.   depersonalization
     c.   reduced accomplishment
     d.   dependence on co-workers

5.   A child who displays childish speech and infantile play after his parents bring
     home a new baby shows signs of
     a.   compensation
     b.   reaction formation
     c.   regression
     d.   sublimation

6.   Persistent but inflexible repsonses to frustration can become
     a.   stereotyped behaviours
     b.   imagined barriers
     c.   negative self-statements
     d.   sublimated and depersonalized

7.   Which of the following behaviours is related to lifestyle diseases?
     a.   drinking alcohol
     b.   smoking tobacco
     c.   illicit drug use
     d.   all of the above are related to lifestyle diseases

8.   Both mountain climbing and marital strife
     a.   are behavioural risk factors
     b.   are appraised as secondary threats
     c.   cause stress reactions
     d.   produce the condition known as pressure

9.   LCUs are used to assess
     a.   burnout
     b.   social readjustment
     c.   microstressors
     d.   what stage of the G.A.S. a person is in

10. Sujata is often ridculed by her boss, who also frequently takes advantage of her. Deep
     inside, Sujata has come to hate her boss, yet on the surface she acts as if she likes him very
     much. It is likely that Sujata is using the defense mechanism called
     a.   reaction formation
     b.   Type B appraisal
     c.   problem-focused coping
     d.   sublimation

11. Lifestyle diseases are of special interest to _____ psychologists.
     a.   health
     b.   community

c.   wellness

d.   psychosomatic

12.   Which of the following is NOT characteristic of the hardy personality?

    a.   commitment

    b.   a sense of control

    c.   accepting challenge

    d.   repression

13.   Unhealthy lifestyles are marked by the presence of a number of

    a.   health refusal factors

    b.   behavioural risk factors

    c.   cultural stressors

    d.   Type B personality traits

14.   The most effective response to a controllable stressor is

    a.   problem-focused coping

    b.   emotion-focused coping

    c.   leaving the field

    d.   depersonalization

15.   Delay, rejection, failure, and loss are all major causes of

    a.   pressure

    b.   frustration

    c.   conflict

    d.   helplessness

16.   There is evidence that the core lethal factor of Type A behaviour is

    a.   time urgency

    b.   anger and hostility

    c.   competitiveness and ambition

    d.   accepting too many responsibilities

17.   A special danger in the transmission of STDs is that many people are _____ at first.

    a.   non-infectious

    b.   androgynous

    c.   androgenital

    d.   asymptomatic

18.   A person is caught between "the frying pan and the fire" in an _____ conflict.

    a.   approach-approach

    b.   avoidance-avoidance

    c.   approach-avoidance

    d.   double appraisal

19.   Which of the following is NOT one of the major health-promoting behaviours listed in the text?

    a.   do not smoke

    b.   get adequate help

    c.   get regular exercise

    d.   avoid eating between meals

20.   Ambivalence and partial approach are very common reactions to what type of conflict?

    a.   approach-approach

    b.   avoidance-avoidance

    c.   approach-avoidance

    d.   multiple avoidance

21.   Which of the following terms does not belong with the others?

    a.   Type A personality

    b.   stage of exhaustion

    c.   displaced aggression

    d.   psychosomatic disorder

22.   Coping statements are a key element in

    a.   stress inoculation

    b.   the K.I.S. technique

    c.   guided imagery

    d.   refusal skills training

23.   Which of the following factors typically minimizes the amount of stress experienced?

    a.   predictable stressors

    b.   repeated stressors

    c.   uncontrollable stressors

    d.   intense stressors

24.   Scapegoating is closely related to which response to frustration?

    a.   leaving the field

    b.   displaced aggression

    c.   circumvention

    d.   reaction formation

25.   The study of the ways in which stress and the immune system affect susceptibility to disease is called

    a.   neuropsychosymptomology

    b.   immunohypochondrology

    c.   psychosomatoneurology

    d.   psychoneuroimmunology

26.   Refusal skills training is typically used to teach young people how to

    a.   avoid drug use

    b.   cope with burnout

    c.   resist stressors at home and at school

    d.   avoid forming habits that lead to heart disease

27.   Which combination is most relevant to managing bodily reactions to stress?

    a.   social support, self-pacing

    b.   exercise, social support

    c.   exercise, negative self-statements

    d.   progressive relaxation, guided imagery

28. Stress reactions are most likely to occur when a stressor is viewed as a _____ during the _____.

    a.   pressure, primary appraisal

    b.   pressure, secondary appraisal

    c.   threat, primary appraisal

    d.   threat, secondary appraisal

29. External symptoms of the body's adjustment to stress are least visible in which stage of the general adaptation syndrome (G.A.S.)?

    a.   alarm

    b.   regulation

    c.   resistance

    d.   exhaustion

30. A perceived lack of control creates a stressful sense of threat when combined with a perceived

    a.   sense of time urgency

    b.   state of sublimation

    c.   need to change secondary risk factors

    d.   lack of competence

31. Which of the following risky behaviours increases from adolescence to adulthood for both males and females?

    a.   binge drinking

    b.   tobacco smoking

    c.   sex without using a condom and multiple sex partners

    d.   all of these risky behaviours increase

32. Expecting to pass a test even if you did not study is an example of

    a.   regression

    b.   rationalization

    c.   denial

    d.   projection

Solutions

Recite and Review

1. behaviour, medical
2. habits
3. disease (or illness)
4. illness (or disease)
5. behaviours, smoking, diet, sleep
6. diseases
7. acquired, immune, virus
8. risk, risk
9. health, campaigns
10. adjust
11. control, intense
12. Stress
13. work, exhaustion
14. primary, threat
15. secondary
16. goal, blocked
17. personal
18. intense
19. vigorous
20. direct, withdrawal
21. Conflict
22. positive, negative
23. positive, negative
24. easiest
25. difficult, leaving
26. mixed, partial
27. approach-avoidance
28. inadequacy
29. reaction, repression
30. positive
31. avoid
32. identical
33. training
34. reduce
35. change, accident
36. hassles
37. psychological
38. disease
39. monitored
40. relaxation
41. heart, time
42. Anger
43. stress
44. general
45. psychosomatic
46. disease (or illness)
47. behaviour, thoughts
48. relaxation, imagery
49. relaxation
50. positive

Connections

1. D
2. A
3. J
4. B
5. I
6. H
7. C
8. F
9. E
10. G
11. F
12. I
13. A
14. K
15. B
16. H
17. D
18. C
19. G
20. E
21. J
22. I
23. H
24. A
25. G
26. B
27. C
28. D
29. E
30. F

Check Your Memory

1. T
2. F
3. T
4. T
5. T
6. T
7. T
8. T
9. F
10. F
11. F
12. T
13. T
14. T
15. F
16. T
17. T
18. T

19. F
20. F
21. T
22. F
23. F
24. F
25. T
26. T
27. F
28. T
29. F
30. T
31. F
32. T
33. T
34. F
35. T
36. F
37. T
38. T
39. T
40. T
41. F
42. T
43. T
44. F
45. T
46. F
47. F
48. T
49. F
50. F
51. T
52. F
53. T

54. T
55. F
56. T
57. T
58. T
59. T
60. T

Final Survey and Review

1. behavioural, medicine
2. lifestyle
3. risk, factors
4. disease-prone
5. promoting, deprivation, stress
6. sexually, transmitted
7. deficiency, immunodeficiency
8. STDs
9. wellness, community, health
10. adapt, demands
11. pressure, stressor
12. threat, competent
13. burnout, depersonalization
14. appraisal, appraisal
15. problem, emotion
16. Frustration, personal
17. External, Personal
18. blocked, motive
19. persistence, circumvention
20. displaced, scapegoating
21. contradictory
22. approach-approach, avoidance-avoidance
23. double, multiple
24. Approach-approach
25. Avoidance

26. ambivalence
27. vacillation
28. defense, mechanisms, anxiety
29. denial, rationalization
30. compensation, sublimation
31. helplessness, punishment
32. depression
33. Mastery
34. Depression, helplessness
35. Social, Readjustment, Rating
36. microstressors
37. psychosomatic
38. Psychosomatic, hypochondria
39. biofeedback, signal
40. regulation
41. Type, A, angry
42. heart, attack
43. hardy
44. adaptation, syndrome
45. alarm, exhaustion
46. immune
47. ineffective, upsetting
48. progressive, guided
49. limits, social
50. negative, coping

Mastery Test

1. B (p. 428)
2. A (p. 431)
3. C (p. 418)
4. D (p. 419)
5. C (p. 426)
6. A (p. 433)
7. D (p. 411)
8. C (p. 417)

9. B (p. 431)

10. A (p. 425)

11. A (p. 410)

12. D (p. 435)

13. B (p. 411)

14. A (p. 419)

15. B (p. 420)

16. B (p. 434)

17. D (p. 414)

18. B (p. 422)

19. D (p. 414)

20. C (p. 423)

21. C (p. 421)

22. A (p. 442)

23. A (p. 418)

24. B (p. 421)

25. D (p. 437)

26. A (p. 413)

27. D (p. 441)

28. C (p. 418)

29. C (p. 416)

30. D (p. 419)

31. D (p. 416)

32. C (p. 425)

Chapter 12

Psychological Disorders

Chapter Overview

Abnormal behaviour is defined by subjective discomfort, deviation from statistical norms, social non-conformity, and cultural or situational contexts. Disordered behaviour is also maladaptive. Major types of psychopathology are described by DSM-IV-TR. Insanity is a legal term, not a mental disorder.

Personality disorders are deeply ingrained maladaptive personality patterns, such as the antisocial personality. Anxiety disorders, dissociative disorders, and somatoform disorders are characterized by high levels of anxiety, rigid defense mechanisms, and self-defeating behaviour patterns.

Anxiety disorders include generalized anxiety disorder, panic disorder (with or without agoraphobia), agoraphobia, specific phobia, social phobia, obsessive-compulsive disorders, and post-traumatic or acute stress disorders. Dissociative disorders may take the form of amnesia, fugue, or identity disorder (multiple personality). Somatoform disorders centre on physical complaints that mimic disease or disability.

Psychodynamic explanations of anxiety disorders emphasize unconscious conflicts. The humanistic approach emphasizes faulty self-images. The behavioural approach emphasizes the effects of learning, particularly avoidance learning. The cognitive approach stresses maladaptive thinking patterns.

Psychosis is a break in contact with reality. Persons suffering from delusional disorders have delusions of grandeur, persecution, infidelity, romantic attraction, or physical disease. The most common delusional disorder is paranoid psychosis.

Schizophrenia is the most common psychosis. Four types of schizophrenia are: disorganized, catatonic, paranoid, and undifferentiated. Explanations of schizophrenia emphasize environmental stress, inherited susceptibility, and biochemical abnormalities.

Mood disorders involve disturbances of emotion. Two moderate mood disorders are dysthymic disorder and cyclothymic disorder. Major mood disorders include bipolar disorders and major depressive disorder. Seasonal affective disorder is another common form of depression. Biological, psychoanalytic, cognitive, and behavioural theories of depression have been proposed. Heredity is clearly a factor in susceptibility to mood disorders.

Two basic approaches to treating major disorders are psychotherapy and medical therapies. Prolonged hospitalization has been discouraged by deinstitutionalization and by partial-hospitalization policies. Community mental health centres attempt to prevent mental health problems.

Suicide is statistically related to such factors as age, sex, marital status, ethnicity and place of residence. However, in individual cases the potential for suicide is best identified by a desire to escape, unbearable psychological pain, frustrated psychological needs, and a constriction of options. Suicide can sometimes be prevented by the efforts of family, friends, and mental health professionals.

Learning Objectives

1. Present information to indicate the magnitude of mental health problems in this country.

2. Define *psychopathology*.

3. Describe the following ways of viewing normality including the shortcoming(s) of each:
   a. subjective discomfort
   b. statistical abnormality
   c. social nonconformity (Include the concept of situational context.)
   d. cultural relativity

4. Discuss gender bias in judging abnormality.

5. State conditions under which a person is usually judged to need help.

6. Generally describe each of the following categories of mental disorders found in the DSM-IV-TR:
   a. psychotic disorders
   b. organic mental disorders
   c. substance related disorders
   d. mood disorders
   e. anxiety disorders
   f. somatoform disorders
   g. dissociative disorders
   h. personality disorders
   i. sexual and gender-identity disorders

7. List the four general categories of risk factors for mental disorders.

8. Define *insanity*.

9. List and briefly describe the ten different types of personality disorders.

10. Describe the distinctive characteristics, causes, and treatment of the antisocial personality.

11. Differentiate anxiety from fear.

12. Outline the four features of anxiety-related problems.

13. State what is usually meant when the term *nervous breakdown* is used. Differentiate this category from an anxiety disorder and an adjustment disorder.

14. Define the key element of most anxiety disorders. Differentiate generalized anxiety disorders from panic disorders.

15. Describe the following conditions:
   a. agoraphobia
   b. specific phobia
   c. social phobia
   d. obsessive-compulsive disorder
   e. stress disorder
      i) post-traumatic stress disorder
      ii) acute stress disorder
   f. dissociative disorders
      i) dissociative amnesia
      ii) dissociative fugue

iii)   dissociative identity disorder

g.   somatoform disorders

   i)   hypochondriasis

   ii)   somatization disorder

   iii)   pain disorder

   iv)   conversion disorder

16.   Discuss how each of the four major perspectives in psychology explains anxiety disorders.

a.   psychodynamic

b.   humanistic (Include the concept of self-image.)

c.   behavioural (Include the terms *self-defeating, paradox, avoidance learning,* and *anxiety reduction hypothesis.*)

d.   cognitive

17.   Define the term *psychosis.*

18.   List five major characteristics of a psychosis.

19.   Define *delusion.* Give an example of a delusion.

20.   Define *hallucination* and name the most common type.

21.   Describe the emotional, communication, and personality changes that may occur in someone with a psychosis.

22.   State what the term *organic psychosis* means.

23.   Briefly describe dementia and Alzheimer's disease, including its incidence, symptoms, and neurological concomitants.

24.   Describe the characteristics of delusional disorders, including each of the five delusional types.

25.   Describe a paranoid psychosis. Explain why treatment of this condition is difficult.

26.   Generally describe schizophrenia.

27.   List and describe the four major types of schizophrenia.

28.   Explain how paranoid delusional disorder and paranoid schizophrenia differ.

29.   Describe the roles of the following three areas as causes of schizophrenia:

a.   environment

   i)   prenatal problems and birth complications

   ii)   psychological trauma

   iii)   disturbed family environment

   iv)   deviant communication patterns

b.   heredity

c.   brain chemistry

   i)   dopamine

   ii)   CT, MRI, and PET scans

30.   Describe the general relationship between violence and mental illness.

31. Discuss the stress-vulnerability model of psychosis.

32. Describe the characteristics of depressive disorders.

33. List and describe the four major mood disorders.

34. Generally describe the likely causes of mood disorders. Include the condition known as SAD.

35. List and describe two basic kinds of treatment for major mental disorders.

36. Define *pharmacotherapy*. List and describe the three classes of drugs used to treat psychopathology.

37. Describe the role of hospitalization and partial hospitalization in the treatment of psychological disorders.

38. Discuss the role of community mental health centres in mental health.

39. Discuss how each of the following factors affects suicide rates: sex, age, ethnicity, place of residence, income, marital status.

40. List the eight major risk factors which typically precede suicide. Discuss why people try to kill themselves.

41. List four common characteristics of suicidal thoughts and feelings.

42. Explain how you can help prevent suicide.

Practice Quizzes

Recite and Review

- *How is normality defined, and what are the major psychological disorders?*

Recite and Review: Pages 449−456

1. Psychopathology refers to mental _____ themselves or to psycholog-ically _____ behaviour.

2. Formal definitions of abnormality usually take into account subjective _____ (private feelings of suffering or unhappiness).

3. Statistical definitions define abnormality as an extremely _____ or _____ score on some dimension or measure.

4. Social non-conformity is a failure to follow societal _____ for acceptable conduct.

5. Frequently, the _____ or situational context that a behaviour takes place in affects judgments of normality and abnormality.

6. _____ of the preceding definitions are relative standards.

7. A key element in judgments of disorder is that a person's _____ must be maladaptive (it makes it difficult for the person to _____ to the demands of daily life).

8. A _____ disorder is a significant impairment in psychological functioning.

9. Major disorders and categories of psychopathology are described in the Diagnostic and Statistical _____ of _____ Disorders (DSM-IV-TR).

10. Psychotic disorders are characterized by a retreat from _____ , by hallucinations and delusions, and by _____ withdrawal.

11. Organic mental disorders are problems caused by _____ injuries and _____ .

12. Substance related disorders are defined as abuse of or dependence on _____ - or behaviour-altering _____ .

13. Mood disorders involve disturbances in affect, or _____ .

14. Anxiety disorders involve high levels of fear or _____ and distortions in behaviour that are _____ related.

15. Somatoform disorders involve physical symptoms that mimic physical _____ or injury for which there is no identifiable _____ .

16. Dissociative disorders include cases of sudden amnesia, multiple _____ , or episodes of depersonalization.

17. Personality disorders are deeply ingrained, unhealthy _____ patterns.

18. Sexual and gender disorders include _____ identity disorders, paraphilias, and _____ dysfunctions.

19. In the past, the term *neurosis* was used to describe milder, _____ related disorders. However, the term is fading from use.

20. Insanity is a _____ term defining whether a person may be held responsible for his or her actions. Sanity is determined in _____ on the basis of testimony by expert witnesses.

• *What is a personality disorder?*

Recite and Review: Pages 456–458

21. Personality disorders are deeply ingrained _____ personality patterns.

22. Antisocial persons (sociopaths) seem to lack a _____ . They are _____ shallow and manipulative.

23. Individuals with an antisocial personality often had a _____ childhood (i.e. were neglected, or suffered physical abuse). Evidence has also been found for neurological _____ in sociopaths.

• *What problems result when a person suffers high levels of anxiety?*

Recite and Review: Pages 458–463

24. Anxiety disorders, dissociative disorders, and somatoform disorders involve high levels of _____ , rigid _____ mechanisms, and self-defeating behaviour patterns.

25. The term nervous breakdown has no formal meaning. However, "emotional breakdowns" do correspond somewhat to adjustment disorders, in which the person is overwhelmed by ongoing _____ _____ .

26. Anxiety disorders include generalized anxiety disorder (chronic _____ and worry) and panic disorder (anxiety attacks, panic, free- _____ anxiety).

27. Panic disorder may occur with or without agoraphobia (fear of _____ places, unfamiliar situations, or leaving the _____).

28. Other anxiety disorders are agoraphobia and _____ phobia (irrational fears of specific objects or situations).

29. In the anxiety disorder called social phobia, the person fears being _____ , evaluated, embarrassed, or humiliated by others in _____ situations.

30. Obsessive-compulsive disorders (obsessions and compulsions), and post-traumatic stress disorder or acute stress disorder (emotional disturbances triggered by severe _____) are also classified as _____ disorders.

31. Dissociative disorders may take the form of dissociative amnesia (loss of _____ and personal identity) or _____ fugue (flight from familiar surroundings).

32. A more dramatic problem is dissociative identity disorder, in which a person develops _____ personalities.

33. Somatoform disorders centre on physical complaints that mimic _____ or disability.

34. In hypochondriasis, persons think that they have specific diseases, when they are, in fact _____ .

35. In a somatization disorder, the person has numerous _____ complaints. The person repeatedly seeks medical _____ for these complaints, but no organic problems can be found.

36. Somatoform pain refers to discomfort for which there is no identifiable _____ cause.

37. In conversion disorders, actual symptoms of disease or disability develop but their causes are really _____ .

- ## *How do psychologists explain anxiety-based disorders?*

Recite and Review: Pages 464—466

38. The psychodynamic approach emphasizes _____ conflicts within the personality as the cause of disabling anxiety.

39. The humanistic approach emphasizes the effects of a faulty _____ .

40. The behavioural approach emphasizes the effects of previous _____ , particularly avoidance _____ .

41. Some patterns in anxiety disorders can be explained by the _____ reduction hypothesis, which states that immediate _____ from anxiety rewards self-defeating behaviours.

42. According to the cognitive view, distorted _____ patterns cause anxiety disorders.

- ## *What are the general characteristics of psychotic disorders?*

Recite and Review: Pages 468—469

43. Psychosis is a _____ in contact with reality.

44. Psychosis is marked by delusions, _____ (false sensations), and sensory changes.

45. Other symptoms of psychosis are disturbed emotions, disturbed communication, and _____ disintegration.

46. An organic psychosis is based on known injuries or _____ of the brain.

47. The most common _____ problem is dementia, a serious mental impairment in old age caused by deterioration of the _____ .

48. One of the common causes of _____ is Alzheimer's disease.

- ## *How do delusional disorders differ from other forms of psychosis?*

Recite and Review: Pages 469—474

49. A diagnosis of delusional disorder is based primarily on the presence of _____ (false beliefs).

50. Delusions may concern grandeur, _____ (harassment or threat), infidelity, _____ attraction, or physical disease.

51. The most common delusional disorder is paranoid psychosis. Because they often have intense and irrational delusions of _____ , paranoids may be violent if they believe they are threatened.

- ## *What forms does schizophrenia take? What causes it?*

Recite and Review: Pages 469—474

52. Schizophrenia is distinguished by a _____ between _____ and emotion, and by delusions, hallucinations, and communication difficulties.

53. Disorganized schizophrenia is marked by extreme _____ disintegration and silly, bizarre, or obscene behaviour. _____ impairment is usually extreme.

54. Catatonic schizophrenia is associated with stupor, _____ (inability to speak), _____ flexibility, and odd postures. Sometimes violent and agitated behaviour also occurs.

55. In paranoid schizophrenia (the most common type), outlandish delusions of grandeur and _____ are coupled with psychotic symptoms and personality breakdown.

56. Undifferentiated schizophrenia is the term used to indicate a _____ of clear-cut patterns of disturbance.

57. Current explanations of schizophrenia emphasize a combination of environmental _____ , inherited susceptibility, and biochemical _____ in the body or brain.

58. A number of environmental factors appear to increase the risk of developing schizophrenia. These include viral _____ during the mother's pregnancy and _____ complications.

59. Early psychological _____ (psychological injury or shock) and a disturbed _____ environment, especially one marked by deviant communication, also increase the risk of schizophrenia.

60. Studies of _____ and other close relatives strongly support heredity as a major factor in schizophrenia.

61. Recent biochemical studies have focused on abnormalities in brain _____ substances, especially dopamine and its receptor sites.

62. Additional abnormalities in brain structure or _____ have been detected in schizophrenic brains by the use of CT scans, MRI scans, and PET scans.

63. The dominant explanation of schizophrenia is the _____ -vulnerability model.

- ## *What are mood disorders? What causes depression?*

Recite and Review: Pages 475—478

64. Mood disorders primarily involve disturbances of mood or _____ .

65. Long-lasting, though relatively moderate, _____ is called a dysthymic disorder.

66. Chronic, though moderate, swings in mood between _____ and _____ are called a cyclothymic disorder.

67. In a bipolar I disorder the person alternates between extreme mania and _____ .

68. In a bipolar II disorder the person is mostly _____ , but has had at least one episode of hypomania (mild _____).

69. The problem known as major depressive disorder involves extreme sadness and despondency, but no evidence of _____ .

70. Major mood disorders more often appear to be endogenous (produced from _____) rather than reactions to _____ events.

71. _____ affective disorder (SAD), which occurs during the _____ months is another common form of depression. SAD is typically treated with phototherapy.

72. Biological, psychoanalytic, cognitive, and _____ theories of depression have been proposed. Heredity is clearly a factor in susceptibility to mood disorders.

73. Psychotherapy is any psychological treatment for behavioural or emotional problems. _____ _____ disorders are more often treated medically, rather than with psychotherapy.

74. Hospitalization is often associated with the administration of _____ therapies, and it is also considered a form of treatment.

75. Prolonged hospitalization has been discouraged by _____ -hospitalization policies.

76. Half-way _____ within the community can help people make the transition from a hospital or institution to _____ living.

- ## *Why do people commit suicide? Can suicide be prevented?*

Recite and Review: Psychology in Action

77. _____ is statistically related to such factors as age, sex, marital status, ethnicity and place of residence.

78. Major risk factors for suicide include _____ or _____ abuse, a prior attempt, depression, hopelessness, antisocial behaviour, suicide by relatives, shame, failure, or rejection, and the availability of a _____ .

79. In individual cases the potential for suicide is best identified by a desire to _____ , unbearable psychological pain, frustrated psychological needs, and a constriction of _____ .

80. Suicidal _____ usually precede suicide threats, which progress to suicide attempts.

81. Suicide can often be prevented by the efforts of family, friends, and mental health professionals to establish _____ and rapport with the person, and by gaining day-by-day commitments from her or him.

Connections

1.	_____ DSM	a.	once considered a disorder
2.	_____ drapetomania	b.	physical symptoms
3.	_____ psychosis	c.	legal problem
4.	_____ mood disorder	d.	outdated term
5.	_____ somatoform disorder	e.	sexual deviation
6.	_____ insanity	f.	diagnostic manual
7.	_____ organic disorder	g.	retreat from reality
8.	_____ neurosis	h.	arctic hysteria
9.	_____ paraphilia	i.	brain pathology
10.	_____ pibloktoq	j.	mania or depression

11.	_____ dependent personality	a.	self-importance
12.	_____ histrionic personality	b.	rigid routines
13.	_____ narcissistic personality	c.	submissiveness
14.	_____ antisocial personality	d.	little emotion
15.	_____ obsessive-compulsive	e.	attention seeking
16.	_____ schizoid personality	f.	unstable self-image
17.	_____ avoidant personality	g.	odd, disturbed thinking
18.	_____ borderline personality	h.	suspiciousness
19.	_____ paranoid personality	i.	fear of social situations
20.	_____ schizotypal personality	j.	no conscience

21.	_____ adjustment disorder	a.	afraid to leave the house
22.	_____ generalized anxiety	b.	fears being observed
23.	_____ panic disorder	c.	conversion disorder
24.	_____ agoraphobia	d.	one month after extreme stress
25.	_____ specific phobia	e.	dissociation
26.	_____ social phobia	f.	less than a month after extreme stress
27.	_____ PTSD	g.	sudden attacks of fear
28.	_____ acute stress disorder	h.	normal life stress
29.	_____ glove anesthesia	i.	chronic worry
30.	_____ fugue	j.	fears objects or activities

31.	_____ schizotypal	a.	incoherence, bizarre thinking
32.	_____ catatonic type	b.	false belief
33.	_____ paranoid type	c.	personality disorder
34.	_____ disorganized type	d.	depression and hypomania
35.	_____ psychological trauma	e.	stuporous or agitated
36.	_____ twin studies	f.	severe mania and depression
37.	_____ dopamine	g.	genetics of schizophrenia
38.	_____ delusion	h.	grandeur or persecution
39.	_____ bipolar I	i.	chemical messenger
40.	_____ bipolar II	j.	risk factor for schizophrenia

Check Your Memory

Check Your Memory: Pages 449—456

1. Psychopathology refers to the study of mental disorders and to disorders themselves.
   True or False

2. One out of every 10 persons will require mental hospitalization during his or her lifetime.
    True or False

3. Statistical definitions do not automatically tell us where to draw the line between normality and abnormality.
    True or False

4. All cultures classify people as abnormal if they fail to communicate with others.
    True or False

5. Gender is a common source of bias in judging normality.
    True or False

6. Being a persistent danger to oneself or others is regarded as a clear sign of disturbed psychological functioning.
    True or False

7. Poverty, abusive parents, low intelligence, and head injuries are risk factors for mental disorder.
    True or False

8. "Organic mental disorders" is one of the major categories in DSM-IV-TR.
    True or False

9. Insanity is a legal term in the Canadian criminal code.
    True or False

10. Koro, locura, and pibloktoq are brain diseases that cause psychosis.
    True or False

11. Multiple personality is a dissociative disorder.
    True or False

12. Neurosis is a legal term, not a type of mental disorder.
    True or False

Check Your Memory: Pages 456—458

13. Histrionic persons are preoccupied with their own self-importance.
    True or False

14. Personality disorders usually appear suddenly in early adulthood.
    True or False

15. The schizoid person shows little emotion and is uninterested in relationships with others.
    True or False

16. Sociopaths usually have a childhood history of emotional deprivation, neglect, and abuse.
    True or False

17. All sociopaths are dangerous criminals.
    True or False

18. Antisocial behaviour typically declines somewhat after age 20.
    True or False

Check Your Memory: Pages 458—463

19. Anxiety is an emotional response to an ambiguous threat.
    True or False

20. Adjustment disorders occur when severe stresses outside the normal range of human experience push people to their breaking points.
    True or False

21. Sudden, unexpected episodes of intense panic are a key feature of generalized anxiety disorder.
    True or False

22. A person who fears he or she will have a panic attack in public places or unfamiliar situations suffers from acrophobia.
    True or False

23. Arachnophobia, claustrophobia, and pathopobia are all specific phobias.
    True or False

24. Many people who have an obsessive-compulsive disorder are checkers or cleaners.
    True or False

25. Post-traumatic stress disorder is a psychological disturbance lasting more than one month after exposure to severe stress.
    True or False

26. Twenty percent of Canadian overseas peacekeepers have developed a dissociative identity disorder.
    True or False

27. Multiple personality is the most common form of schizophrenia.
    True or False

28. Depersonalization and fusion are the goals of therapy for dissociative identity disorders.
    True or False

29. The word somatoform means "body form."
    True or False

30. An unusual lack of concern about the appearance of a sudden disability is a sign of a conversion reaction.
    True or False

Check Your Memory: Pages 464–466

31. Anxiety disorders appear to be partly hereditary.
    True or False

32. The psychodynamic approach characterizes anxiety disorders as a product of id impulses that threaten a loss of control.
    True or False

33. Carl Rogers interpreted emotional disorders as the result of a loss of meaning in one's life.
    True or False

34. Disordered behaviour is paradoxical, because it makes the person more anxious and unhappy in the long run.
    True or False

35. The cognitive view attributes anxiety disorders to distorted thinking that leads to avoidance learning.
    True or False

Check Your Memory: Pages 466–468

36. The most common psychotic hallucination is hearing voices.
    True or False

37. Even a person who displays flat affect may continue to privately feel strong emotion.
    True or False

38. Extremely psychotic behaviour tends to occur in brief episodes.
    True or False

39. Severe brain injuries or diseases sometimes cause psychoses.
    True or False

40. Children must eat leaded paint flakes before they are at risk for lead poisoning.
    True or False

41. Alzheimer's disease is a type of dementia caused by extra cell activity in the cerebellum.
    True or False

Check Your Memory: Pages 468—469

42. In delusional disorders, people have auditory hallucinations of grandeur or persecution.
    True or False

43. Delusions of persecution are a key symptom of paranoid psychosis.
    True or False

44. A person who believes that his body is diseased and rotting has a erotomanic type of delusional disorder.
    True or False

Check Your Memory: Pages 469—474

45. One person out of 100 will become schizophrenic.
    True or False

46. Schizophrenia is the most common dissociative psychosis.
    True or False

47. Silliness, laughter, and bizarre behaviour are common in disorganized schizophrenia.
    True or False

48. Periods of immobility and odd posturing are characteristic of paranoid schizophrenia.
    True or False

49. At various times, patients may shift from one type of schizophrenia to another.
    True or False

50. Exposure to influenza during pregnancy produces children who are more likely
    to become schizophrenic later in life.
    True or False

51. If one identical twin is schizophrenic, the other twin has a 46 percent chance
    of also becoming schizophrenic.
    True or False

52. Excess amounts of the neurotransmitter substance PCP are suspected as a cause of schizophrenia.
    True or False

53. The brains of schizophrenics tend to be more responsive to dopamine than the brains of normal persons.
    True or False

54. PET scans show that activity in the frontal lobes of schizophrenics tends to be abnormally low.
    True or False

Check Your Memory: Pages 475—478

55. The two most basic types of mood disorder are bipolar I and bipolar II.
    True or False

56. You have a higher chance of becoming depressed if you live in Edmonton than if you live in Beirut.
    True or False

57. In bipolar disorders, people experience both mania and depression.
    True or False

58. If a person is moderately depressed for at least two weeks, a dysthymic disorder exists.
    True or False

59. A cyclothymic disorder is characterized by moderate levels of depression and manic behaviour.
    True or False

60. Endogenous depression appears to be generated from within, with little connection to external events.
    True or False

61. Behavioural theories of depression emphasize the concept of learned helplessness.
    True or False

62. Overall, women are twice as likely as men are to become depressed.
    True or False

63. SAD is most likely to occur during the winter, in countries lying near the equator.
    True or False

64. In the approach known as partial hospitalization, patients live at home.
    True or False

65. Most halfway houses are located in community mental health centres.
    True or False

Check Your Memory: Psychology In Action

66. More men than women complete suicide.
    True or False

67. In Canada, all native groups show extremely high suicide rates.
    True or False

68. Suicide rates steadily decline after young adulthood.
    True or False

69. Most suicides involve despair, anger, and guilt.
    True or False

70. People who threaten suicide rarely actually attempt it—they're just crying wolf.
    True or False

71. Only a minority of people who attempt suicide really want to die.
    True or False

72. The risk of attempted suicide is high if a person has a concrete, workable plan for doing it.
    True or False

Final Survey and Review

• *How is normality defined, and what are the major psychological disorders?*

1. _____ refers to mental disorders themselves or to psychologically unhealthy behaviour.

2. Formal definitions of abnormality usually take into account _____ discomfort (private feelings of suffering or unhappiness).

3. _____ definitions define abnormality as an extremely high or low score on some dimension or measure.

4. _____ _____ is a failure to follow societal standards for acceptable conduct.

5. Frequently, the cultural or situational _____ that a behaviour takes place in affects judgments of normality and abnormality.

6. All of the preceding definitions are _____ standards.

7. A key element in judgments of disorder is that a person's behaviour must be _____ (it makes it difficult for the person to adapt to the environment).

8. A mental disorder is a significant impairment in _____ functioning.

9. Major disorders and categories of psychopathology are described in the _____ *and* _____ *Manual of Mental Disorders* (DSM-IV-TR).

10. _____ disorders are characterized by a retreat from reality, by _____ and delusions, and by social withdrawal.

11. _____ mental disorders are problems caused by brain injuries and diseases.

12. _____ _____ disorders are defined as abuse of or dependence on mood- or behaviour-altering drugs.

13. _____ disorders involve disturbances in _____ , or emotion.

14. _____ disorders involve high levels of fear or anxiety and distortions in behaviour that are anxiety related.

15. _____ disorders involve physical symptoms that mimic physical disease or injury for which there is no identifiable cause.

16. _____ disorders include cases of sudden _____ , multiple personality, or episodes of depersonalization.

17. _____ disorders are deeply ingrained, unhealthy personality patterns.

18. Sexual and gender disorders include gender _____ disorders, paraphilias, and sexual _____ .

19. In the past, the term _____ was used to describe milder, anxiety related disorders. However, the term is fading from use.

20. _____ is a legal term defining whether a person may be held responsible for his or her actions. Sanity is determined in court on the basis of testimony by expert witnesses.

• *What is a personality disorder?*

21. Personality disorders are deeply _____ maladaptive personality patterns.

22. _____ persons (sociopaths) seem to lack a conscience. They are emotionally shallow and _____ .

23. Antisocial personality is linked to traumatic _____ experiences and _____ problems.

• *What problems result when a person suffers high levels of anxiety?*

24. Anxiety disorders, _____ disorders, and _____ disorders are characterized by high levels of anxiety, rigid defense mechanisms, and self-defeating behaviour patterns.

25. The term nervous _____ has no formal meaning. However, people do experience _____ disorders, in which the person is overwhelmed by ongoing life stresses.

26. Anxiety disorders include _____ anxiety disorder (chronic anxiety and worry) and _____ disorder (anxiety attacks, panic, free-floating anxiety).

27. Panic disorder may occur with or without _____ (fear of public places or leaving the home).

28. Other anxiety disorders are _____ (fear of public places, _____ situations, or leaving the home) and specific phobia (irrational fears of specific objects or situations).

29. In the anxiety disorder called _____ _____ , the person fears being observed, _____ , embarrassed, or humiliated by others in social situations.

30. _____ -compulsive disorders, and _____ stress disorder (PTSD) or _____ stress disorder (emotional disturbances triggered by severe stress) are also classified as anxiety disorders.

31. Dissociative disorders may take the form of dissociative _____ (loss of memory and personal identity) or dissociative _____ (confused identity and flight from familiar surroundings).

32. A more dramatic problem is dissociative _____ _____ , in which a person develops multiple personalities.

33. _____ disorders centre on physical complaints that mimic disease or disability.

34. In _____ , persons think that they have specific diseases, when they are, in fact healthy.

35. In a _____ disorder, the person has numerous physical complaints. The person repeatedly seeks medical treatment for these complaints, but no organic problems can be found.

36. _____ _____ refers to discomfort for which there is no identifiable physical cause.

37. In _____ disorders, actual symptoms of disease or disability develop but their causes are actually psychological.

• *How do psychologists explain anxiety-based disorders?*

38. The _____ approach emphasizes unconscious conflicts within the personality as the cause of disabling anxiety.

39. The _____ approach emphasizes the effects of a faulty self-image.

40. The _____ approach emphasizes the effects of previous learning, particularly _____ learning.

41. Some patterns in anxiety disorders can be explained by the anxiety _____ hypothesis, which states that immediate relief from anxiety rewards _____ behaviours.

42. According to the _____ view, distorted thinking patterns cause anxiety disorders.

• *What are the general characteristics of psychotic disorders?*

43. _____ is a break in contact with _____ .

44. Psychosis is marked by _____ (false beliefs), hallucinations, and _____ changes.

45. Other symptoms of psychosis are disturbed emotions, disturbed _____ , and personality _____ .

46. An _____ psychosis is based on known injuries or diseases of the brain.

47. The most common organic problem is _____ , a serious mental impairment in old age caused by deterioration of the brain.

48. One of most common causes of dementia is _____ disease.

• *How do delusional disorders differ from other forms of psychosis?*

49. A _____ of _____ disorder is based primarily on the presence of delusions.

50. Delusions may concern _____ (personal importance), persecution, infidelity, romantic attraction, or physical _____ .

51. The most common delusional disorder is _____ psychosis. Because they often have intense and irrational delusions of persecution, afflicted persons may be _____ if they believe they are threatened.

- ### *What forms does schizophrenia take? What causes it?*

52. Schizophrenia is distinguished by a split between thought and _____ , and by delusions, hallucinations, and _____ difficulties.

53. _____ schizophrenia is marked by extreme personality _____ and silly, bizarre, or obscene behaviour. Social impairment is usually extreme.

54. _____ schizophrenia is associated with stupor, mutism, waxy _____ , and odd postures. Sometimes violent and agitated behaviour also occurs.

55. In _____ schizophrenia (the most common type), outlandish delusions of _____ and persecution are coupled with psychotic symptoms and personality breakdown.

56. _____ schizophrenia is the term used to indicate a lack of clear-cut patterns of disturbance.

57. Current explanations of schizophrenia emphasize a combination of _____ stress, inherited susceptibility, and _____ abnormalities in the body or brain.

58. A number of _____ factors appear to increase the risk of developing schizophrenia. These include viral infection during the mother's pregnancy and birth complications.

59. Early _____ trauma and a disturbed family environment, especially one marked by _____ communication, also increase the risk of schizophrenia.

60. Studies of twins and other close relatives strongly support _____ as a major factor in schizophrenia.

61. Recent biochemical studies have focused on abnormalities in brain transmitter substances, especially _____ and its _____ sites.

62. Additional abnormalities in brain structure or function have been detected in schizophrenic brains by the use of _____ scans, _____ scans, and _____ scans.

63. The dominant explanation of schizophrenia is the stress-_____ model.

- ### *What are mood disorders? What causes depression?*

64. Mood disorders primarily involve disturbances of _____ or emotion.

65. Long-lasting, though relatively moderate, depression is called a _____ disorder.

66. Chronic, though moderate, swings in mood between depression and elation are called a _____ disorder.

67. In a _____ _____ disorder the person alternates between extreme _____ and depression.

68. In a _____ _____ disorder the person is mostly depressed, but has had at least one episode of _____ (mild mania).

69. The problem known as _____ _____ disorder involves extreme sadness and despondency, but no evidence of mania.

70. Major mood disorders more often appear to be _____ (produced from within) rather than reactions to external events.

71. Seasonal _____ disorder (SAD), which occurs during the winter months is another common form of depression. SAD is typically treated with _____ (exposure to bright light).

72. _____ , psychoanalytic, _____ , and behavioural theories of depression have been proposed. Heredity is clearly a factor in susceptibility to mood disorders.

73. _____ is any psychological treatment for behavioural or emotional problems. Major mental disorders are more often treated medically.

74. Psychiatric _____ is often associated with the administration of medical therapies, and it is also considered a form of treatment.

75. Prolonged hospitalization has been discouraged by _____ policies.

76. _____ houses within the community can help people make the transition from a hospital or institution to independent living.

• *Why do people commit suicide? Can suicide be prevented?*

77. Suicide is _____ related to such factors as age, sex, marital status, ethnicity and place of _____ .

78. Major _____ _____ for suicide include drug or alcohol abuse, a prior attempt, depression, hopelessness, _____ behaviour, suicide by relatives, shame, failure, or rejection, and the availability of a firearm.

79. In individual cases the potential for suicide is best identified by a desire to escape, unbearable psychological _____ , _____ psychological needs, and a constriction of options.

80. Suicidal thoughts usually precede suicide _____ , which progress to suicide _____ .

81. Suicide can often be prevented by the efforts of family, friends, and mental health professionals to establish communication and _____ with the person, and by gaining day-by-day _____ from her or him.

Mastery Test

1. The difference between an acute stress disorder and PTSD is
    a. how long the disturbance lasts
    b. the severity of the stress
    c. whether the anxiety is free-floating
    d. whether the dissociative behaviour is observed

2. A person is at greatest risk of becoming schizophrenic if he or she has
    a. schizophrenic parents
    b. a schizophrenic fraternal twin
    c. a schizophrenic mother
    d. a schizophrenic sibling

3. A core feature of all abnormal behaviour is that it is
    a. statistically extreme
    b. associated with subjective discomfort
    c. ultimately maladaptive
    d. marked by a loss of contact with reality

4. Excess amounts of dopamine in the brain, or high sensitivity to dopamine provides one major explanation for the problem known as
    a. PTSD
    b. schizophrenia
    c. major depression
    d. SAD

269

5. The descriptions "acro," and "claustro," and "pyro" refer to
    a. common obsessions
    b. specific phobias
    c. free-floating anxieties
    d. hypochondriasis

6. Glove anesthesia strongly implies the existence of a _____ disorder.
    a. organic
    b. depersonalization
    c. somatization
    d. conversion

7. In the stress-vulnerability model of psychosis, vulnerability is primarily attributed to
    a. heredity
    b. exposure to influenza
    c. psychological trauma
    d. disturbed family life

8. A patient believes that she has a mysterious disease that is causing her body to "rot away." What type of symptom is she suffering from?
    a. bipolar
    b. delusion
    c. neurosis
    d. cyclothymic

9. Phototherapy is used primarily to treat
    a. postseasonal depression
    b. SAD
    c. catatonic depression
    d. affective psychoses

10. Psychopathology is defined as an inability to behave in ways that
    a. foster personal well-being
    b. match social norms
    c. lead to personal achievement
    d. do not cause anxiety

11. Which of the following is NOT characteristic of suicidal thinking?
    a. desires to escape
    b. psychological pain
    c. frustrated needs
    d. too many options

12. Fear of using the rest room in public is
    a. a social phobia
    b. an acute stress disorder
    c. a panic disorder

    d.   an adjustment disorder

13. A person who displays personality disintegration, waxy flexibility, and delusions of persecution suffers from _____ schizophrenia.

    a.   disorganized

    b.   catatonic

    c.   paranoid

    d.   undifferentiated

14. There are major gaps in your memory of events; you feel like you are a robot or a stranger to yourself. It is likely that you are suffering from

    a.   paraphilia

    b.   Alzheimer's disease

    c.   a borderline personality disorder

    d.   a dissociative disorder

15. A major problem with statistical definitions of abnormality is

    a.   calculating the normal curve

    b.   choosing dividing lines

    c.   that they do not apply to groups of people

    d.   that they do not take norms into account

16. DSM-IV-TR primarily describes and classifies _____ disorders.

    a.   mental

    b.   organic

    c.   psychotic

    d.   cognitive

17. A person who is a frequent "checker" may have which disorder?

    a.   agoraphobic

    b.   somatization

    c.   free-floating fugue

    d.   obsessive-compulsive

18. The most direct explanation for the anxiety reducing properties of self-defeating behaviour is found in

    a.   an overwhelmed ego

    b.   avoidance learning

    c.   the loss of meaning in one's life

    d.   the concept of existential anxiety

19. A person with a(an) _____ personality disorder might be described as "charming" by people who don't know the person well.

    a.   avoidance

    b.   schizoid

    c.   antisocial

    d.   dependent

20. One of the most powerful situational contexts for judging the normality of behaviour is
    a. culture
    b. gender
    c. statistical norms
    d. private discomfort

21. A person who is manic most likely suffers from a(an) _____ disorder.
    a. anxiety
    b. somatoform
    c. organic
    d. mood

22. The principal problem in paranoid psychosis is
    a. delusions
    b. hallucinations
    c. disturbed emotions
    d. personality disintegration

23. A problem that may occur with or without agoraphobia is
    a. dissociative disorder
    b. somatoform disorder
    c. panic disorder
    d. obsessive-compulsive disorder

24. Hearing voices that do not exist is an almost sure sign of a _____ disorder.
    a. psychotic
    b. dissociative
    c. personality
    d. delusional

25. A conversion reaction is a type of _____ disorder.
    a. somatoform
    b. dissociative
    c. obsessive-compulsive
    d. post-traumatic

26. The existence, in the past, of "disorders" such as "drapetomania" and "nymphomania" suggests that judging normality is greatly affected by
    a. gender
    b. cultural disapproval
    c. levels of functioning
    d. subjective discomfort

27. Which of the following terms does NOT belong with the others?
    a. neurotic disorder
    b. somatoform disorder
    c. personality disorder

    d.   dissociative disorder

28. Threats to one's self-image are a key element in the _____ approach to understanding anxiety and disordered functioning.

    a.   Freudian

    b.   humanistic

    c.   existential

    d.   behavioural

29. Which of the following is NOT classified as an anxiety disorder?

    a.   adjustment disorder

    b.   panic disorder

    c.   agoraphobia

    d.   obsessive-compulsive disorder

30. Cyclothymic disorder is most closely related to

    a.   reactive depression

    b.   major depressive disorder

    c.   bipolar disorder

    d.   SAD

31. Which of the following individuals has a higher risk of developing SAD?

    a.   a student

    b.   an individual born in the arctic

    c.   an individual from the south who moved to the north

    d.   a descendent of Icelandic settlers

Solutions

Recite and Review

1. disorders, unhealthy
2. discomfort
3. high, low
4. standards
5. cultural
6. All
7. behaviour, adapt
8. mental
9. Manual, Mental
10. reality, social
11. brain, diseases
12. mood, drugs
13. emotion
14. anxiety, anxiety
15. disease, cause
16. personality
17. personality
18. gender, sexual
19. anxiety
20. legal, court
21. maladaptive
22. conscience, emotionally
23. traumatic, problems
24. anxiety, defense
25. life, stresses
26. anxiety, floating
27. public, home
28. specific
29. observed, social
30. stress, anxiety
31. memory, dissociative
32. multiple

33. disease
34. healthy
35. physical, treatment
36. physical
37. psychological
38. unconscious
39. self-image
40. learning, learning
41. anxiety, relief
42. thinking
43. break
44. hallucinations
45. personality
46. diseases
47. organic, brain
48. dementia
49. delusions
50. persecution, romantic
51. persecution
52. split, thought
53. personality, social
54. mutism, waxy
55. persecution
56. lack
57. stress, abnormalities
58. infection, birth
59. trauma, family
60. twins
61. transmitter
62. activity
63. stress
64. emotion
65. depression
66. depression, elation
67. depression
68. depressed, mania

69. mania
70. within, external
71. Seasonal, winter
72. behavioural
73. Major, mental
74. medical
75. partial
76. houses, independent
77. Suicide
78. alcohol, drugs, firearm
79. escape, options
80. thoughts
81. communication

Connections

1. F
2. A
3. G
4. J
5. B
6. C
7. I
8. D
9. E
10. H
11. C
12. E
13. A
14. J
15. B
16. D
17. I
18. F
19. H
20. G

21. H
22. I
23. G
24. A
25. J
26. B
27. D
28. F
29. C
30. E
31. C
32. E
33. H
34. A
35. J
36. G
37. I
38. B
39. F
40. D

Check Your Memory

1. T
2. F
3. T
4. T
5. T
6. T
7. T
8. F
9. F
10. F
11. T
12. F
13. F

14. F
15. T
16. T
17. F
18. F
19. T
20. F
21. F
22. F
23. T
24. T
25. T
26. F
27. F
28. F
29. T
30. T
31. T
32. T
33. F
34. T
35. F
36. F
37. T
38. T
39. T
40. F
41. T
42. F
43. T
44. F
45. T
46. F
47. T
48. F
49. T

50. T
51. T
52. F
53. T
54. T
55. F
56. F
57. T
58. F
59. T
60. T
61. T
62. T
63. F
64. T
65. F
66. T
67. F
68. F
69. T
70. F
71. T
72. T

Final Survey and Review

1. Psychopathology
2. subjective
3. Statistical
4. Social, non-conformity
5. context
6. relative
7. maladaptive
8. psychological
9. Diagnostic, Statistical
10. Psychotic, hallucinations

11. Organic

12. Substance, related

13. Mood, affect

14. Anxiety

15. Somatoform

16. Dissociative, amnesia

17. Personality

18. identity, dysfunctions

19. neurosis

20. Insanity

21. ingrained

22. Antisocial, manipulative

23. childhood, neurological

24. dissociative, somatoform

25. breakdown, adjustment

26. generalized, panic

27. agoraphobia

28. agoraphobia, unfamiliar

29. social, phobia, evaluated

30. Obsessive, post-traumatic, acute

31. amnesia, fugue

32. identity, disorder

33. Somatoform

34. hypochondriasis

35. somatization

36. Somtoform, pain

37. conversion

38. psychodynamic

39. humanistic

40. behavioural, avoidance

41. reduction, self-defeating

42. cognitive

43. Psychosis, reality

44. delusions, sensory

45. communication, disintegration

46. organic

47. dementia

48. Alzheimer's

49. diagnosis, delusional

50. grandeur, disease

51. paranoid, violent

52. emotion, communication

53. Disorganized, disintegration

54. Catatonic, flexibility

55. paranoid, grandeur

56. Undifferentiated

57. environmental, biochemical

58. environmental

59. psychological, deviant

60. heredity

61. dopamine, receptor

62. CT, MRI, PET

63. vulnerability

64. mood

65. dysthymic

66. cyclothymic

67. bipolar, I, mania

68. bipolar, II, hypomania

69. major, depressive

70. endogenous

71. affective, phototherapy

72. Biological, cognitive

73. Psychotherapy

74. hospitalization

75. partial-hospitalization

76. Half-way

77. statistically, residence

78. risk, factors, antisocial

79. pain, frustrated

80. threats, attempts

81. rapport, commitments

Mastery Test

1. A (p. 461)

2. A (p. 472)

3. C (p. 451)

4. B (p. 471)

5. B (p. 460)

6. D (p. 463)

7. A (p. 474)

8. B (p. 468)

9. B (p. 477)

10. A (p. 449)

11. D (p. 481)

12. A (p. 460)

13. D (p. 469)

14. D (p. 462)

15. B (p. 449)

16. A (p. 451)

17. D (p. 461)

18. B (p. 465)

19. C (p. 456)

20. A (p. 450)

21. D (p. 475)

22. A (p. 468)

23. C (p. 460)

24. A (p. 466)

25. A (p. 463)

26. B (p.450)

27. A (p. 454)

28. B (p. 464)

29. A (p. 459)

30. C (p. 475)

31. C (p. 477)

Chapter 13

Therapies

Chapter Overview

Psychotherapies may be classified as individual, group, insight, action, directive, non-directive, or supportive, and combinations of these. Primitive and superstitious approaches to mental illness have included trepanning and demonology. More humane treatment began in 1793 with the work of Philippe Pinel in Paris.

Freudian psychoanalysis seeks to release repressed thoughts and emotions from the unconscious. Brief psychodynamic therapy has largely replaced traditional psychoanalysis.

Client-centred (or person-centred) therapy is a non-directive humanistic technique dedicated to creating an atmosphere of growth. Existential therapies focus on the meaning of life choices. Gestalt therapy attempts to rebuild thinking, feeling, and acting into connected wholes.

Behaviour therapists use behaviour modification techniques such as aversion therapy, systematic desensitization, operant shaping, extinction, and token economies.

Cognitive therapists attempt to change troublesome thought patterns. In rational-emotive behaviour therapy, clients learn to recognize and challenge their own irrational beliefs.

Group therapies, such as psychodrama and family therapy, may be based on individual therapy methods or special group techniques. Sensitivity groups, encounter groups, and large-group awareness trainings also try to promote constructive changes.

All psychotherapies offer a caring relationship, emotional rapport, a protected setting, catharsis, explanations for one's problems, a new perspective, and a chance to practice new behaviours. Many basic counselling skills underlie the success of therapies. Successful therapists may also need to overcome cultural barriers to be effective with people from diverse backgrounds.

Three medical approaches to the treatment of psychological disorders are pharmaco-therapy, electroconvulsive therapy, and psychosurgery.

Cognitive and behavioural techniques such as covert sensitization, thought stopping, covert reinforcement, and desensitization can aid self-management. In most communities, competent therapists can be located through public sources or by referrals.

Learning Objectives

1. Define *psychotherapy*.
2. Describe each of the following approaches to therapy:
   a. individual therapy
   b. group therapy
   c. insight therapy
   d. action therapy
   e. directive therapy
   f. non-directive therapy

      g.   time-limited therapy

      h.   supportive therapy

3.   Discuss what a person can expect as possible outcomes from psychotherapy.

4.   Briefly describe the history of the treatment of psychological problems, including in your description trepanning, demonology, exorcism, ergotism, and Pinel.

5.   Explain why the first formal psychotherapy was developed.

6.   List the four basic techniques used in psychoanalysis and explain their purpose.

7.   Name and describe the therapy that is frequently used today instead of psychoanalysis. Describe the criticism that helped prompt the switch.

8.   Contrast client-centred (humanistic) therapy and psychoanalysis.

9.   Describe client-centred therapy including the four conditions that should be maintained for successful therapy.

10.   Explain the approach of existential therapy and compare and contrast it with client-centred therapy.

11.   Briefly describe Gestalt therapy.

12.   Discuss the limitations of media phone-in psychologists and describe what the APA recommends should be the extent of their activities.

13.   Discuss the advantages and disadvantages of telephone therapy, cybertherapy, and videoconferencing therapy.

14.   Contrast the goal of behaviour therapy with the goal of insight therapies.

15.   Define *behaviour modification* and state its basic assumption.

16.   Explain the relationship of aversion therapy to classical conditioning.

17.   Describe aversion therapy and explain how it can be used to stop smoking and drinking.

18.   Explain how use of a hierarchy, reciprocal inhibition, and relaxation are combined to produce systematic desensitization.

19.   State for what desensitization is used and give an example of desensitization therapy and vicarious desensitization therapy.

20.   Explain how virtual reality exposure may be used to treat phobias. Very briefly describe eye-movement desensitization and the results of studies of EMDR.

21.   List and briefly describe the seven operant principles most frequently used by behaviour therapists.

22.   Explain how nonreward and time out can be used to bring about extinction of a maladaptive behaviour.

23.   Describe a token economy including its advantages and possible disadvantages. Include the terms token and target behaviour in your description.

24.   Describe what sets cognitive therapists apart from behaviour therapists.

25.   List and describe three thinking errors which underlie depression and explain what can be done to correct such thinking.

26.   Describe the effectiveness of cognitive therapy for depression.

27. Describe rational-emotive behaviour therapy. List the three core ideas which serve as the basis of most irrational beliefs.

28. Describe the advantages of group therapy.

29. Briefly describe each of the following group therapies:
    a. psychodrama (include role-playing, role reversal, and mirror technique)
    b. family therapy
    c. group awareness training (include sensitivity groups, encounter groups, and large group awareness training)

30. Evaluate the effectiveness of encounter groups and sensitivity groups. Include the concept of the therapy placebo effect.

31. Discuss the effectiveness of psychotherapy. Describe the rate at which doses of therapy help people improve.

32. List the eight goals of psychotherapy, and state the four means used to accomplish the goals.

33. List ten characteristics of effective therapists.

34. List and briefly describe the nine points or tips which can help a person when counselling a friend.

35. Explain what the phrase "culturally skilled counsellor" means.

36. List the three main types of somatic therapy.

37. Define *pharmacotherapy* and discuss the advantages and disadvantages of the use of pharmacotherapy in the treatment of disorders.

38. List the three major classes of drugs used in pharmacotherapy, including their effects and the types of disorders for which they are each most useful. Include the term *tardive dyskinesia* in your discussion.

39. Describe the risk-benefit controversy for drugs such as Clozaril and Risperdal.

40. Briefly describe the risks associated with self-medication with herbal extracts.

41. Describe the advantages and disadvantages of electroconvulsive therapy. Include a discussion of how the ECT debate is resolved.

42. Describe the past and current uses of psychosurgery in the treatment of psychosis. Include a description of prefrontal lobotomy and deep lesioning techniques.

43. Describe the role of community mental health centres in the treatment of psychological disorders.

44. Describe how covert sensitization, thought-stopping, and covert reinforcement can be used to reduce unwanted behaviour.

45. Give an example of how you can overcome a common fear or break a bad habit using the steps given for desensitization.

46. List and describe four indicators that may signal the need for professional psychological help.

47. List six methods a person can use for finding a therapist.

48. Describe how one can choose a psychotherapist. Include the concepts of peer counsellors, self-help groups, and bibliotherapy.

49. Summarize what is known about the importance of the personal qualities of the therapist and the client for successful therapy.

Practice Quizzes

Recite and Review

• *How do psychotherapies differ? How did modern therapies originate?*

Recite and Review: Pages 489–491

1. Psychotherapy is any psychological techniques used to facilitate _____ changes in a person's personality, _____ , or adjustment.

2. _____ therapies seek to produce personal understanding. Action therapies try to directly change troublesome thoughts, feelings, or behaviours.

3. Directive therapists provide strong _____ . Non-directive therapists assist, but do not _____ their clients.

4. Supportive therapies provide on-going support, rather than actively promoting personal _____ .

5. Therapies may be conducted either individually or in groups, and they may be _____ limited (restricted to a set number of sessions).

6. Approximately _____ percent of Canadians consulted a psychologist in the 1990s. Most of the clients seen by psychologists are women. Users tend to be middle-aged, single, _____ , widowed, and have higher education and _____ .

7. Primitive approaches to mental illness were often based on _____ .

8. Trepanning involved boring a hole in the _____ .

9. Demonology attributed mental disturbance to supernatural forces and prescribed _____ as the cure.

10. In some instances, the actual cause of bizarre behaviour may have been ergotism or _____ fungus _____ .

11. More humane treatment began in 1793 with the work of Philippe Pinel who created the first _____ _____ in Paris.

• *Is Freudian psychoanalysis still used?*

Recite and Review: Pages 492–493

12. Sigmund Freud's psychoanalysis was the first formal _____ .

13. Psychoanalysis was designed to treat cases of hysteria (physical symptoms without known _____ causes).

14. Psychoanalysis seeks to release repressed thoughts, memories, and emotions from the _____ and resolve _____ conflicts.

15. The psychoanalyst uses _____ association, _____ analysis, and analysis of resistance and transference to reveal health-producing insights.

16. Some critics have argued that traditional psychoanalysis may frequently receive credit for _____ remissions of symptoms. However, psychoanalysis has been shown to be better than no treatment at all.

17. _____ psychodynamic therapy (which relies on psychoanalytic theory but is brief and focused) is as effective as other major therapies.

- ## *What are the major humanistic therapies?*

Recite and Review: Pages 494—497

18. _____ therapies try to help people live up to their potentials and to give tendencies for mental health to emerge.

19. Carl Rogers's client-centred (or _____ -centred) therapy is non-directive and is dedicated to creating an atmosphere of _____ .

20. In client-centred therapy, unconditional _____ regard, _____ (feeling what another is feeling), authenticity, and reflection are combined to give the client a chance to solve his or her own problems.

21. Existential therapies focus on the _____ one makes in life.

22. Clients in existential therapy are encouraged through confrontation and encounter to exercise free _____ , to take responsibility for their _____ , and to find _____ in their lives.

23. Frederick Perls's Gestalt therapy emphasizes immediate _____ of thoughts and feelings.

24. The goal of Gestalt therapy is to rebuild thinking, feeling, and acting into connected _____ and to help clients break through emotional blocks.

25. Media psychologists, such as those found on the radio are supposed to restrict themselves to _____ listeners, rather than actually doing _____ .

26. Telephone therapists and cybertherapists working on the _____ may or may not be competent. Even if they are, their effectiveness may be severely limited.

27. In an emerging approach called telehealth, _____ is being done at a distance, through the use of videoconferencing (two-way _____ links).

- ## *What is behaviour therapy?*

Recite and Review: Pages 498—499

28. Behaviour therapists use various behaviour modification techniques that apply _____ principles to change human behaviour.

29. Classical conditioning is a basic form of _____ in which existing reflex responses are _____ with new conditioned stimuli.

30. In aversion therapy, classical conditioning is used to associate maladaptive behaviour with _____ or immediate discomfort in order to inhibit undesirable responses.

31. To be most effective, aversive _____ or event must be response-contingent (closely connected with negative behaviour).

- ## *How is behaviour therapy used to treat phobias, fears, and anxieties?*

Recite and Review: Pages 500—501

32. Classical conditioning also underlies _____ desensitization, a technique used to reduce fears, phobias, and anxieties.

33. In desensitization, gradual _____ and reciprocal inhibition (using one emotional state to block another) break the link between fear and particular situations.

34. Typical steps in desensitization are: Construct a fear hierarchy; learn to produce total _____ ; and perform items on the hierarchy (from least to most disturbing).

35. Desensitization may be carried out in real settings or it may be done by vividly _____ scenes from the fear hierarchy.

36. Desensitization is also effective when it is administered vicariously; that is, when clients watch _____ perform the feared responses.

37. In a newly developed technique, virtual _____ exposure is used to present _____ stimuli to patients undergoing desensitization.

38. Another new technique called eye-movement desensitization shows promise as a treatment for traumatic _____ and _____ disorders.

- ## *What role does reinforcement play in behaviour therapy?*

Recite and Review: Pages 502—504

39. Behaviour modification also makes use of operant principles, such as positive reinforcement, non-reinforcement, extinction, punishment, shaping, stimulus _____ , and _____ out.

40. Non-reward can extinguish troublesome behaviours. Often this is done by simply identifying and eliminating _____ .

41. Time out is an extinction technique in which attention and approval are withheld following undesirable _____ .

42. Time out can also be done by _____ a person from the setting in which misbehaviour occurs, so that it will not be reinforced.

43. To apply positive reinforcement and operant shaping, symbolic rewards known as tokens are often used. Tokens allow _____ reinforcement of selected target _____ .

44. Full-scale use of _____ in an institutional setting produces a token economy.

45. Toward the end of a token economy program, patients are shifted to social rewards such as recognition and _____ .

- ## *Can therapy change thoughts and emotions?*

Recite and Review: Pages 505—507

46. Cognitive therapy emphasizes changing _____ patterns that underlie emotional or behavioural problems.

47. The goals of cognitive therapy are to correct distorted thinking and/or teach improved coping _____ .

48. Aron Beck's cognitive therapy for depression corrects major distortions in thinking, including _____ perception, overgeneralization, and all-or-nothing _____ .

49. In a variation of cognitive therapy called rational-emotive behaviour therapy (REBT), clients learn to recognize and challenge their own irrational _____ which lead to upsetting consequences.

- ## *Can psychotherapy be done with groups of people?*

Recite and Review: Pages 507—509

50. Group therapy may be a simple extension of _____ methods or it may be based on techniques developed specifically for groups.

51. In psychodrama, individuals use _____ playing, _____ reversals, and the mirror technique to gain insight into incidents resembling their real-life problems.

52. In family therapy, the family group is treated as a _____ so that the entire _____ system is changed for the better.

53. Although they are not literally _____ , sensitivity groups and encounter groups attempt to encourage positive personality change.

54. In recent years, commercially offered large-group awareness _____ have become popular.

55. The therapeutic benefits of large-group techniques are questionable and may reflect nothing more than a _____ placebo effect.

• *What do various therapies have in common?*

Recite and Review: Pages 509—513

56. Psychotherapy does help people with certain psychological _____ and medical conditions such as _____ , hypertension, arthritis, diabetes and chronic low-back _____ .

57. To alleviate personal problems, all psychotherapies offer a caring relationship and _____ rapport in a protected _____ .

58. All therapies encourage catharsis and they provide explanations for the client's _____ .

59. In addition, psychotherapy provides a new perspective and a chance to practice new _____ .

60. Many basic _____ skills are used in therapy. These include listening actively and helping to clarify the problem.

61. Effective therapists also focus on feelings and avoid giving unwanted _____ .

62. It helps to accept the person's perspective, to reflect thoughts and feelings, and to be patient during _____ .

63. In counselling it is important to use _____ questions when possible and to maintain confidentiality.

64. Many _____ barriers to effective counselling and therapy exist.

65. Culturally skilled _____ have the knowledge and skills needed to intervene successfully in the lives of clients from diverse cultural backgrounds.

66. The culturally skilled counsellor must be able to establish rapport with a person from a _____ cultural background and adapt traditional theories and techniques to meet the needs of clients from non-European ethnic or racial groups, such as Native people.

• *How do psychiatrists treat psychological disorders?*

Recite and Review: Pages 513—515

67. Three _____ (bodily) approaches to treatment of psychosis are pharmacotherapy (use of _____), electroconvulsive therapy (ECT) (brain shock for the treatment of depression), and psychosurgery (surgical alteration of the _____).

68. Pharmacotherapy is done with _____ tranquilizers (anti-anxiety drugs), antipsychotics (which reduce delusions and _____), and antidepressants (_____ elevators).

69. All psychiatric drugs involve a trade-off between _____ and benefits.

70. Community mental health centres were created to help avoid or minimize _____ .

71. Community mental health centres also have as their goal the prevention of mental health problems through education, consultation, and _____ intervention.

• *How are behavioural principles applied to everyday problems? How would a person go about finding professional help?*

Recite and Review: Psychology in Action

72. In covert sensitization, aversive _____ are used to discourage unwanted behaviour.

73. Thought stopping uses mild _____ to prevent upsetting thoughts.

74. Covert reinforcement is a way to encourage desired _____ by mental rehearsal.

75. Desensitization pairs _____ with a hierarchy of upsetting images in order to lessen fears.

76. In most communities, a competent and reputable therapist can usually be located through public sources of information or by a _____ .

77. Practical considerations such as _____ and qualifications enter into choosing a therapist. However, the therapist's personal characteristics are of equal importance.

78. Self-help _____ , made up of people who share similar problems, can sometimes add valuable support to professional treatment.

Connections

1.	_____ trepanning	a.	tainted rye
2.	_____ exorcism	b.	old relationships
3.	_____ ergotism	c.	hysteria
4.	_____ Pinel	d.	total acceptance
5.	_____ Freud	e.	waiting list control
6.	_____ dream analysis	f.	client-centred
7.	_____ transference	g.	Bicêtre
8.	_____ spontaneous remission	h.	latent content
9.	_____ Rogers	i.	possession by the devil
10.	_____ unconditional postive regard	j.	release of evil spirits

11.	_____ authenticity	a.	telehealth
12.	_____ existentialist	b.	operant extinction
13.	_____ distance therapy	c.	no facades
14.	_____ Gestalt therapy	d.	thinking error
15.	_____ rapid smoking	e.	choice and responsibility
16.	_____ desensitization	f.	token economy
17.	_____ time out	g.	whole experiences
18.	_____ target behaviours	h.	aversion therapy
19.	_____ overgeneralization	i.	irrational beliefs
20.	_____ rational-emotive behaviour therapy	j.	fear hierarchy

21.	_____ psychodrama	a.	public education
22.	_____ family therapy	b.	enhanced self-awareness
23.	_____ sensitivity group	c.	emotional release
24.	_____ encounter group	d.	positive imagery
25.	_____ media psychologist	e.	shared problems
26.	_____ therapeutic alliance	f.	systems approach
27.	_____ catharsis	g.	aversive imagery
28.	_____ covert sensitization	h.	role reversals
29.	_____ covert reinforcement	i.	caring relationship
30.	_____ self-help group	j.	intense interactions

Check Your Memory

Check Your Memory: Pages 489–491

1. A particular psychotherapy could be both insight- and action-oriented.
   True or False

2. With the help of psychotherapy, chances of improvement are fairly good for phobias and low self-esteem.
   True or False

3. Psychotherapy is sometimes used to encourage personal growth for people who are already functioning well.
   True or False

4. Personal autonomy, a sense of identity, and feelings of personal worth are elements of mental health.
   True or False

5. One reason for not using psychological services is not having enough money to pay for the services.
   True or False

6. Exorcism sometimes took the form of physical torture.
   True or False

7. Trepanning was the most common treatment for ergotism.
   True or False

8. Pinel was the first person to successfully treat ergotism.
   True or False

9. The problem Freud called hysteria is now called a somatoform disorder.
   True or False

Check Your Memory: Pages 492–493

10. During free association, patients try to remember the earliest events in their lives.
    True or False

11. Freud called transference the royal road to the unconscious.
    True or False

12. The manifest content of a dream is its surface or visible meaning.
    True or False

13. In an analysis of resistance, the psychoanalyst tries to understand a client's resistance to forming satisfying relationships.
    True or False

14. Therapists use direct interviewing as part of brief psychodynamic therapy.
    True or False

15. If members of a waiting list control group improve at the same rate as people in therapy, it demonstrates that the therapy is effective.
    True or False

Check Your Memory: Pages 494—497

16. Through client-centred therapy, Carl Rogers sought to explore unconscious thoughts and feelings.
    True or False

17. The client-centred therapist does not hesitate to react with shock, dismay, or disapproval to a client's inappropriate thoughts or feelings.
    True or False

18. In a sense, the person-centred therapist acts as a psychological mirror for clients.
    True or False

19. Existential therapy emphasizes our ability to freely make choices.
    True or False

20. According to the existentialists, our choices must be courageous.
    True or False

21. Existential therapy emphasizes the integration of fragmented experiences into connected wholes.
    True or False

22. Fritz Perls was an originator of telehealth.
    True or False

23. Gestalt therapy may be done individually or in a group.
    True or False

24. Gestalt therapists urge clients to intellectualize their feelings.
    True or False

25. The APA suggests that media psychologists should discuss only problems of a general nature.
    True or False

26. Only trained professionals do telephone and internet therapies.
    True or False

27. The problem with doing therapy by videoconferencing is that facial expressions are not available to the therapist or the client.
    True or False

Check Your Memory: Pages 498—499

28. Aversion therapy is based primarily on operant conditioning.
    True or False

29. For many children, the sight of a hypodermic needle becomes a conditioned stimulus for fear because it is often followed by pain.
    True or False

30. Rapid smoking creates an aversion because people must hyperventilate to smoke at the prescribed rate.
    True or False

31. About one half of all people who quit smoking begin again.
    True or False

32. In aversion therapy for alcohol abuse, the delivery of shock must appear to be response-contingent to be most effective.
    True or False

Check Your Memory: Pages 500—501

33. During desensitization, the steps of a hierarchy are used to produce deep relaxation.
    True or False

34. Relaxation is the key ingredient of reciprocal inhibition.
    True or False

35. Clients typically begin with the most disturbing item in a desensitization hierarchy.
    True or False

36. Programs that treat fear of flying with systematic desensitization and direct exposure to airplines and flying have a high success rate.
    True or False

37. Desensitization is most effective when people are directly exposed to feared stimuli.
    True or False

38. Live or filmed models are used in vicarious desensitization.
    True or False

Check Your Memory: Pages 502—504

39. Operant punishment is basically the same thing as non-reinforcement.
    True or False

40. Shaping involves reinforcing ever closer approximations to a desired response.
    True or False

41. An undesirable response can be extinguished by reversing stimulus control.
    True or False

42. Misbehaviour tends to decrease when others ignore it.
    True or False

43. To be effective, tokens must be tangible rewards, such as slips of paper or poker chips.
    True or False

44. The value of tokens is based on the fact that they can be exchanged for other reinforcers.
    True or False

45. A goal of token economies is to eventually switch patients to social reinforcers.
    True or False

Check Your Memory: Pages 505—507

46. Cognitive therapy is especially successful in treating depression.
    True or False

47. Depressed persons tend to magnify the importance of events.
    True or False

48. Cognitive therapy is as effective as drugs for treating many cases of depression.
    True or False

49. Stress inoculation is a form of rational-emotive behaviour therapy.
    True or False

50. The A in the ABC analysis of REBT stands for "anticipation."
    True or False

51. The C in the ABC analysis of REBT stands for "consequence."
    True or False

Check Your Memory: Pages 507–509

52. The mirror technique is the principal method used in family therapy.
    True or False

53. Family therapists try to meet with the entire family unit during each session of therapy.
    True or False

54. A "trust walk" is a typical sensitivity group exercise.
    True or False

55. Sensitivity groups attempt to tear down defenses and false fronts.
    True or False

56. Large-group awareness training has been known to create emotional crises where none existed before.
    True or False

Check Your Memory: Pages 509–513

57. People are more likely to persist with drug therapy than psychotherapy.
    True or False

58. Half of all people who begin psychotherapy feel better after 8 sessions.
    True or False

59. Emotional rapport is a key feature of the therapeutic alliance.
    True or False

60. Therapy gives clients a chance to practice new behaviours.
    True or False

61. Competent counsellors do not hesitate to criticize clients, place blame when it is deserved, and probe painful topics.
    True or False

62. "Why don't you . . . Yes, but . . ." is a common game used to avoid taking responsibility in therapy.
    True or False

63. Closed questions tend to be most helpful in counselling another person.
    True or False

64. Cultural barriers to effective counselling include differences in language, social class, and non-verbal communication.
    True or False

65. A necessary step toward becoming a culturally skilled counsellor is to adopt the culture of your clients as your own.
    True or False

Check Your Memory: Pages 513–515

66. Major mental disorders are primarily treated with psychotherapy.
    True or False

67. When used for long periods of time, major tranquilizers can cause a neurological disorder.
    True or False

68. Two percent of all patients taking clozaril suffer from a serious blood disease.
    True or False

69. ECT treatments are usually given in a series of 20 to 30 sessions, occurring once a day.
    True or False

70. ECT is most effective when used to treat depression.
    True or False

71. The prefrontal lobotomy is the most commonly performed type of psychosurgery today.
    True or False

72. Psychosurgeries performed by deep lesioning can be reversed if necessary.
    True or False

73. Crisis intervention is typically one of the services provided by community mental health centres.
    True or False

Check Your Memory: Psychology in Action

74. Disgusting images are used in thought stopping.
    True or False

75. To do covert sensitization, you must first learn relaxation exercises.
    True or False

76. Covert reinforcement should be visualized before performing steps in a fear hierarchy.
    True or False

77. The tension-release method is used to produce deep relaxation.
    True or False

78. Significant changes in your work, relationships, or use of drugs or alcohol can be signs that you should seek professional help.
    True or False

79. In Canada, your visits to a psychologist will be covered by the Medicare program but psychiatric services will not be covered.
    True or False

80. For some problems, paraprofessional counsellors and self-help groups are as effective as professional psychotherapy.
    True or False

81. All major types of psychotherapy are about equally successful.
    True or False

Final Survey and Review

• *How do psychotherapies differ? How did modern therapies originate?*

1. _____ is any psychological technique used to facilitate positive changes in a person's _____ , behaviour, or adjustment.

2. Insight therapies seek to produce personal understanding. _____ therapies try to directly change troublesome thoughts, feelings, or behaviours.

3. _____ therapists provide strong guidance. _____ therapists assist, but do not guide their clients.

4. _____ therapies provide on-going assistance, rather than actively promoting personal change.

5. Therapies may be conducted either _____ or in _____ , and they may be time _____ (restricted to a set number of sessions).

6. Most Canadians who did psychotherapy in the 1990s were women. Users also tend to be _____ , single, separated, widowed, and have a higher _____ and income.

7. _____ approaches to mental illness were often based on superstition.

8. _____ involved boring a hole in the skull.

9. _____ attributed mental disturbance to supernatural forces and prescribed exorcism as the cure.

10. In some instances, the actual cause of bizarre behaviour may have been _____ , a type of _____ poisoning.

11. More humane treatment began in 1793 with the work of Philippe _____ who created the first mental hospital in _____ .

- ## *Is Freudian psychoanalysis still used?*

12. Sigmund _____ _____ was the first formal psychotherapy.

13. Psychoanalysis was designed to treat cases of _____ (physical symptoms without known physical causes).

14. Psychoanalysis seeks to release _____ thoughts, memories, and emotions from the unconscious and resolve unconscious conflicts.

15. The psychoanalyst uses free _____ , dream analysis, and analysis of _____ and transference to reveal health-producing insights.

16. Some critics have argued that traditional psychoanalysis may frequently receive credit for spontaneous _____ of symptoms. However, psychoanalysis has been shown to be better than no treatment at all.

17. Brief _____ therapy (which relies on _____ theory but is brief and focused) is as effective as other major therapies.

- ## *What are the major humanistic therapies?*

18. Humanistic therapies try to help people live up to their _____ and to give tendencies for mental health to emerge.

19. Carl _____ client-centred (or person-centred) therapy is non- _____ and is dedicated to creating an atmosphere of growth.

20. In client-centred therapy, _____ positive regard, empathy, authenticity, and _____ (restating thoughts and feelings) are combined to give the client a chance to solve his or her own problems.

21. _____ therapies focus on the choices one makes in life.

22. Clients in existential therapy are encouraged through _____ and _____ to exercise free will, to take responsibility for their choices, and to find meaning in their lives.

23. Frederick Perls's _____ therapy emphasizes immediate awareness of thoughts and feelings.

24. The goal of Perls's approach is to rebuild thinking, feeling, and acting into connected wholes and to help clients break through _____ _____ .

25. _____ psychologists, such as those found on the radio are supposed to restrict themselves to educating listeners, rather than actually doing therapy.

26. Telephone therapists and _____ working on the Internet may or may not be competent. Even if they are, their effectiveness may be severely limited.

27. In an emerging approach called _____ , therapy is being done at a distance, through the use of _____ (two-way audio-video links).

• *What is behaviour therapy?*

28. _____ therapists use various behaviour _____ techniques that apply learning principles to change human behaviour.

29. _____ conditioning is a basic form of learning in which existing _____ responses are associated with new conditioned stimuli.

30. In _____ therapy, classical conditioning is used to associate maladaptive behaviour with pain in order to inhibit undesirable responses.

31. To be most effective, an aversive stimuli or event must be _____ (closely connected with negative behaviour).

• *How is behaviour therapy used to treat phobias, fears, and anxieties?*

32. Classical conditioning also underlies systematic _____ , a technique used to reduce fears, phobias, and anxieties.

33. In this approach, gradual exposure and reciprocal _____ (e.g. relaxation blocking _____) break the link between fear and particular situations.

34. Typical steps are: Construct a fear _____ ; learn to produce total relaxation; and perform items on the _____ (from least to most disturbing).

35. Desensitization may be carried out in real settings or it may be done by vividly imagining scenes from the _____ _____ .

36. Desensitization is also effective when it is administered _____ ; that is, when clients watch models perform the feared responses.

37. In a newly developed technique, _____ reality _____ is used to present fear stimuli to patients undergoing desensitization.

38. Another new technique called _____ desensitization shows promise as a treatment for traumatic memories and stress disorders.

• *What role does reinforcement play in behaviour therapy?*

39. Behaviour modification also makes use of _____ principles, such as positive reinforcement, non-reinforcement, _____ (eliminating responses), punishment, _____ (molding responses), stimulus control, and time out.

40. _____ can extinguish troublesome behaviours. Often this is done by simply identifying and eliminating reinforcers.

41. Time out is an _____ technique in which attention and approval are withheld following undesirable responses.

42. Time out can also be done by removing a person from the _____ in which misbehaviour occurs, so that it will not be _____ .

43. To apply positive reinforcement and operant shaping, symbolic rewards known as _____ are often used. These allow immediate reinforcement of selected _____ behaviours.

44. Full-scale use of symbolic rewards in an institutional setting produces a _____ _____ .

45. Toward the end of such programs, patients are shifted to _____ rewards such as recognition and approval.

- ### *Can therapy change thoughts and emotions?*

46. _____ therapy emphasizes changing thinking patterns that underlie emotional or behavioural problems.

47. Its goals are to correct distorted thinking and/or teach improved _____ skills.

48. Aron _____ therapy for depression corrects major distortions in thinking, including selective perception, _____ , and all-or-nothing thinking.

49. In a variation called _____ _____ therapy (REBT), clients learn to recognize and challenge their own irrational beliefs which lead to upsetting consequences.

- ### *Can psychotherapy be done with groups of people?*

50. _____ therapy may be a simple extension of individual methods or it may be based on techniques developed specifically for _____ .

51. In _____ , individuals use role playing, role _____ , and the mirror technique to gain insight into incidents resembling real-life problems.

52. In _____ therapy, the _____ group is treated as a unit so that the entire family system is changed for the better.

53. Although they are not literally psychotherapies, sensitivity groups and _____ groups attempt to encourage positive personality change.

54. In recent years, commercially offered large-group _____ trainings have become popular.

55. The therapeutic benefits of large-group techniques are questionable and may reflect nothing more than a therapy _____ effect.

- ### *What do various therapies have in common?*

56. _____ does help people with certain psychological disorders and _____ conditions such as headaches, _____ , arthritis, diabetes, and chronic low-back _____ .

57. To alleviate personal problems, all psychotherapies offer a caring relationship and emotional _____ in a _____ setting.

58. All therapies encourage _____ (emotional release) and they provide explanations for the client's problems.

59. In addition, psychotherapy provides a new _____ and a chance to practice new behaviours.

60. Many basic counselling skills are used in therapy. These include listening _____ and helping to _____ the problem.

61. Effective therapists also focus on _____ and avoid giving unwanted advice.

62. It helps to accept the person's _____ , to _____ thoughts and feelings, and to be patient during silences.

63. In counselling it is important to use open questions when possible and to maintain _____ .

64. Many cultural _____ to effective counselling and therapy exist.

65. _____ _____ counsellors have the knowledge and skills needed to intervene successfully in the lives of clients from diverse cultural backgrounds.

66. The aware counsellor must be able to establish _____ with a person from a different cultural background and _____ traditional theories and techniques to meet the needs of clients from non-European ethnic or racial groups such as Native people.

- ### *How do psychiatrists treat psychological disorders?*

67. Three somatic approaches to treatment of psychosis are _____ (use of drugs), _____ therapy (ECT), and psychosurgery.

68. Pharmacotherapy is done with minor tranquilizers (anti-anxiety drugs), _____ (which control delusions and hallucinations), and _____ (mood elevators).

69. All psychiatric drugs involve a trade-off between risks and _____ .

70. _____ _____ health centres were created to help avoid or minimize hospitalization.

71. These centres also have as their goal the _____ of mental health problems through education, consultation, and crisis _____ .

- ### *How are behavioural principles applied to everyday problems?*

72. In _____ sensitization, aversive images are used to discourage unwanted behaviour.

73. _____ _____ uses mild punishment to prevent upsetting thoughts.

74. Covert _____ is a way to encourage desired responses by mental rehearsal.

75. _____ pairs relaxation with a hierarchy of upsetting images in order to lessen fears.

- ### *How would a person go about finding professional help?*

76. In most communities, a _____ and reputable therapist can usually be located through public sources of information or by a referral.

77. Practical considerations such as cost and qualifications enter into choosing a therapist. However, the therapist's _____ _____ are of equal importance.

78. _____ groups made up of people who share similar _____ can sometimes add valuable support to professional treatment.

Mastery Test

1. To demonstrate that spontaneous remissions are occurring, you could use a
   a. patient-defined hierarchy
   b. waiting list control group
   c. target behaviour group
   d. short-term dynamic correlation

2. In desensitization, relaxation is induced to block fear, a process known as
   a. systematic adaptation
   b. vicarious opposition
   c. stimulus control
   d. reciprocal inhibition

3. Role reversals and the mirror technique are methods of
   a. psychodrama
   b. person-centred therapy
   c. family therapy
   d. brief psychodynamic therapy

4. One thing that both trepanning and exorcism have in common is that both were used
   a. to treat ergotism
   b. by Pinel in the Bicêtre Aslyum
   c. to remove spirits
   d. to treat cases of hysteria
5. Unconditional positive regard is a concept particularly associated with
   a. Beck
   b. Frankl
   c. Perls
   d. Rogers
6. Many of the claimed benefits of large-group awareness trainings appear to represent a therapy _____ effect,
   a. remission
   b. education
   c. placebo
   d. transference
7. Personal change is LEAST likely to be the goal of
   a. supportive therapy
   b. action therapy
   c. desensitization
   d. humanistic therapy
8. Inducing seizures is a standard part of using
   a. Gestalt therapy
   b. antidepressants
   c. ECT
   d. cybertherapy
9. Which counselling behaviour does not belong with the others listed here?
   a. paraphrasing
   b. judging
   c. reflecting
   d. active listening
10. In psychoanalysis, the process most directly opposite to free association is
   a. resistance
   b. transference
   c. symbolization
   d. remission
11. Identification of target behaviours is an important step in designing
   a. a desensitization hierarchy
   b. activating stimuli
   c. token economies

> d. encounter groups

12. A person who wants to lose weight looks at a dessert and visualizes maggots crawling all over it. The person is obviously using
    a. systematic adaptation
    b. covert sensitization
    c. stress inoculation
    d. systematic desensitization

13. Which of the following is NOT a humanistic therapy?
    a. client-centred
    b. Gestalt
    c. existential
    d. cognitive

14. Not many emergency room doctors drive without using their seatbelts. This observation helps explain the effectiveness of
    a. systematic desensitzation
    b. aversion therapy
    c. covert reinforcement
    d. the mirror technique

15. Telephone counsellors have little chance of using which element of effective psychotherapy?
    a. empathy
    b. non-directive reflection
    c. the therapeutic alliance
    d. accepting the person's frame of reference

16. Which of the following is a self-management technique?
    a. thought stopping
    b. vicarious reality exposure
    c. REBT
    d. EMDR

17. A good example of a non-directive insight therapy is _____ therapy.
    a. client-centred
    b. Gestalt
    c. psychoanalytic
    d. brief psychodynamic

18. Which statement about psychotherapy is true?
    a. Most therapists are equally successful.
    b. Most techniques are equally successful.
    c. Therapists and clients need not agree about the goals of therapy.
    d. Effective therapists instruct their clients not to discuss their therapy with anyone else.

19. Analysis of resistances and transferences is a standard feature of
    a. client-centred therapy
    b. Gestalt therapy

    c.   REBT

    d.   psychoanalysis

20. Both classical and operant conditioning are the basis for
    a. desensitization
    b. token economies
    c. behaviour therapy
    d. aversion therapy

21. Rational-emotive behaviour therapy is best described as
    a. insight, non-directive, individual
    b. insight, supportive, individual
    c. action, supportive, group
    d. action, directive, individual

22. Deep lesioning is a form of
    a. ECT
    b. psychosurgery
    c. pharmacotherapy
    d. PET

23. Identifying and removing rewards is a behavioural technique designed to bring about
    a. operant shaping
    b. extinction
    c. respondent aversion
    d. token inhibition

24. Culturally skilled counsellors must be aware of their own cultural backgrounds, as well as
    a. the percentage of ethnic populations in the community
    b. that of their clients
    c. the importance of maintaining confidentiality
    d. the life goals of minorities

25. A behavioural therapist would treat acrophobia with
    a. desensitization
    b. aversion therapy
    c. covert sensitization
    d. cybertherapy

26. Which technqiue most closely relates to the idea of non-directive therapy?
    a. confrontation
    b. dream analysis
    c. role reversal
    d. reflection

27. Fifty percent of psychotherapy patients say they feel better after the first _____ sessions.
    a. 4
    b. 8

c.   12

d.   20

28. Overgeneralization is a thinking error that contributes to

a.   depression

b.   somatization

c.   phobias

d.   emotional reprocessing

29. Death, freedom, and meaning are special concerns of

a.   REBT

b.   cognitive therapy

c.   existential therapy

d.   psychodrama

30. An intense awareness of present experience and breaking through emotional impasses is the heart of

a.   action therapy

b.   Gestalt therapy

c.   time-limited therapy

d.   REBT

31. The ABC's of REBT stand for

a.   anticipation, behaviour, conduct

b.   action, behaviour, conflict

c.   activating experience, belief, consequence

d.   anticipation, belief, congruent experience

32. Which of the following is NOT a "distance therapy"?

a.   REBT

b.   telephone therapy

c.   cybertherapy

d.   telehealth

33. Virtual reality exposure is a type of

a.   psychodrama

b.   ECT therapy

c.   cognitive therapy

d.   desensitization

34. ECT is most often used to treat

a.   psychosis

b.   anxiety

c.   hysteria

d.   depression

35. Which of the following is most often associated with community mental health programs?
    a.   pharmacotherapy
    b.   covert reinforcement
    c.   crisis intervention
    d.   REBT

Solutions

Recite and Review

1. positive, behaviour
2. Insight
3. guidance, guide
4. change
5. time
6. 2.15, separated, income
7. superstition
8. skull
9. exorcism
10. ergot, poisoning
11. mental, hospital
12. psychotherapy
13. physical
14. unconscious, unconscious
15. free, dream
16. spontaneous
17. Brief
18. Humanistic
19. person, growth
20. positive, empathy
21. choices
22. will, choices, meaning
23. awareness
24. wholes
25. educating, therapy
26. Internet
27. therapy, audio-video
28. learning
29. learning, associated
30. pain
31. stimuli
32. systematic
33. exposure
34. relaxation
35. imagining
36. models
37. reality, fear
38. memories, stress
39. control, time
40. reinforcers
41. responses
42. removing
43. immediate, behaviours
44. tokens
45. approval
46. thinking
47. skills
48. selective, thinking
49. beliefs
50. individual
51. role, role
52. unit, family
53. psychotherapies
54. trainings
55. therapy
56. disorders, headaches, pain
57. emotional, setting
58. problems
59. behaviours
60. counselling
61. advice
62. silences
63. open
64. cultural
65. counsellors
66. different
67. somatic, drugs, brain
68. minor, hallucinations, mood
69. risks
70. hospitalization
71. crisis
72. images
73. punishment
74. responses
75. relaxtion
76. referral
77. cost (or fees)
78. groups

Connections

1. J
2. I
3. A
4. G
5. C
6. H
7. B
8. E
9. F
10. D
11. C
12. E
13. A
14. G
15. H
16. J
17. B
18. F
19. D
20. I
21. H
22. F
23. B

24. J	**27.** F	**63.** F
25. A	**28.** F	**64.** T
26. I	**29.** T	**65.** F
27. C	**30.** F	**66.** F
28. G	**31.** T	**67.** T
29. D	**32.** T	**68.** T
30. E	**33.** F	**69.** F
	34. T	**70.** T
	35. F	**71.** F
Check Your Memory	**36.** T	**72.** F
	37. T	**73.** T
1. T	**38.** T	**74.** F
2. T	**39.** F	**75.** F
3. T	**40.** T	**76.** F
4. T	**41.** F	**77.** T
5. T	**42.** T	**78.** T
6. T	**43.** F	**79.** T
7. F	**44.** T	**80.** T
8. F	**45.** T	**81.** T
9. T	**46.** T	
10. F	**47.** T	
11. F	**48.** T	**Final Survey and Review**
12. T	**49.** F	
13. F	**50.** F	**1.** Psychotherapy, personality
14. T	**51.** T	**2.** Action
15. F	**52.** F	**3.** Directive, Non-directive
16. F	**53.** F	**4.** Supportive
17. F	**54.** T	**5.** individually, groups, limited
18. T	**55.** F	**6.** middle-aged, education
19. T	**56.** T	**7.** Primitive
20. T	**57.** F	**8.** Trepanning
21. F	**58.** T	**9.** Demonology
22. F	**59.** T	**10.** ergotism, fungus
23. T	**60.** T	**11.** Pinel, Paris
24. F	**61.** F	**12.** Freud's, psychoanalysis
25. T	**62.** T	**13.** hysteria
26. F		**14.** repressed

15. association, resistance

16. remissions

17. psychodynamic, psychoanalytic

18. potentials

19. Roger's, directive

20. unconditional, reflection

21. Existential

22. confrontation, encounter

23. Gestalt

24. emotional, blocks

25. Media

26. cybertherapists

27. telehealth, videoconferencing

28. Behaviour, modification

29. Classical, reflex

30. aversion

31. response-contingent

32. desensitization

33. inhibition, fear

34. hierarchy, hierarchy

35. fear, hierarchy

36. vicariously

37. virtual, exposure

38. eye-movement

39. operant, extinction, shaping

40. Non-reward (or non-reinforcement)

41. extinction

42. setting, reinforced

43. tokens, target

44. token, economy

45. social

46. Cognitive

47. coping

48. Beck's, overgeneralization

49. rational-emotive, behaviour

50. Group, groups

51. psychodrama, reversals

52. family, family

53. encounter

54. awareness

55. placebo

56. Psychotherapy, medical, hypertension, pain

57. rapport, protected

58. catharsis

59. perspective

60. actively, clarify

61. feelings

62. perspective, reflect

63. confidentiality

64. barriers

65. Culturally, skilled

66. rapport, adapt

67. pharmacotherapy, electroconvulsive

68. antipsychotics, antidepressants

69. benefits

70. Community, mental

71. prevention, intervention

72. covert

73. Thought, stopping

74. reinforcement

75. Desensitzation

76. competent

77. personal, characteristics

78. Self-help, problems

Mastery Test

1. B (p. 493)

2. D (p. 500)

3. A (p. 508)

4. C (p. 491)

5. D (p. 494)

6. C (p. 509)

7. A (p. 489)

8. C (p. 514)

9. B (p. 511)

10. A (p. 492)

11. C (p. 504)

12. B (p. 516)

13. D (p. 494)

14. B (p. 498)

15. C (p. 496)

16. A (p. 517)

17. A (p. 494)

18. B (p. 509)

19. D (p. 492)

20. C (p. 498, 502)

21. D (p. 506)

22. B (p. 514)

23. B (p. 503)

24. B (p. 512)

25. A (p. 499)

26. D (p. 489)

27. B (p. 509)

28. A (p. 505)

29. C (p. 494)

30. B (p. 495)

31. C (p. 506)

32. A (p. 496)

33. D (p. 501)

34. D (p. 514)

35. C (p. 515)

Chapter 14

Social Behaviour

Chapter Overview

Social psychology is the study of behaviour in social situations. Affiliating with others is related to needs for approval, support, friendship, information, and reassurance. Social comparison theory holds that we affiliate to evaluate our actions, feelings, and abilities.

Interpersonal attraction is increased by frequent contact, physical attractiveness, competence, similarity, and self-disclosure. Romantic love is marked by mutual absorption between lovers, who also like one another. Evolutionary psychology attributes human mating patterns to the reproductive challenges faced by men and women since the dawn of time.

Attribution theory summarizes how we make inferences about behaviour . The fundamental attributional error is to think that the actions of others are the result of internal causes. Because of an actor-observer bias, we tend to attribute our own behaviour to external causes.

Social influence refers to how our behaviour is changed by the behaviour of others. Examples are conformity, groupthink, obedience, and complying with direct requests. Self-assertion involves clearly stating your wants and needs to others. Learning to be assertive can be aided by role-playing.

Attitudes have belief, emotional, and action components. Attitudes are formed through direct contact, interacting with others, child-rearing, group pressures, peer-group influences, the mass media, and chance conditioning. Attitude change is related to reference group membership, to deliberate persuasion, and to personal experiences. Effective persuasion occurs when characteristics of the communicator, the message, and the audience are well matched. Cognitive dissonance theory explains how attitudes are maintained and changed. Brainwashing is forced attitude change. Some cults recruit new members with high-pressure techniques similar to brainwashing.

Prejudice is a negative attitude held toward out-group members. Prejudice can be attributed to scapegoating, personal prejudice, group norms, and authoritarian personality traits. Intergroup conflict leads to hostility and stereotyping. Status inequalities tend to build prejudices. Equal-status contact and superordinate goals tend to reduce these problems.

Ethologists blame aggression on instincts. Biological explanations emphasize brain mechanisms and physical factors. Aggression tends to follow frustration, especially when aggression cues are present. Social learning theory relates aggressive behaviour to the influence of aggressive models.

Four decision points that must be passed before we give help to others are: noticing, defining an emergency, taking responsibility, and selecting a course of action. Helping is less likely at each point when other potential helpers are present. Giving help tends to encourage others to help, too.

Multiculturalism is an attempt to give equal status to different ethnic, racial, and cultural groups. Cultural awareness is a key element in promoting greater social harmony.

Learning Objectives

1. Define *social psychology*.

2. State the needs that appear to be satisfied by affiliation and describe research indicating humans have a need to affiliate.

3. Describe social comparison theory.

4. List and describe the factors that affect interpersonal attraction. Include a description of homogamy.

5. Explain self-disclosure and discuss the effects of varying degrees of disclosure on interpersonal relationships.

6. Describe Rubin's studies of romantic love. Discuss the differences between loving and liking and between male and female friendships (including the term *mutual absorption*).

7. Define the term *evolutionary psychology* and describe how it explains the different mating preferences of males and females.

8. Define the following terms:
   a. social roles
   b. ascribed roles
   c. achieved roles
   d. role conflict
   e. group structure
   f. group cohesiveness
   g. status
   h. norm

9. Define *attribution* and state the difference between external and internal causes.

10. Explain what the fundamental attribution error is. Include the concept of the double-standard.

11. State the meaning of *social influence*.

12. Describe Asch's experiment on conformity.

13. Define *groupthink* and explain how it may contribute to poor decision-making.

14. Explain how group sanctions and unanimity affect conformity.

15. Describe Milgram's study of obedience.

16. Identify the factors which affect the degree of obedience.

17. Explain how compliance differs from simple conformity.

18. Describe the following methods of gaining compliance:
    a. foot-in-the-door
    b. door-in-the-face
    c. low-ball technique

19. Describe passive compliance and briefly explain how it applies to everyday behaviour .

20. Describe assertiveness training. Include the concept of self-assertion and contrast it with aggression.

21. Define *attitude*. Describe the belief, emotional, and action components of an attitude.

22. List, describe, and give examples of six ways in which attitudes are acquired.

23. Differentiate between reference groups and membership groups.

24. Define *persuasion* and list three factors in understanding the success or failure of persuasion.

25. List nine conditions that encourage attitude change.

26. Explain cognitive dissonance theory.

27. List five strategies for reducing dissonance.

28. Describe the effect of reward or justification on dissonance.

29. Differentiate between brainwashing and other forms of persuasion.

30. Explain how beliefs may unfreeze, change, and refreeze, and indicate how permanent the attitude changes brought about by brainwashing are.

31. Describe how cults are able to recruit, convert, and retain their members.

32. Define and differentiate between prejudice and discrimination.

33. Explain how scapegoating relates to prejudice.

34. Distinguish between personal and group prejudices.

35. Describe the characteristic beliefs (including ethnocentrism) and childhood experiences of the authoritarian personality.

36. Present the major characteristics of social stereotypes and indicate how they may lead to intergroup conflicts. Include a description of symbolic prejudice.

37. Explain how status inequalities may lead to the development of stereotypes and how equal-status contact may reduce intergroup tension. Give an example of each situation.

38. Define *superordinate goals*. Include an explanation of how they can reduce conflict and hostility.

39. Explain how a jigsaw classroom utilizes superordinate goals and helps reduce prejudice.

40. Define *aggression*. Discuss how instincts and biology affect aggression.

41. State the frustration-aggression hypothesis. Indicate why it may or may not be true.

42. Discuss how frustration, in the presence of aversive stimuli, can encourage aggression.

43. Identify proactive aggression and reactive aggression.

44. Explain how the weapons effect encourages aggression.

45. Discuss how social learning theory explains aggression.

46. Explain how television may serve as a disinhibiting factor with respect to aggression, and present evidence to support the viewpoint that watching television can cause a desensitization to violence.

47. Briefly list six ways in which parents can buffer the impact of television on children's behaviour .

48. Give an example of bystander apathy, and indicate the major factor which determines whether or not help will be given.

49. Describe four conditions that need to exist before bystanders are likely to give help. Indicate how the presence of other people can influence apathy.

50. Discuss how heightened and empathetic arousal affect helping behaviour . Include the concept of the empathy-helping relationship.

51. State three ways in which prosocial behaviour can be encouraged.

52. Define the term *multiculturalism*.

53. Discuss seven ways in which a person can become more tolerant.

54. Explain how a person can develop cultural awareness.

Practice Quizzes

Recite and Review

- ### *Why do people affiliate? What factors influence interpersonal attraction?*

Recite and Review: Pages 528–533

1. Social psychology studies how individuals behave, think, and feel in _____ situations.

2. The need to affiliate is tied to needs for _____ , support, friendship, and _____ .

3. Additionally, research indicates that we sometimes affiliate to _____ anxiety and uncertainty.

4. Social comparison theory holds that we affiliate to _____ our actions, feelings, and abilities.

5. Children are attracted to those who are similar in _____ , age, race and _____ activity. Older children (those starting high school) are more attracted to those who _____ out and who are aggressive.

6. Initial acquaintance and _____ are influenced by physical attractiveness (beauty), competence (high ability), and _____ (being alike).

7. A large degree of _____ on many dimensions is characteristic of _____ selection, a pattern called homogamy.

8. Self-disclosure (_____ oneself to others) occurs to a greater degree if two people like one another.

9. Self-disclosure follows a reciprocity _____ : Low levels of self-disclosure are met with low levels in return, whereas moderate self-disclosure elicits more personal replies.

10. Overdisclosure tends to inhibit _____ by others. What is considered overdisclosure will vary from culture to culture.

11. Self-disclosure between friends will typically increase in _____ school.

12. Romantic love can be distinguished from liking by the use of attitude scales. Dating couples _____ and _____ their partners but only _____ their friends.

13. Romantic love is also associated with greater _____ absorption between people.

14. Evolutionary psychology attributes human _____ patterns to the differing reproductive challenges faced by men and women since the dawn of time. However, women may change their criteria of selection as they become more capable of _____ themselves.

- ### How does group membership affect individual behaviour ?

Recite and Review: Pages 534−536

15. One's position in _____ defines a variety of roles to be played.

16. _____ _____ , which may be achieved or ascribed, are particular behaviour patterns associated with social positions.

17. When two or more _____ roles are held, role conflict may occur.

18. Positions within _____ typically carry higher or lower levels of status. High status is associated with special privileges and respect.

19. Group structure refers to the organization of _____ , communication pathways, and power within a group.

20. Group cohesiveness is basically the degree of _____ among group members.

21. Norms are _____ of conduct enforced (formally or informally) by _____ . Group membership helps people deal with daily _____ .

22. Attribution theory is concerned with how we make inferences about the _____ of behaviour.

23. Behaviour can be attributed to internal _____ or external _____ .

24. The fundamental attributional _____ is to ascribe the actions of others to _____ causes. This is part of the actor-observer bias, in which we ascribe the behaviour of others to _____ causes, and our own behaviour to _____ causes.

- ### What have social psychologists learned about conformity, obedience, compliance and self-assertion?

Recite and Review: Pages 536−544

25. Social influence refers to alterations in _____ brought about by the behaviour of _____ .

26. Conformity to group pressure is a familiar example of social influence. Virtually everyone _____ to a variety of broad social and cultural _____ .

27. Conformity pressures also exist within small _____ . The famous Asch experiments demonstrated that various _____ pressures encourage conformity.

28. Groupthink refers to compulsive conformity in group _____ _____ . Victims of groupthink seek to maintain each other's approval, even at the cost of critical thinking.

29. Obedience to _____ has been investigated in a variety of experiments, particularly those by Stanley Milgram.

30. _____ in Milgram's studies decreased when the victim was in the same room, when the victim and subject were face to face, when the authority figure was absent, and when others refused to obey.

31. Compliance with direct _____ by a person who has little or no social _____ is another means by which behaviour is influenced.

32. Three strategies for inducing compliance are the _____ -in-the-door technique, the door-in-the- _____ approach, and the low-ball technique.

33. Recent research suggests that in addition to excessive obedience to _____ , many people show a surprising passive compliance to unreasonable _____ .

34. Self-assertion involves clearly stating one's _____ and _____ to others.

35. Aggression expresses one's feelings and desires, but it _____ others.

36. Learning to be _____ is accomplished by role-playing and rehearsing assertive actions.

● *How are attitudes acquired and changed?*

Recite and Review: Pages 545–549

37. Attitudes are learned tendencies to respond in a _____ or _____ way.

38. Attitudes are made up of a belief component, an emotional component, and an _____ component.

39. Attitudes may be formed by _____ contact, interaction with others, the effects of _____ -rearing practices, and social pressures from group membership.

40. Peer group influences, the mass _____ , and _____ conditioning (accidental learning) also appear to be important in attitude formation.

41. The _____ consequences of actions, how we think others will _____ our actions, and habits all influence whether attitudes are converted to actions.

42. Attitudes held with conviction are most likely to be _____ in behaviour.

43. People tend to change their attitudes to match those of their reference group (a group the person _____ with and refers to for guidance).

44. Effective persuasion occurs when characteristics of the communicator, the _____ , and the audience are well matched.

45. In general, a likable and believable communicator who repeats a credible message that arouses _____ in the audience and states clear-cut _____ will be persuasive.

46. Maintaining and changing attitudes is closely related to needs for _____ in thoughts and actions. Cognitive dissonance theory explains the dynamics of such needs.

47. Cognitive dissonance occurs when there is a _____ between thoughts or between thoughts and actions.

48. The amount of reward or justification (reasons) for one's actions influences whether _____ occurs.

49. We are motivated to _____ dissonance when it occurs, often by changing beliefs or attitudes.

● *Is brainwashing actually possible? How are people converted to cult membership?*

Recite and Review: Pages 549–551

50. Brainwashing is a form of _____ attitude change. It depends on control of the target person's total environment.

51. Three steps in brainwashing are unfreezing (loosening) old attitudes and beliefs, _____ , and refreezing (rewarding and strengthening) new attitudes and beliefs.

52. Many cults recruit new members with high-pressure indoctrination techniques resembling _____ .

53. Cults attempt to catch people when they are vulnerable. Then they combine isolation, displays of _____ , discipline and rituals, intimidation, and escalating commitment to bring about _____ .

• *What causes prejudice and intergroup conflict? What can be done about these problems?*

Recite and Review: Pages 551—556

54. Prejudice is a _____ attitude held toward members of various out-groups.

55. Racism, ageism, and sexism are specific types of prejudice based on race, age, and _____ .

56. One theory attributes prejudice to scapegoating, which is a type of displaced _____ .

57. A second account says that prejudices may be held for personal reasons such as direct threats to a person's well being (personal prejudice) or simply through adherence to group _____ (group prejudice).

58. Prejudiced individuals tend to have an authoritarian _____ , characterized by rigidity, inhibition, intolerance, and _____ -simplification.

59. Authoritarians tend to be very ethnocentric (they use their own _____ as a basis for judging all others).

60. Intergroup _____ gives rise to hostility and the formation of social stereotypes (over-simplified images of members of various groups).

61. Symbolic prejudice, or prejudice expressed in _____ ways, is common today.

62. _____ inequalities (differences in power, prestige, or privileges) tend to build prejudices.

63. Equal-status contact (social interaction on an equal footing) tends to _____ prejudice.

64. Superordinate _____ (those that rise above all others) usually reduce intergroup conflict.

65. On a small scale, jigsaw _____ (which encourage cooperation through _____ interdependence) have been shown to be an effective way of combating prejudice.

• *How do psychologists explain human aggression?*

Recite and Review: Pages 557—560

66. Ethologists explain aggression as a natural expression of inherited _____ .

67. Biological explanations emphasize brain mechanisms and physical factors that _____ the threshold (trigger point) for aggression.

68. According to the frustration- _____ hypothesis, frustration and _____ are closely linked.

69. Aggression has been divided into _____ types: _____ aggression and reactive aggression.

70. Frustration is only one of many aversive _____ that can arouse a person and make aggression more likely. Aggression is especially likely to occur when _____ cues (stimuli associated with aggression) are present.

71. Social learning theory has focused attention on the role of aggressive _____ in the development of aggressive behaviour .

72. Aggressive _____ on television encourage aggression because they desensitize (lower the sensitivity of) _____ to violence and disinhibit (remove restraints against) aggressive impulses.

- **Why are bystanders so often unwilling to help in an emergency?**

Recite and Review: Pages 561−563

73. Prosocial behaviour is _____ , constructive, or altruistic toward others.

74. Bystander apathy is the unwillingness of bystanders to offer _____ to others during emergencies.

75. Four decision points that must be passed before a person gives help are: _____ , defining an emergency, taking responsibility, and selecting a course of action.

76. Helping is _____ likely at each point when other potential helpers are present.

77. Helping is encouraged by general arousal, empathic _____ , being in a good mood, low effort or _____ , and perceived similarity between the victim and the helper.

- **What can be done to lower prejudice and promote social harmony?**

Recite and Review: Psychology in Action

78. Multiculturalism is an attempt to give _____ status to different ethnic, racial, and cultural groups.

79. Greater tolerance can be encouraged by neutralizing stereotypes with individuating information (which helps see others as _____).

80. Tolerance comes from looking for commonalties with others and by avoiding the effects of just-world _____ , self-fulfilling prophecies, and _____ competition.

81. _____ awareness is a key element in promoting greater social harmony.

Connections

1.	_____ superordinate	a.	privilege and importance
2.	_____ ascribed role	b.	rule or standard
3.	_____ achieved role	c.	aggression target
4.	_____ status	d.	above all others
5.	_____ cohesiveness	e.	over-simplified image
6.	_____ norm	f.	uncomfortable clash
7.	_____ stereotype	g.	group centred
8.	_____ ethnocentric	h.	unequal treatment
9.	_____ scapegoat	i.	assigned role
10.	_____ discrimination	j.	thought reform
11.	_____ brainwashing	k.	degree of attraction
12.	_____ dissonance	l.	voluntary role

13.	_____ attribution	a.	relating self to others
14.	_____ authoritarianism	b.	honest expression of needs
15.	_____ need to affiliate	c.	following authority
16.	_____ social comparison	d.	aggression cue
17.	_____ symbolic prejudice	e.	yielding to requests
18.	_____ weapons effect	f.	rewards and punishments
19.	_____ conformity	g.	altruistic behaviour
20.	_____ group sanctions	h.	desire to associate
21.	_____ obedience	i.	matching behaviour
22.	_____ compliance	j.	F Scale
23.	_____ assertiveness	k.	modern bias
24.	_____ prosocial	l.	cause of one's behaviour

Check Your Memory

Check Your Memory: Pages 528—533

1. The need to affiliate is a basic human characteristic.
   True or False

2. People who are frightened prefer to be with others who are in similar circumstances.
   True or False

3. Social comparisons are used to confirm objective evaluations and measurements.
   True or False

4. Useful social comparisons are usually made with persons similar to ourselves.
   True or False

5. When entering high school children are less attracted to good students.
   True or False

6. Physical proximity leads us to think of people as competent, and therefore worth knowing.
   True or False

7. The halo effect is the tendency to generalize a positive or negative first impression to other personal characteristics.
   True or False

8. Collectivist cultures, such as China, show a stronger halo effect towards physically attractive people.
   True or False

9. The risk of divorce is higher than average for couples who have large differences in age and education.
   True or False

10. In choosing mates, women rank physical attractiveness as the most important feature.
    True or False

11. Self-disclosure is a major step toward friendship.
    True or False

12. Overdisclosure tends to elicit maximum self-disclosure from others.
    True or False

13. Individuals from cultures where self-disclosure is not encouraged will have a lot of difficulty working with a psychologist who expects self-disclosure.
    True or False

14. The statement, "I find it easy to ignore _____'s faults" is an item on the Liking Scale.
    True or False

15. Where their mates are concerned, men tend to be more jealous over a loss of emotional commitment than they are over sexual infidelities.
    True or False

Check Your Memory: Pages 534–536

16. *Son*, *husband*, and *teacher* are achieved roles.
    True or False

17. Persons of higher status are more likely to touch persons of lower status than the reverse.
    True or False

18. A group could have a high degree of structure but low cohesiveness.
    True or False

19. Like non-natives, natives used teasing, shaming and ridiculing to encourage conforming behaviours in the group.
    True or False

20. Canadian researchers found that all foreign-born people in their study lacked a social support network.
    True or False

21. If someone always salts her food before eating, it implies that her behaviour has an external cause.
    True or False

22. Attributing the actions of others to external causes is the most common attributional error.
    True or False

23. Unlike non-disabled children, physically disabled children do not have an actor-observer bias.
    True or False

24. Good performances by women are more often attributed to luck than skill.
    True or False

Check Your Memory: Pages 536–544

25. Conformity situations occur when a person becomes aware of differences between his or her own behaviour and that of a group.
    True or False

26. Most subjects in the Asch conformity experiments suspected that they were being deceived in some way.
    True or False

27. Seventy-five percent of Asch's subjects yielded to the group at least once.
    True or False

28. People who are anxious and those who have just witnessed someone else being ridiculed are more likely to conform to group pressure.
    True or False

29. Groupthink is more likely to occur when people emphasize the task at hand, rather than the bonds between group members.
    True or False

30. Rejection, ridicule, and disapproval are group norms that tend to enforce conformity.
    True or False

31. Research has shown that teenagers are more likely to do risky things to be popular rather than conform to the norms of the group.
    True or False

32. A unanimous majority of 3 is more powerful than a majority of 8 with 1 person dissenting.
    True or False

33. Milgram's famous shock experiment was done to study compliance and conformity.
    True or False

34. Over half of Milgram's "teachers" went all the way to the maximum shock level.
    True or False

35. Being face-to-face with the "learner" had no effect on the number of subjects who obeyed in the Milgram experiments.
    True or False

36. People are less likely to obey an unjust authority if they have seen others disobey.
    True or False

37. The foot-in-the-door effect is a way to gain compliance from another person.
    True or False

38. The low-ball technique involves changing the terms that a person has agreed to, so that they are less desirable from the person's point of view.
    True or False

39. Many people have difficulty asserting themselves because they have learned to be obedient and "good."
    True or False

40. Self-assertion involves the rights to request, reject, and retaliate.
    True or False

41. In order to be assertive, you should never admit that you were wrong.
    True or False

42. Girls will become less assertive around boys only if they do not know the boys.
    True or False

Check Your Memory: Pages 545—549

43. Attitudes predict and direct future actions.
    True or False

44. What you think about the object of an attitude makes up its belief component.
    True or False

45. If both parents belong to the same political party, their child probably will too.
    True or False

46. A person who deviates from the majority opinion in a group tends to be excluded from conversation.
    True or False

47. Heavy TV viewers feel safer than average because they spend so much time in security at home.
    True or False

48. An attitude held with conviction is more likely to be acted upon.
    True or False

49. Our attitudes are more likely to match those held by members of our reference groups than our membership groups.
    True or False

50. Persuasion refers to a deliberate attempt to change a person's reference groups.
    True or False

51. Persuasion is less effective if the message appeals to the emotions.
    True or False

52. For a poorly informed audience, persuasion is more effective if only one side of the argument is presented.
    True or False

53. Someone who has not made up his mind on an issue will be more difficult to persaude than someone who already holds a strong opinion on the issue.
    True or False

54. Acting contrary to one's attitudes or self-image causes cognitive dissonance.
    True or False

55. Public commitment to an attitude or belief makes it more difficult to change.
    True or False

56. The greater the reward or justification for acting contrary to one's beliefs, the greater the cognitive dissonance felt.
    True or False

57. Dissonance is especially likely to be felt when a person causes an undesired event to occur.
    True or False

Check Your Memory: Pages 549—551

58. Roughly 16 percent of American POWs in the Korean war signed false confessions.
    True or False

59. True brainwashing requires a captive audience.
    True or False

60. In brainwashing, the target person is housed with other people who hold the same attitudes and beliefs that he or she does.
    True or False

61. In most cases, the effects of brainwashing are very resistant to further change.
    True or False

62. A cult is a group in which the belief system is more important than the leader who espouses it.
    True or False

63. Cults play on emotions and discourage critical thinking.
    True or False

64. Cult members are typically isolated from former reference groups.
    True or False

Check Your Memory: Pages 551—556

65. Sexism is a type of prejudice.
    True or False

66. The term *racial profiling* refers to giving preferential treatment to some students seeking admission to college.
    True or False

67. Scapegoating could be one explanation for why the Jumping Frenchmen of Maine are being teased and startled.
    True or False

68. A person who views members of another group as competitors for jobs displays group prejudice.
    True or False

69. A negative correlation has been found between academic success and prejudice against homosexuals and stereotyping of gender-based occupations.
    True or False

70. Authoritarian persons tend to be prejudiced against all out-groups.
    True or False

71. The *F* in F scale stands for fanatic.
    True or False

72. An authoritarian would agree that people can be divided into the weak and the strong.
    True or False

73. Social stereotypes can be positive as well as negative.
    True or False

74. Symbolic prejudice is the most obvious and socially unacceptable form of bigotry.
    True or False

75. The key to creating prejudice in Jane Elliot's experiment was her use of scapegoating to cause group conflict.
    True or False

76. Equal-status contact tends to reduce prejudice and stereotypes.
    True or False

77. Superordinate groups help people of opposing groups to see themselves as members of a single larger group.
    True or False

Check Your Memory: Pages 557–560

78. Ethologists argue that humans learn to be aggressive by observing aggressive behaviour in lower animals.
    True or False

79. Specific areas of the brain are capable of initiating or ending aggression.
    True or False

80. Physical aggression is normally not displayed in young children before the age of 3.
    True or False

81. Higher levels of the hormone testosterone are associated with more aggressive behaviour by both men and women.
    True or False

82. The frustration-aggression hypothesis says that being aggressive is frustrating.
    True or False

83. People exposed to aversive stimuli tend to become less sensitive to aggression cues.
    True or False

84. Murders are less likely to occur in homes where guns are kept.
    True or False

85. Social learning theorists assume that instinctive patterns of human aggression are modified by learning.
    True or False

86. Aggressive crimes in TV dramas occur at a much higher rate than they do in real life.
    True or False

Check Your Memory: Pages 561–563

87. Bystanders offered no immediate help in the Kitty Genovese case and in the case of the Montreal woman.
    True or False

88. In an emergency, the more potential helpers present, the more likely a person is to get help.
    True or False

89. The first step in giving help is to define the situation as an emergency.
    True or False

90. A person sitting alone will donate less when asked to contribute to a charity than
    if they had been sitting in a group.
    True or False

91. Emotional arousal, especially empathic arousal, lowers the likelihood that one person will help another.
    True or False

92. You are more likely to help a person who seems similar to yourself.
    True or False

93. In many emergency situations it can be more effective to shout "Fire!" rather than "Help!"
    True or False

Check Your Memory: Psychology in Action

94. Multiculturalism is an attempt to blend multiple ethnic backgrounds into one universal culture.
    True or False

95. The emotional component of prejudicial attitudes may remain even after a person
    intellectually renounces prejudice.
    True or False

96. Recent research has shown that looking at real cultural differences among groups
    can, in fact, promote good interethnic relations.
    True or False

97. Individuating information forces us to focus mainly on the labels attached to a person.
    True or False

98. From a scientific point of view, "race" is a matter of social labelling, not a biological reality.
    True or False

99. People who hold just-world beliefs assume that people generally get what they deserve.
    True or False

100. Each ethnic group has strengths that members of other groups could benefit from emulating.
    True or False

Final Survey and Review

- ## *Why do people affiliate? What factors influence interpersonal attraction?*

1. _____ _____ studies how individuals behave, think, and feel in social situations.

2. The _____ to _____ is tied to additional needs for approval, support, friendship, and information.

3. Additionally, research indicates that we sometimes affiliate to reduce _____ and uncertainty.

4. Social _____ theory holds that we affiliate to evaluate our actions, feelings, and abilities.

5. Children are attracted to those who are _____ in sex, age, race and preferred activity. Older children (those starting high school) are more likely to be attracted to those who stand out and who are _____ .

6. Initial acquaintance and attraction are influenced by _____ attractiveness (beauty), _____ (high ability), and similarity.

7. A large degree of similarity on many dimensions is characteristic of mate selection, a pattern called _____ .

8. _____ (revealing oneself to others) occurs to a greater degree if two people like one another.

9. Self-disclosure follows a _____ norm: Low levels of self-disclosure are met with low levels in return, whereas moderate self-disclosure elicits more personal replies.

10. _____ (excessive) tends to inhibit self-disclosure by others. What is considered overdisclosure will _____ from culture to culture.

11. Self-disclosure between friends will typically _____ in high school.

12. Romantic love can be distinguished from liking by the use of _____ _____ . Dating couples love and like their partners but only like their friends.

13. Romantic love is also associated with greater mutual _____ between people.

14. _____ psychology attributes human mating patterns to the differing _____ challenges faced by men and women since the dawn of time. However, women may change their _____ of selection as they become more capable of supporting themselves.

- ## *How does group membership affect individual behaviour ?*

15. One's position in groups defines a variety of _____ to be played.

16. Social roles, which may be _____ or _____ , are particular behaviour patterns associated with social positions.

17. When two or more contradictory roles are held, role _____ may occur.

18. Positions within groups typically carry higher or lower levels of _____ . _____ is associated with special privileges and respect.

19. Group _____ refers to the organization of roles, _____ pathways, and power within a group.

20. Group _____ is basically the degree of attraction among group members.

21. _____ are standards of conduct enforced (formally or informally) by groups. Group _____ helps people deal with the stresses of life.

22. _____ theory is concerned with how we make inferences about the causes of behaviour .

23. Behaviour can be attributed to _____ causes or _____ causes.

24. The _____ _____ error is to ascribe the actions of others to internal causes. This is part of an _____ bias, in which we ascribe the behaviour of others to internal causes, and our own behaviour to external causes.

- ## What have social psychologists learned about conformity, obedience, compliance, and self-assertion?

25. _____ _____ refers to alterations in behaviour brought about by the behaviour of others.

26. _____ to group pressure is a familiar example of social influence. Virtually everyone conforms to a variety of broad social and _____ norms.

27. Conformity pressures also exist within small groups. The famous _____ experiments demonstrated that various group _____ encourage conformity.

28. _____ refers to compulsive conformity in group decision making. Its victims seek to maintain each other's _____ , even at the cost of critical thinking.

29. _____ to authority has been investigated in a variety of experiments, particularly those by Stanley _____ .

30. Obedience in his studies _____ when the victim was in the same room, when the victim and subject were face to face, when the _____ figure was absent, and when others refused to obey.

31. _____ with direct requests by a person who has little or no social power is another means by which behaviour is influenced.

32. Three strategies for getting people to comply are the foot-in-the- _____ technique, the _____ -in-the-face approach, and the _____ technique.

33. Recent research suggests that in addition to excessive obedience to authority, many people show a surprising _____ compliance to unreasonable requests.

34. _____ involves clearly stating one's wants and needs to others.

35. _____ expresses one's feelings and desires, but it hurts others.

36. Learning to be assertive is accomplished by _____ and rehearsing assertive actions.

- ## How are attitudes acquired and changed?

37. Attitudes are _____ _____ to respond in a positive or negative way.

38. Attitudes are made up of a _____ component, an _____ component, and an action component.

39. Attitudes may be formed by direct _____ , interaction with others, the effects of child-rearing practices, and social pressures from _____ _____ .

40. _____ group influences, the mass media, and chance _____ (accidental learning) also appear to be important in attitude formation.

41. The immediate _____ of actions, how we think others will evaluate our actions, and _____ all influence whether attitudes are converted to actions.

42. Attitudes held with _____ are most likely to be expressed in behaviour .

43. People tend to change their attitudes to match those of their _____ group (a group the person identifies with and refers to for guidance).

44. Effective persuasion occurs when characteristics of the _____ , the message, and the _____ are well matched.

45. In general, a likable and believable _____ who repeats a credible message that arouses emotion in the _____ and states clear-cut conclusions will be persuasive.

46. Maintaining and changing attitudes is closely related to needs for consistency in thoughts and actions. Cognitive _____ theory explains the dynamics of such needs.

47. Cognitive _____ occurs when there is a clash between _____ or between thoughts and actions.

48. The amount of _____ or _____ (reasons) for one's actions influences whether dissonance occurs.

49. We are motivated to reduce dissonance when it occurs, often by changing _____ or _____ , rather than behaviour .

● *Is brainwashing actually possible? How are people converted to cult membership?*

50. Brainwashing is a form of forced attitude change. It depends on _____ of the target person's total _____ .

51. Three steps in brainwashing are _____ (loosening) old attitudes and beliefs, change, and _____ (rewarding and strengthening) new attitudes and beliefs.

52. Many cults recruit new members with high-pressure _____ techniques resembling brainwashing.

53. Cults attempt to catch people when they are vulnerable. Then they combine isolation, displays of affection, discipline and _____ , intimidation, and escalating _____ to bring about conversion.

● *What causes prejudice and intergroup conflict? What can be done about these problems?*

54. Prejudice is a negative attitude held toward members of various _____ .

55. _____ , _____ , and _____ are specific types of prejudice based on race, age, and gender.

56. One theory attributes prejudice to _____ , which is a type of _____ aggression.

57. A second account says that prejudices may be held for personal reasons such as direct threats to a person's well being (_____ prejudice) or simply through adherence to group norms (_____ prejudice).

58. Prejudiced individuals tend to have an _____ personality, characterized by rigidity, inhibition, intolerance, and over-simplification.

59. Authoritarians tend to be very _____ (they use their own group as a basis for judging all others).

60. Intergroup conflict gives rise to hostility and the formation of _____ _____ (over-simplified images of members of various groups).

61. _____ prejudice, or prejudice expressed in disguised ways, is common today.

62. Status _____ (differences in power, prestige, or privileges) tend to build prejudices.

63. _____ contact (social interaction on an equal footing) tends to reduce prejudice.

64. _____ goals (those that rise above all others) usually reduce intergroup conflict.

65. On a small scale, _____ classrooms (which encourage cooperation through mutual _____) have been shown to be an effective way of combating prejudice.

- ### *How do psychologists explain human aggression?*

66. _____ explain aggression as a natural expression of inherited instincts.

67. Biological explanations emphasize brain mechanisms and physical factors that lower the _____ (trigger point) for aggression.

68. According to the _____ -aggression hypothesis, _____ and aggression are closely linked.

69. Aggression has been divided into two types: _____ aggression and _____ aggression.

70. Frustration is only one of many _____ stimuli that can arouse a person and make aggression more likely. Aggression is especially likely to occur when aggression _____ (stimuli associated with aggression) are present.

71. _____ _____ theory has focused attention on the role of aggressive models in the development of aggressive behaviour .

72. Aggressive models on television encourage aggression because they _____ (lower the sensitivity of) viewers to violence and _____ (remove restraints against) aggressive impulses.

- ### *Why are bystanders so often unwilling to help in an emergency?*

73. Prosocial behaviour is helpful, constructive, or _____ toward others.

74. Bystander _____ is the unwillingness of bystanders to offer help to others during emergencies.

75. Four decision points that must be passed before a person gives help are: noticing, defining an _____ , taking _____ , and selecting a course of action.

76. Helping is less likely at each point when other _____ _____ are present.

77. Helping is encouraged by general arousal, _____ arousal, being in a good mood, low effort or risk, and perceived _____ between the victim and the helper.

- ### *What can be done to lower prejudice and promote social harmony?*

78. _____ is an attempt to give equal status to different ethnic, racial, and cultural groups.

79. Greater tolerance can be encouraged by neutralizing stereotypes with _____ information (which helps see others as individuals).

80. Tolerance comes from looking for commonalties with others and by avoiding the effects of _____ beliefs, _____ prophecies, and social competition.

81. Cultural _____ is a key element in promoting greater social harmony.

Mastery Test

1. Homogamy is directly related to which element of interpersonal attraction?
    a. competence
    b. similarity
    c. beauty
    d. proximity

2. The weapons effect refers to the fact that weapons can serve as aggression
    a. thresholds
    b. cues
    c. models
    d. inhibitors

3. Suspicion and reduced attraction are associated with
    a. reciprocity
    b. self-disclosure
    c. competence and proximity
    d. overdisclosure

4. The identification with one's group increases for both Anglophone and Francophone military students during their years of training demonstrates the role of
    a. personal prejudice.
    b. group prejudice.
    c. the prejudiced personality.
    d. symbolic prejudice.

5. One thing that *reduces* the chances that a bystander will give help in an emergency is
    a. heightened arousal
    b. empathic arousal
    c. others who could help
    d. similarity to the victim

6. One consequence of seeing aggression portrayed on TV is a loss of emotional response, called
    a. disinhibition
    b. disassociation
    c. deconditioning
    d. desensitization

7. If you are speaking to a well-informed audience, it is important to _____ if you want to persuade them.
    a. repeat your message
    b. give both sides of the argument
    c. be likable
    d. appeal to their emotions

8. "President of the United States" is
    a. an ascribed role
    b. an achieved role
    c. a structural norm
    d. a cohesive role

9. Where attribution is concerned, wants, needs, motives, or personal characteristics are perceived as
    a. external causes
    b. situational attributions
    c. discounted causes
    d. internal causes

10. Asch is to _____ experiments as Milgram is to _____ experiments.
    a. compliance, assert
    b. conformity, obedience
    c. autokinetic, social power

    d.   groupthink, authority

11. Social psychology is the scientific study of how people

    a.   behave in the presence of others

    b.   form into groups and organizations

    c.   form and maintain interpersonal relationships

    d.   make inferences about the behaviour of others

12. "A person who first agrees with a small request is later more likely to comply with a larger demand." This statement summarizes the

    a.   low-ball technique

    b.   set-the-hook technique

    c.   door-in-the-face effect

    d.   foot-in-the-door effect

13. Which view of human aggression is most directly opposed to that of the ethologists?

    a.   social learning

    b.   brain mechanisms

    c.   attributional

    d.   innate releaser

14. Creating superordinate goals is an important way to

    a.   reduce group conflict

    b.   break the frustration-aggression link

    c.   promote bystander intervention

    d.   reverse self-fulfilling prophecies

15. A key element in the effectiveness of jigsaw classrooms is

    a.   deindividuation

    b.   the promotion of self-fulfilling prophecies

    c.   mutual interdependence

    d.   selecting competent student leaders

16. Group structure involves all but one of the following elements. Which does NOT belong?

    a.   roles

    b.   communication pathways

    c.   allocation of power

    d.   social comparisons

17. Research has shown that teenagers are more likely to engage in risky behaviours because

    a.   they want to be popular

    b.   their high level of hormones promotes such risky behaviours

    c.   they want to conform to the norms of their group

    d.   they are trapped by the foot-in-the-door phenomenon

18. Groupthink is a type of _____ that applies to decision making in groups.

    a.   conformity

    b.   social comparison

    c. social power
    d. obedience

19. A good antidote for social stereotyping is
    a. adopting just-world beliefs
    b. creating self-fulfilling prophecies
    c. accepting status inequalities
    d. seeking individuating information

20. An important difference between brainwashing and other types of persuasion is that brainwashing
    a. requires a captive audience
    b. is almost always permanent
    c. changes actions, not attitudes and beliefs
    d. is reversed during the refreezing phase

21. In Milgram's studies, the smallest percentage of subjects followed orders when
    a. the teacher and learner were in the same room
    b. the teacher received orders by phone
    c. the teacher and learner were face to face
    d. the experiment was conducted off campus

22. The most basic attributional error is to attribute the behaviour of others to _____ causes, even when they are caused by _____ causes.
    a. inconsistent, consistent
    b. internal, external
    c. random, distinctive
    d. situational, personal

23. In an experiment, most women waiting to receive a shock preferred to wait with others who
    a. were about to be shocked
    b. did not share their fears
    c. were trained to calm them
    d. had been shocked the day before

24. Evolutionary theories attribute mate selection, in part, to the _____ faced by men and women of past generations.
    a. food-gathering habits
    b. tribal customs
    c. maternal instincts
    d. differing reproductive needs

25. People tend to act like "what is beautiful is good." However, beauty has little connection to
    a. talents
    b. intelligence
    c. ability
    d. all of the preceding traits

26. Which of the following gives special privileges to a member of a group?

    a.   convergent norms

    b.   high cohesiveness

    c.   actor-observer bias

    d.   high status

27. Your actions are most likely to agree with one of your attitudes when

    a.   the actions reverse an old habit

    b.   the attitude is held with conviction

    c.   you know that others disagree with your position

    d.   you score high on an attitude scale

28. When we are subjected to conformity pressures, the _____ of a majority is more important than the number of people in it.

    a.   unanimity

    b.   cohesion

    c.   proximity

    d.   comparison level

29. If it is easier for caucasian Canadians to get automobile insurance than it is for African Canadians, then African Canadians have experienced

    a.   discrimination

    b.   scapegoating

    c.   ethnocentrism

    d.   personal prejudice

30. The Bennington College study showed that attitudes are affected very much by

    a.   membership groups

    b.   child-rearing

    c.   reference groups

    d.   chance conditioning

31. If you respond aggressively to someone's insults you are displaying what type of aggression?

    a.   symbolic

    b.   proactive

    c.   aversive

    d.   reactive

Solutions

Recite and Review

1. social
2. approval, information
3. reduce
4. evaluate
5. sex, preferred, stand
6. attraction, similarity
7. similarity, mate
8. revealing
9. norm
10. self-disclosure
11. high
12. like, love, like
13. mutual
14. mating, supporting
15. groups
16. Social, roles
17. contradictory
18. groups
19. roles
20. attraction
21. standards, groups, stresses
22. causes
23. causes, causes
24. error, internal, internal, external
25. behaviour, others
26. conforms, norms
27. groups, group
28. decision, making
29. authority
30. Obedience
31. requests, power
32. foot, face
33. authority, requests
34. wants, needs
35. hurts
36. assertive
37. positive, negative
38. action
39. direct, child
40. media, chance
41. immediate, evaluate
42. expressed
43. identifies
44. message
45. emotion, conclusions
46. consistency
47. clash
48. dissonance
49. reduce
50. forced
51. changing
52. brainwashing
53. affection, conversion
54. negative
55. gender (or sex)
56. aggression
57. norms
58. personality, over
59. group
60. conflict
61. disguised
62. Status
63. reduce
64. goals
65. classrooms, mutual
66. instincts
67. lower
68. aggression, aggression
69. two, proactive
70. stimuli, aggression
71. models
72. models, viewers
73. helpful
74. help
75. noticing
76. less
77. arousal, risk
78. equal
79. individuals
80. beliefs, social
81. Cultural

Connections

1. D
2. I
3. L
4. A
5. K
6. B
7. E
8. G
9. C
10. H
11. J
12. F
13. L
14. J
15. H
16. A
17. K
18. D
19. I
20. F

21. C
22. E
23. B
24. G

Check Your Memory

1. T
2. T
3. F
4. T
5. T
6. F
7. T
8. T
9. T
10. F
11. T
12. F
13. T
14. F
15. F
16. F
17. T
18. T
19. T
20. T
21. F
22. F
23. F
24. T
25. T
26. F
27. T
28. T

29. F
30. F
31. F
32. T
33. F
34. T
35. F
36. T
37. T
38. T
39. T
40. F
41. F
42. T
43. T
44. T
45. T
46. T
47. F
48. T
49. T
50. F
51. F
52. T
53. F
54. T
55. T
56. F
57. T
58. T
59. T
60. F
61. F
62. F
63. T

64. T
65. T
66. F
67. T
68. F
69. T
70. T
71. F
72. T
73. T
74. F
75. T
76. T
77. T
78. F
79. T
80. F
81. T
82. F
83. F
84. F
85. F
86. T
87. T
88. F
89. T
90. F
91. F
92. T
93. T
94. F
95. T
96. T
97. F
98. T

99. T

100. T

Final Survey and Review

1. Social, psychology
2. need, affiliate
3. anxiety
4. comparison
5. similar, aggressive
6. physical, competence
7. homogamy
8. Self-disclosure
9. reciprocity
10. Overdisclosure, vary
11. increase
12. attitude, scales
13. absorption
14. Evolutionary, reproductive, criteria
15. roles
16. achieved, ascribed
17. conflict
18. status, High, status
19. structure, communication
20. cohesiveness
21. Norms, membership
22. Attribution
23. internal, external
24. fundamental, attributional, actor-observer
25. Social, influence
26. Conformity, cultural
27. Asch, sanctions
28. Groupthink, approval
29. Obedience, Milgram
30. decreased, authority

31. Compliance
32. door, door, low-ball
33. passive
34. Self-assertion
35. Aggression
36. role-playing
37. learned, tendencies
38. belief, emotional
39. contact, group, membership
40. Peer, conditioning
41. consequences, habits
42. conviction
43. reference
44. communicator, audience
45. communicator, audience
46. dissonance
47. dissonance, thoughts
48. reward, justification
49. beliefs, attitudes
50. control, environment
51. unfreezing, refreezing
52. indoctrination
53. rituals, commitment
54. out-groups
55. Racism, ageism, sexism
56. scapegoating, displaced
57. personal, group
58. authoritarian
59. ethnocentric
60. social, stereotypes
61. Symbolic
62. inequalities
63. Equal-status
64. Superordinate
65. jigsaw, interdependence
66. Ethologists

67. threshold
68. frustration, frustration
69. proactive, reactive
70. aversive, cues
71. Social, learning
72. desensitize, disinhibit
73. altruistic
74. apathy
75. emergency, responsibility
76. potential, helpers
77. empathic, similarity
78. Multiculturalism
79. individuating
80. just-world, self-fulfilling
81. awareness

Mastery Test

1. B (p. 531)
2. B (p. 558)
3. D (p. 531)
4. B (p. 552)
5. C (p. 561)
6. D (p. 559)
7. B (p. 547)
8. B (p. 534)
9. D (p. 535)
10. B (p. 537, 539)
11. A (p. 528)
12. D (p. 542)
13. A (p. 559)
14. A (p. 555)
15. C (p. 555)
16. D (p. 534)
17. C (p. 539)
18. A (p. 538)

19. D (p. 564)
20. A (p. 549)
21. B (p. 541)
22. B (p. 535)
23. A (p. 528)
24. D (p. 532)
25. D (p. 529)
26. D (p. 535)
27. B (p. 546)
28. A (p. 539)
29. A (p. 551)
30. C (p. 546)
31. D (p. 558)